The Creative Container Gardener

The Creative Container Gardener

How to Create a Theme-Based Garden in a Small Space

Elaine Stevens

TEN SPEED PRESS
Berkeley, California

A Kirsty Melville book

TEN SPEED PRESS
P.O. Box 7123
Berkeley, CA 94707

Published by arrangement with Whitecap Books, 351 Lynn Avenue, North Vancouver, B.C. Canada V7J 2C4

Edited by Elaine Jones
Technical editing by Carolyn Jones
Cover design by Tracy Dean
Interior design by Warren Clark
Thematic illustrations by Bernie Lyon
Technical illustrations by Doris Fancourt-Smith
Cover photograph by Bert Klassen
Typeset by Warren Clark

Library of Congress Cataloguing-in-Publication Data
Stevens, Elaine.
    The creative container gardener / Elaine Stevens.
        p. cm.
    Includes bibliographical references and index.
    ISBN 0-89815-697-1
    1. Container gardening. I. Title.
SB418.S89 1995   95–70
635.9'86—dc20   Printed in Canada   CIP

Contents

This is for you, Mum

Acknowledgments

MANY PEOPLE HAVE HELPED TO MAKE THIS BOOK A REALITY, AND I AM indebted to them all, especially to those who shared their knowledge, ideas, and enthusiasms so generously along the way. Special thanks go to Bernie Lyon and Doris Fancourt-Smith for their marvelous illustrations, and to all the staff at Whitecap Books for editing, designing, and producing the finished product: not only did they contribute their talents and professional expertise, but they also supported me with humor and patience throughout. For additional help with various aspects of the book I would like to thank: staff, master gardeners, and volunteers at VanDusen Botanical Display Gardens, especially Carolyn Jones, Barbara Fox, and Gerry Gibbens; staff and FOGs of the UBC Botanical Garden, especially Judy Newton and Wilf Nicholls; Mary and Tom Fisher of Cultus Bay nursery; Michael Luco of Earthrise garden store; Michael Kluckner and Christine Allen; Norm Watts; Peter Fancourt-Smith; Ted Eaton; Paddy Wales; Mike Carroll; and Gary Anderson.

I owe a large debt of gratitude to the many friends who have supported me positively, patiently, and enthusiastically throughout, and helped me cope with the unexpected challenges the book has presented. It has been an adventure, and I have learned a lot. Last, but not least, a special thanks to the many knowledgeable gardeners in my family who share my passion for plants and enthusiasm for nurturing the land.

Preface

THERE ARE LOTS OF GLOSSY BOOKS ON CONTAINER GARDENING, FULL OF expensive statuary, sumptuous Italian terracotta pots, and exotic plants. This is not that kind of book. This is for people who are actually wrestling with the dilemma of what to do with their patio, balcony, window box, basement stairwell, or pot, and are looking for entertaining ideas and straightforward solutions. People often think that container gardening is an easy way to grow plants, but in fact it can be more challenging than working with a larger space. The smaller the space, the simpler the design has to be.

This book is intended to stimulate your imagination and help you deal with challenging corners, so that you can create your own unique and personal outdoor living space. It leads you step-by-step through the process of creating a garden in a small area, usually where there is no natural soil. It includes planting ideas for many very different types of gardens, discusses the bylaws and regulations that might influence your choices, looks at the many pots and containers you can make and use, and features plants that suit various spaces, places, personalities, and moods. In short, it's a practical book for people with a sense of adventure and no time to waste.

Introduction

AROUND THE WORLD, CONTAINER GARDENING FLOURISHES. HIGH IN THE Swiss Alps, window boxes full of red and pink geraniums brighten the outside of mountain chalets; in Japan, where simplicity is an art, one ancient Bonsai pine, carefully tended, may be the only feature of a tiny courtyard; and in rural Provence, fragrant thyme and lavender plants tumble over the edges of old stone troughs and ceramic pots. Wherever you look, there are gardeners with an eye for design and color, and a love for growing plants.

In North America we are fortunate to be able to observe these and many other gardening traditions at first hand. From the lush perennial borders of England to the elegant conceptual forms of classical Chinese gardens, this continent holds some of the best planting ideas from around the world within its multicultural boundaries. This has allowed me a lot of freedom to explore gardening ideas for this book.

Here you can see some of the wonderful opportunities container gardening offers to break away from the dull and boring, to think creatively and flexibly, and to explore and express imaginative ideas in a small space. This is gardening with no holds barred, and it offers you a chance to fulfill your gardening yearnings and fantasies, whatever they may be: perhaps a balcony overflowing with pastel-colored sweet peas and white Casablanca lilies to scent the night air; or a water garden, complete with the soft sounds of a fountain, brightly colored fish, and a fragrant water lily in full bloom; or even a rustic boardwalk and prairie grasses that remind you of childhood summers by the lake, long gone. With imagination, anything is possible.

One of the great advantages of gardening in a small space is that it is easy to change your theme from one season or one year to the next. Maybe one year you will want to grow bulbs in the spring, followed by vegetables in the summer, and Michaelmas daisies and asters in the fall. It's easy to switch. Just make sure your plants have the right amount of sun, give them the right container and the soil, water, and nutrients they need, and let them grow. If you follow the guidelines in this book, you can create your own magical container garden, whatever your lifestyle and wherever you live.

Any outdoor space can become a beautiful garden. Some of the most visually appealing spots are those that have been created out of awkward corners: around basement doorways, under windows, on highrise balconies, and on patios overlooked by unattractive neighboring structures. Any negative feature can be turned into a positive one with a few good ideas and a bit of hard work.

You don't need to have a lot of space or money, but you do need some imaginative and creative ideas, good planning, and patience. Each place has potential; it's simply a matter of finding it and helping it to come to life. In this way, you can create a garden that is an expression of your personality and interests. It may be very small, or it may be large enough for entertaining, relaxing, eating meals, and enjoying the outdoors. Whatever its size, it's possible to make it interesting and beautiful without having to spend a lot of money.

A short history of patios, balconies, and containers

For over five thousand years, gardeners with limited space have grown plants in pots. The ancient Egyptians even put potted palms onto burning funeral barges as they sent their deceased loved ones downriver. One of the best known of the Egyptian gardeners was the pharaoh Ramses III (1198–1166 B.C.), who introduced many new plants into cultivation and grew trees and shrubs in decorated vases. Earthenware pots were used to highlight the symmetry of a garden design, grow less common plants, and define or separate garden spaces.

Egyptian gardening ideas spread from Egypt to neighboring Mediterranean countries, such as Cyprus, where one of the most curious gardening cults of the ancient world, the Adonis cult, sprang up. According to one version of the legend, a Cypriot prince called Adonis (who was later adopted by the Greeks as a god) was gored to death by a boar sent by the warrior god Ares, who was jealous of the handsome younger man. The goddess Aphrodite, hurrying to help Adonis, stepped on the thorn of a rose bush. The rose, which had been white until then, changed to a deep red, and from the blood of Adonis rose the anemone flower which blooms on Cypriot hillsides today.

In honor of the tragically short life of such a beautiful youth, the women of Cyprus made rooftop gardens in the summer, surrounding an image of Adonis with pots planted with wheat, barley, fennel, and lettuce seeds. The seeds germinated quickly but they were not watered and so they died prematurely, just like Adonis. Thus the "gardens of Adonis" came to symbolize the joys of youth that flower all too briefly before fading away. This is a nice image to remember if you forget to water your pots one day, and come home to find everything wilted.

The Romans took to the idea of container gardening with enthusiasm. They were great innovators as well as borrowers and developed many new techniques for making terracotta pots. They also invented topiary and greenhouses, and were skilled in the art of grafting and pruning trees. The Romans built their houses or villas around enclosed courtyards, known as atriums or peristyles, and filled them with topiary, formal gardens, fountains, statues, columns, vases, pottery urns, and artifacts. They painted the courtyard walls with trompe-l'oeil trees and flowers to make the space look bigger and grew a wide range of utilitarian, medicinal, and fragrant plants. Pots were used to decorate the roofs and balconies of Roman households, and the people experimented with many different shapes and sizes of pots. Today container gardens are still immensely popular in Italy, whether they are in courtyards or on roofs, terraces, or patios.

The patio is a Spanish development of the Roman atrium. It was a major feature in medieval Spanish architecture, and became a standard element in houses during the Spanish Renaissance. Because of the heat of the summers in Spain, arcades were built to surround the patio, and these were richly decorated. When they colonized Latin America, the Spanish took the idea of the patio with them and gradually incorporated it into Spanish-American architecture. From here it became popular throughout North America. When we think about a patio today we usually mean a small outdoor area, larger than a balcony, beside or partially enclosed by the house, with room for a seating area and plants. A patio can be at ground level, first-floor level, or even higher.

Balconies and windows are well represented in history and literature, although not necessarily for their horticultural use. Shakespeare's Romeo and Juliet, for instance, were obviously thinking of other things when they met on Juliet's balcony by moonlight; and the fairy-tale heroine Rapunzel was more interested in letting her hair down for the prince than in planting geraniums and petunias in her window boxes. Of all the balcony gardens in history, perhaps the most famous are the hanging gardens of Babylon. Unfortunately, since they were destroyed and no record of them exists today, we can only imagine how wonderful they were from the many legends that persist about them.

Although the suggestions in this book are unlikely to help you re-create these ancient gardens, or to find your prince, I hope they will help you to break away from conventional ideas and make your garden whatever you want it to be.

How to use this book

While choosing a theme is obviously very important, many a good idea can come to grief if you are not sure how to make it work. To help you take your inspirations from concept to finished product, I have put the ideas first, to inspire you, and the practical details second, to help you do it right. First, however, there are a few things to consider before you look at the themes, since they will influence what you can do.

The first thing to think about is the size and shape of the space itself. It is a good idea to estimate approximately the amount of room you can allot to plants and containers, and how much you will allow for furniture, garden ornaments, and other garden features. This will determine how many containers you will have, their size, and how many plants you will be buying.

Privacy may be an extremely important factor, especially if your balcony, patio, or suite is overlooked, right next to your neighbors' back door, or completely exposed to the street. In these cases, you will probably need to provide some screening—either trellis or fencing for vines and other climbers, or screening plants, such as bamboo. These will confine and enclose the space, which is an advantage, but they may also limit the amount of light that gets through to the plants, which may possibly be a disadvantage.

The exposure of your site is also important. If it gets plenty of sun, you will have a very different garden from the person whose garden is in shade. In some cases it may be possible to make a shade garden in a sunny spot, but only if you can create enough shade for the plants to do well. It is harder to make a sunny-theme garden out of a shady spot and, even if you do, it may not seem right. Balconies can be exposed to strong winds and weather extremes, especially those on the upper floors of a highrise. You can create windbreaks by using trellis or hardy trees and shrubs, and you should choose plants that do well in these conditions.

Since there are so many different kinds of areas readers might be working with, I have not provided exact planting plans. These would, inevitably, only work for a few people. Instead, I have tried to convey the essence of each idea, with suggestions for adapting the ideas to many different spots. There are practical lists of materials and plants; instructions on how to make useful or decorative garden features and orna-ments, such as lumières ("Santa Fe style") and alpine troughs ("There are fairies at the bottom of the garden"); and practical, relevant information on different aspects of gardening, such as espaliering an apple tree ("The urban apple orchard") and making a penjing ("A touch of the Orient"). Each theme also includes instructions for making one specifically planted container that uses materials particularly suited to that idea. This will give you an excellent starting point to develop your own theme garden.

The extensive plant lists include descriptions of size, color, fragrance, growth hab-its, and blooming times. Hardiness zones for each plant are given, according to the United States Department of Agriculture (USDA) hardiness zones classifications (your local garden center can tell you which zone you live in). For more information on zones, see "Practical Details: Plant selection."

The second section of the book, "Practical Details," covers issues such as budget; bylaws, rules, and regulations; exposure to sun or shade; tools and equipment; con-tainers, planters, trellis, fencing, and seating; making and using fertilizers and com-post; and selecting, feeding, watering, and caring for plants in containers.

The key to working with small spaces is to be ruthless and disciplined, to decide upon a theme or idea, and to develop it clearly. Try to resist the temptation to add conflicting colors or styles until you become familiar with the plants and materials you are using. For example, if you have decided to create a white garden, the drama and simplicity of the effect will be lost if you put in a backdrop of scarlet runner beans, or scatter seeds of brightly colored Shirley poppies among the plants.

Although the information given here is specifically for outdoor spaces that do not have any natural soil, the ideas can be applied equally well to any contained and enclosed space. Many ideas can be combined beautifully and successfully, and will bring greater interest and variety. This could mean growing fruits, vegetables, and herbs, surrounded by a trellis for fragrant sweet peas; or maybe creating a fragrant cutting garden, with a large pot in one corner for water plants. If the effect you are trying to achieve doesn't work, that's all right too, for we learn more from our failures than our successes.

Some of the most challenging places to work with are standard concrete apartment balconies. They tend to be exposed to general view, and are usually too narrow for seating. However, containers and hanging devices can make them look very attractive. For instance, there are many metal hoops and hangers that are made especially to hook over railings, so that plants can be suspended along the edges of a balcony. Free-standing metal or wooden shelves can provide multilayered places for pots, and vines and climbers can be grown through them to soften the balcony edges and block unsightly views. Shelving can even be used as a framework for hanging a water fountain (see "Water, water everywhere"). Long, narrow window boxes can be suspended inside the railing and filled with compact and trailing plants that look attractive from inside the apartment.

Containers made from various materials and in many different sizes and shapes add much to the visual appeal of a small space, especially when they are arranged attractively and filled with interesting plants. Then they become important architectural elements that help define the feeling of the landscape. Ideally they will be both attractive and practical.

Different themes lend themselves well to different kinds of planters, and this is discussed within the various themes and ideas given in the book. Although a variety of containers can be used for planters, the most durable, and the ones most commonly used on patios and balconies, are wooden planters and terracotta, glazed earthenware, and concrete pots.

There is no need to let the cost of containers stop you from making a garden. If your budget is really restricted you can use a selection of inexpensive containers. Some of them are even free! Recycled plastic pots, plastic milk crates, tin cans with holes punched in them, wooden crates, old boots and shoes, wire or wicker baskets, cracked mugs and tea cups, wash buckets, hats, fishing creels, and many other objects can be turned into planters. Go to junk and second-hand stores, search garage sales, and you will be amazed at the things you can find. If you use your imagination and think of the theme, you will find all sorts of containers that are appropriate for it, and you will have a true collector's garden by the time you are finished.

As you read through the information on each theme it is helpful to bear these points in mind, so that when you are ready to plan your own garden you will be able to adapt the ideas to your space and make practical decisions. Above all, remember that good planning will save you time, money, and effort and will help you have a good time gardening. There are few hard and fast rules when it comes to plants and gardening, so let your imagination be your guide, as you begin a new Container Gardening adventure.

Garden Themes, Plans and Ideas

A taste of Provence

Mediterranean herbs bring taste and fragrance to the garden

FOR MANY PEOPLE, THE VERY BEST USE OF A SMALL SPACE IS TO GROW fragrant and tasty herbs for the kitchen. Even a single container can provide you with enough parsley, sage, rosemary, and thyme for everyday cooking. If you devote your whole balcony or patio to herbs, you may have enough left over to share with your friends, and you will have the added bonus of a sweet-smelling garden, reminiscent of herb-covered hillsides in the south of France.

In Provence, wild and cultivated herbs are still harvested before dawn and sold in local street markets: lavender by the basketful, bunches of freshly cut kitchen herbs, dried herbs for medicines, and bouquets of roses that are cut and arranged before the dewdrops have dried on their petals. So many of the herbs we use every day for culinary, cosmetic, and medicinal purposes are native to these sun-drenched Mediterranean hills and will grow well in containers, in a hot and sunny spot, with a minimum of fuss and care.

As long as you have at least six hours of sunshine a day, a Mediterranean herb garden is easy and fun to create. It can be left to its own devices most of the time once it is established, especially since so many herbs contain large quantities of volatile oils and other chemicals that repel pests and diseases. You can drift through the afternoons, reclining in a comfy wicker chair among your herbs, reading the latest bestseller. On summer weekends you can enjoy a late brunch or lengthy lunch at a small table laid for two, shaded from the sun by a brightly colored patio umbrella. A good bottle of French wine and some elegant food liberally spiced with your own produce will complete the picture.

Cooking with herbs is a satisfying and rewarding experience. Herbs bring richness and flavor to the simplest of dishes: even the humble omelet can be elevated to a gourmet dish with the addition of a generous handful of chopped herbs, such as parsley, chives, basil, and oregano. Thus the first thing to decide when planning your herb garden is the herbs you actually like, use, and want to have, whether for their fragrance, their beauty, or their flavor.

Another important factor is the climate in which you live. Even though they come from a mild and sunny place, many Mediterranean herbs adapt well to cooler northern latitudes when they are planted in the right spot, and some cooking herbs, such as dill and parsley, actually prefer cooler growing conditions. Tender perennials, such as bay and rosemary, will only survive out of doors in areas where the winter is mild. If they are kept in pots year round, they can be brought indoors during the winter.

If cold winters are likely to kill even the hardier herbs and you have limited space for herbs indoors during the winter, you may prefer to concentrate on growing annuals and biennials, such as fennel, dill, parsley, basil, pot marigold, and German chamomile, and use them in abundance during summer months. Tender annuals, such as basil, will do really well as long as they are kept indoors until the temperature outside is reliably warm, day and night.

A sunny patio provides an ideal spot for growing herbs in a variety of planters and containers. If you want to re-create the casual and seemingly haphazard plantings found throughout the south of France, search for old, recycled materials for the patio itself—brick, flagstones, concrete pavers—and find pots and troughs that have the same sense of rustic antiquity. Stone troughs may be too expensive for most budgets, but simple concrete containers are relatively inexpensive and can be aged nicely by painting them with yogurt, which encourages moss to grow on shaded spots. It can also be fun to make your own rustic-looking hypertufa troughs (see "There are fairies at the bottom of the garden"). Boxwood hedges and topiary help to make a herb garden look formal, and the boxwood makes a very effective edging, especially if it is kept carefully clipped. (To make a herbal topiary, see "Clipped for style.")

For a herb garden on a balcony, it is worth raising planters so that the soil level is at waist height. This allows room for storage under the plants, and the tantalizing fragrance of herbs will be closer to your nose. Tender plants can be lifted out, still in their containers, and brought indoors during cold winter weather. Herbs in balcony planters will be equally effective whether they are planted informally, as on a wild hillside, or formally, as in an eighteenth-century French garden, with clipped hedging, topiary, and herbs arranged symmetrically. Topiaries can be underplanted with bulbs for the spring and chamomile or thyme for summer blooming. Lavender is an excellent edging plant; dwarf lavender cultivars are particularly attractive when they are planted in front of roses, and the roses underplanted with garlic and chives to keep the aphids away.

Some herbs are notorious spreaders that will invade quickly, crowding out more compact plants. This is particularly true of some members of the mint family, such as peppermint and spearmint. Be sure to grow them in their own containers, separated from the other herbs. You can also experiment with unusual cultivars of perennial kitchen favorites, such as lemon or caraway thyme, pineapple sage, apple mint, and bronze fennel, although some of them are less hardy than their better-known relatives. The seeds of hardy flowering annuals, such as pot marigolds, nasturtiums, and borage, can be scattered among the perennials, and will provide edible flowers for salad all summer long.

If you only have room for a few smaller containers, there are some attractive terracotta pots on the market made especially for growing herbs. They have side pockets, ideal for growing different herbs within the one container. You can also use a half-barrel, a square wooden planter box, or a stone or concrete container. If you want your container to look formal, try planting a topiary bay or rosemary in the center and edge it with lavender or thyme, adding kitchen herbs to fill in the gaps. Whether your planting is formal or informal, if you are growing your favorite herbs you will have a fragrant and useful pot all summer long.

Setting the scene

The following checklist will help you start creating a Provençal herb garden on your balcony or patio.

- Six to eight hours of sunshine a day.
- A variety of weathered troughs, terracotta pots, and planters suitable for the herbs you choose and the space you have. Try to include some raised planters, or raise plants up using shelving, hooks on walls, or a balcony railing.
- Recycled brick, flagstones, or concrete pavers for old-looking flooring.
- Basic soil mix and organic fertilizer.
- Watering and lighting systems.
- Basic gardening tools and storage.
- A variety of herbs and complementary plants; your selection will depend upon how formal or informal you would like your garden to be.
- If there is room, a table and chairs. Consider a wicker chair with soft cushions covered in colorful Provençal fabric, a small table with a blue or red checkered cloth, and a canvas patio umbrella. For extra seating you could use folding chairs.

To add to the feeling of the south of France, include any other props you can, such as French terracotta pots, bright red geraniums, whitewashed walls, and brightly painted doors and windows.

A selection of favorite herbs to grow

Most culinary herbs are easy to obtain and they thrive in regular potting mix, as long as there is a reasonable depth of soil; eight inches (20 cm) is a minimum. Regular watering and a good dose of organic fertilizer every few weeks during the growing season will keep the plants healthy and growing well. Aromatic oils and other chemicals in many herbs act as natural insecticides, so most of them will be relatively untroubled by insects and diseases, especially if chives and garlic are planted at regular intervals. When choosing your plants, try to find a garden center or grower in your area who specializes in herbs so that you can experiment with some of the more unusual cultivars of common favorites, as mentioned above, such as tricolored sage, apple mint, caraway thyme, and bronze fennel. The herbs listed below are all tried and true favorites and form an excellent basis for any herb garden.

You will be able to use many of your herbs throughout the year if you cut and dry them during the summer when they are at peak potency and freshness. The best time to harvest the aerial parts of a plant (leaves and flowers) is just as they come into flower. Pick them in the morning as soon as the dew is off the leaves and petals. Tie them into small bunches (five or six stems only) with rubber bands and hang them to dry in a warm, dry place out of direct sunlight. As soon as they are dry, transfer them to sealed containers and store in a cool, dry place in the dark.

Many of these herbs can be used as part of your home medicine chest, as well as in the kitchen, and some of their principal medicinal uses are itemized following the plant list.

Basil (*Ocimum basilicum*). This popular culinary herb has white flowers and finely flavored, large, succulent leaves. It is a very tender annual and should not be put outside until the weather is reliably warm day and night: usually in early June. It grows in sun or partial shade in a moderately rich, well-watered soil. Basil is the main ingredient in pesto sauce, is great in salads, and is widely used in many dishes. It does not dry well, so is best used fresh. If you want to preserve some for winter use, make it into pesto sauce and freeze the sauce.

Bay laurel (*Laurus nobilis*). The shiny, pungent leaves of the bay tree are widely used as a flavoring in soups, stews, and casserole dishes. Bay can be kept pruned to whatever size you like in a topiary form, or left to grow into a shrub. It is unlikely to grow to more than 5 feet (1.5 m) in a container. It is a tender perennial and will need to be brought indoors once the nighttime temperature starts to drop in the fall. It should also be protected from scorching sun and cold winds. Grow in rich, well-drained soil. Zones 9–10.

Bee balm, bergamot (*Monarda didyma*). The flowers of bee balm are among the most striking in the herb garden. It has big, wild-looking, shaggy, red, pink, or mauve flower heads that attract bees and hummingbirds, and highly fragrant, broad, pointed, spicy leaves. It is a perennial and will grow in partial shade or sun, reaching a height of 2 to 3 feet (60 to 90 cm). It prefers a rich, moist, well-drained soil. Leaves can be floated on drinks and the flowers make an unusual addition to salads. Zones 3–9.

Borage (*Borago officinalis*). Borage is one of those easy-to-grow annuals that self-seeds cheerfully from year to year. It has blue-green leaves and bright blue, star-shaped flowers that hang in clusters and look most attractive in salads. The leaves taste slightly of cucumber and can be used in salads and vinegars and as tea. It grows to 3 feet (90 cm) and its leaves and stems are covered with bristly little hairs. It grows well in almost any soil and prefers sun.

Chamomile, German (*Chamaemelum nobile* syn. *Matricaria chamomilla*). Chamomile has delicate, finely divided leaves and tiny, daisylike flowers that rise above the foliage to about 10 inches (25 cm). It has a sweet, distinct scent and the flowers are most commonly used for a soothing, relaxing tea. German chamomile is an annual and grows easily almost anywhere, but prefers slightly acid, fairly rich soil. It likes lots of sun but will tolerate some shade.

Chives (*Allium schoenoprasum*). Chive is garlic's mild-flavored relative. It is a rapidly multiplying bulb that grows in bright green clumps of tapered, round, hollow leaves. It produces rose-purple flower heads in late spring and early summer. The leaves and flowers have a delicate onion flavor and are used in many dishes, especially in soups and salads. It grows from 12 to 18 inches (30 to 45 cm), and likes rich soil in sun or partial shade. Zones 3–9.

Coriander, cilantro, or Chinese parsley (*Coriandrum sativum*). Coriander is a delicately leafed annual that produces umbels of tiny, white flowers tinged with lavender. The whole plant is strongly aromatic, and the dried seeds are scented like orange peel. The fresh herb is widely used in cooking, and is especially popular in China, East India, and Mexico. The seeds are ground for use in curries, and are baked into breads and cakes. It grows from 2 to 3 feet (60 to 90 cm) and likes a well-drained soil and lots of sun.

Dill (*Anethum graveolens*). Dill is an annual that grows to 5 feet (1.5 m), with fine, delicate leaves, decorative yellow flower umbels and aromatic seeds. The leaves and seeds are used in cooking, especially in fish dishes, sour-cream dressings, and sauces, and the seeds are used for tea. Dill grows very easily from seed. Plant it in the sun in average, well-drained soil and protect it from strong winds.

Fennel (*Foeniculum vulgare*). Fennel is a tender perennial that grows anywhere from 3 to 5 feet (0.9 to 1.5 m) tall, with feathery green leaves and umbels of tiny yellow flowers that ripen into aromatic brown seeds. The leaves, stems, and seeds of fennel have a strong licorice flavor and are widely used in salads and for cooking, especially with fish. The seeds make a pleasant-tasting tea. If fennel will not suvive the winter where you live, grow it as an annual. It grows easily from seed in well-drained soil, prefers sun, and should be protected from strong winds. Zones 5–9.

Garlic (*Allium sativum*). One of the most widely used of all the herbs, garlic has a rich, pungent flavor and is used by cooks around the world. It is a bulb that grows easily in good soil, but only where the climate is warm and sunny. Separate one whole head into individual cloves and plant them in October or November for best results, if it is appropriate in your area, or as early as possible in the spring. The plant grows to 2 feet (60 cm), with flat, long, pointed leaves. Garlic is said to repel insects, and many people plant it around their roses to keep aphids away. Sun or partial shade.

Lavender (*Lavandula angustifolia*). There are many kinds of lavender, and all have highly aromatic leaves and flowers. Lavender blooms from midsummer into the fall, and prefers sun and a well-drained soil. Prune back to just above the previous year's growth in early spring to maintain an attractive, compact plant. Dwarf cultivars such as 'Hidcote' and 'Munstead' grow to about 18 inches (45 cm), while the species plant grows up to 3 feet (90 cm). Lavender is grown mainly for its soothing, relaxing scent, but the flowers are excellent as a flavoring for desserts, vinegar, and tea. Zones 5–9.

Lemon balm (*Melissa officinalis*). This popular perennial has lemon-scented, heart-shaped leaves and a distinct lemon flavor. It grows from 18 inches to 3 feet (45 to 90 cm) in height and prefers partial shade, although it can be grown in the sun. It forms a spreading clump and likes rich, moist, well-drained soil. It also self-seeds easily. The leaves make a refreshing drink and can be used to flavor teas, fruit salads, cakes, and cookies. Zones 4–9.

Marigold, English or pot (*Calendula officinalis*). This cheerful annual blooms all summer and into the fall. Its bright yellow and orange petals make an excellent flavoring for soups and salads, and the dried petals can be used as a substitute for saffron, especially in rice dishes and breads. The plant grows from 1 to 2 feet tall (30 to 60 cm) and prefers full sun and a rich soil mix.

Mint (*Mentha* spp.). The culinary members of the mint family are perennials with square stems, pointed leaves, and whorls of flowers in summer. They spread rapidly from creeping stems and must be contained or they will become invasive. They are easily propagated and grow best in light shade in rich, moist, slightly acid soil. They reach 1 to 3 feet (30 to 90 cm) in height, and are used for their cooling, delicious taste, especially in salads, desserts, cold drinks, and teas. The two most commonly used are peppermint (*M. piperita*) and its milder relative, spearmint (*M. spicata*). Zones 4–9.

Parsley (*Petroselinum crispum*). Parsley is a self-seeding biennial that is usually grown as an annual. You can start it from seed or buy seedlings from the garden center. It does well in sun or light shade and prefers a rich, well-drained soil. Rich in vitamins and minerals, it is one of the most important culinary herbs and is used widely to add flavor to food. It grows 8 to 10 inches (20 to 25 cm) high, and makes an excellent after-dinner tea for settling the digestion. Chewing on a little parsley after you have eaten raw garlic helps take away the odor of the garlic and sweetens the breath.

Rosemary (*Rosmarinus officinalis*). Rosemary is an attractive, shrubby perennial with fragrant, needlelike leaves and dainty flowers in blue, lavender, pink, or white, depending on the cultivar. It is an indispensable plant in the herb garden, but must be taken indoors for the winter in most areas. It prefers full sun, a protected spot, and sandy, well-drained soil. It can grow to a height of 6 feet (1.8 m) under ideal conditions, although it is unusual to see it taller than 3 feet (0.9 m). It is widely used in cooking, especially in combination with lamb and potatoes. Zones 8–10.

Sage (*Salvia officinalis***).** Sage is a shrubby, woody, strongly aromatic perennial with gray leaves. In early or late summer, depending on the weather, it bears purple-blue flowers that the bees love. It grows to 2 feet (60 cm), and its pungent leaves are used to flavor poultry and pork stuffings, pasta and rice, and vinegar. It also makes a pleasant tea. It is relatively hardy and likes full sun and a well-drained soil. Zones 4–9.

Savory (*Satureja* **spp.).** Summer savory (*S. hortensis*) is an annual; winter savory (*S. montana*) is a perennial. Both grow 10 to 12 inches (25 to 30 cm) high and have a peppery, aromatic taste, a bit like thyme, although the annual has a more delicate, pungent flavor. Both are used for flavoring in soups and stews. Savory has long, narrow leaves and small pink, white, or lavender flowers in summer. Winter savory prefers to grow in a fairly dry, ordinary soil and summer savory needs a richer, moister soil. They both prefer sun. Winter savory, zones 4–9.

Tarragon, French (*Artemisia dracunculus* **'***Sativus***').** This wonderful kitchen herb is always grown from cuttings or root divisions. It is a perennial and grows 18 inches to 2 feet (45 to 60 cm) tall, spreading slowly. The leaves have a distinctively hot but subtle flavor and are especially good with chicken. Plant it in good, well-drained soil in the sun. Tarragon's elusive flavor is often lost when the herb is dried. My preferred method is to cut the herb when it is at its peak in midsummer, take all the fragile leaves off the stems, and dry them flat, in a warm, dry, dark place, as quickly as possible. Store in a glass container with a little salt in the bottom to absorb any moisture. Zones 4–9.

Thyme (*Thymus* **spp.).** There are many types and flavors of this important perennial and kitchen herb. All the thymes have small, strongly scented leaves that release their scent when crushed, as do most herbs. *Thymus vulgaris,* the common thyme, reaches about 12 inches (30 cm) in height; its white, pink, or mauve flowers on small flower spikes are borne in late spring or early summer and are attractive to bees. Thyme grows well from seeds, cuttings, and layerings and prefers full sun and dry, sandy soil. It is widely used in Europe as a flavoring in soups and stews. Try adding a few leaves of lemon thyme, *T. citriodorus,* to your salads for a little extra zip. Zones 5–9.

The kitchen medicine chest

It is nice to be able to reach into the kitchen cupboard, rather than the medicine chest, to treat some common ailments, especially if you can use your own herbs. You will be making most of the herbs into tea. To do this, pour 1 cup (250 ml) of boiling water over 1 to 3 tablespoons (15 to 45 ml) of the herb. Infuse, covered, for ten to fifteen minutes. Strain and drink.

Here is a short list of some of the things you can do with the plants listed above:

- To soothe the digestive system after a meal and dispel any gas or flatulence, the following herbs can be used singly or in combination: dried parsley, peppermint leaves, fennel seeds, dill seeds, basil leaves, rosemary leaves, and thyme leaves.
- To treat and prevent colds and flu: eat one or two raw cloves of garlic a day. Honest. (And then you'll need some parsley, for sure.)
- For a sore throat: gargle with a tea of sage leaves.
- To relieve coughing and as a general antibacterial: a tea of thyme leaves.
- To help you sleep at night: a tea of lemon balm leaves and/or chamomile flowers.
- As a tonic to the nervous system, and to ease muscular pains: a tea of rosemary leaves and/or lavender flowers.
- To soothe insect bites: a tea of lemon balm leaves applied to the bites.
- To heal and soothe delicate skin: infuse the petals of pot marigold in olive oil and rub the oil onto the damaged skin.
- For babies with colic: a tea of fennel seeds, dill seeds, and lavender flowers.

Additional plants

Other plants that look attractive in the herb garden include spring bulbs, such as snowdrops, daffodils, grape hyacinths, and tulips, and the traditional rose of the medieval herb garden, *Rosa gallica* 'Officinalis', also known as the apothecary's rose.

An excellent edging shrub is *Buxus sempervirens* 'Suffruticosa' (dwarf common boxwood). This perennial evergreen shrub can be kept trimmed to 8 inches (20 cm) and forms a tight, dense mass of bright green oval leaves. It bears insignificant flowers in late spring or early summer. Hardier plants include *Teucrium chamaedrys* (wall germander), *Santolina chamaecyparissus* syn. *S. incana* (cotton lavender), *Fragaria vesca* (alpine strawberry), and *Origanum vulgare* 'Aureum' (golden marjoram).

A herbal window box for a sunny spot

Window boxes are very versatile. Besides being hung under a window, they can be attached to a wall or balcony, within easy reach for summer picking. The plants given below can easily be interchanged with others if you prefer.

Materials

- Container: a wooden planter approximately 4 feet (1.2 m) long by 1 foot (30 cm) wide by 10 inches (25 cm) deep, and painted a light gray color.
- Potting mixture: basic soil mix and organic fertilizer.
- Plants: choose your favorites from the herbs listed above or add your own. You will need biennial and perennial plants and some packets of seeds and/or annual seedlings. Your box might include rosemary, thyme, sage, parsley, fennel, oregano, chives, and lavender plants, and pot marigold, borage, and chamomile seeds.

Method

Fill the planter with soil to within an inch (2.5 cm) of the top of the planter. Plant the herbs so that they are evenly spaced and pleasingly arranged: be creative! Scatter the seeds of the annuals among the plants and water well.

Aftercare

Water every day and fertilize every other week during the growing season with fish or seaweed fertilizer. Cut herbs as needed and enjoy.

The multicultural vegetable garden

Growing your own vegetables brings fresh taste and flavor to the table

IF YOU HAVE EVER GROWN YOUR OWN VEGETABLES YOU WILL KNOW THAT they are better than anything you can buy in the stores. Fresh, flavorful, and energy-packed, home-grown vegetables taste of the warmth of the sun and the richness of the soil. Vegetables that go straight from the garden to the kitchen lose none of their vitamins and minerals along the way, and they will be sweeter, juicier, and more tender than commercial produce. These are compelling reasons to have your own vegetable patch. But perhaps one of the best reasons of all is that it is so satisfying to sow, nurture, and grow edible plants for your own table.

Many vegetables remind us of different cultures and parts of the world. Just as Italian cooking is unthinkable without tomatoes, so French cooking wouldn't exist without garlic. In China the markets and restaurants are full of succulent, tender young Chinese greens, and in Germany the people have raised the humble cabbage to culinary heights, preparing it fermented, for sauerkraut, and in many other interesting ways.

Today we eat vegetables grown in many other parts of the world, both in and out of season, and usually pay scant attention to their cultural origins. Yet it is a treat to come across gardens where the origins of the gardeners are instantly apparent because of the fruits and vegetables they grow. This yields such memorable sights as a huge tropical greenhouse filled with banana plants, thriving in the middle of a Canadian winter, and a city patio covered with red-hot chili peppers, destined to be made into the best salsa in town.

Although you may not share the passions of the retired Portuguese-born farmer who grows bananas, or the ex-Cuban scientist who grows chilis, you will have your own cultural roots, shoots, and preferences that seek expression. Your mini-garden, where space is so limited, is the perfect place to do this, and to experiment with other personal favorites: perhaps a planter full of waving corn, with bright tubs of red chili peppers and tomatoes; or a green garden full of exotic salad ingredients for summer and hardier greens, such as Chinese greens, broccoli, Brussels sprouts, and cabbages, for the fall. Maybe, if you're Irish, a crop of potatoes; or a bed of leeks for the Welsh; or Brussels sprouts for the English.

Since your vegetable garden will be small and constantly on show, you'll want to plan the selection of vegetables carefully and plant it with an eye for color and design. This is a good opportunity to try new cultivars of old favorites that have been hybridized to grow in small containers. Vegetables mature and are harvested throughout the season, so you will be able to replant continuously—a chance to have fun and experiment. A sunny, protected patio or balcony can become a microclimate where vegetables can be planted earlier and harvested later than would otherwise be possible.

It is possible to grow a wide selection of vegetables in a container garden, just as it is in the average family vegetable plot. Since space is limited, it is most important to make sure the soil stays healthy and pests and diseases are kept under control. As many balcony gardeners know from experience, aphids, carrot rust fly, mildew, black spot, and other insects and diseases are just as likely to find a tenth-floor balcony or roof garden as they are to invade a garden at ground level.

Vegetable gardening lends itself well to raised beds, which are easily achieved by constructing wood-sided planters. A good width for balcony vegetable planters is 30 inches (75 cm). This allows plenty of space to grow short rows of vegetables. The planters can be assembled in modules of various sizes, depending upon the space available. Each planter needs at least an eight-inch (20 cm) depth of soil to grow most vegetables successfully; ten to twelve inches (25 to 30 cm) is a much better depth, and essential for root crops. Round five-gallon (23-L) containers are excellent for sun-loving vegetables such as tomatoes and green peppers, and the different containers look quite decorative, especially if they have been set into baskets and are overflowing with ripening produce.

An old wooden chair and table set among the planters can provide a comfortable resting spot to admire your growing harvest. If you have room, and an extra half-barrel, line it with heavy-gauge plastic and collect rain for watering your plants. Place an old watering can next to the barrel and your vegetable garden will be as aesthetically pleasing as it is functional.

If there is only room for a few pots, you may not be able to feed the family all summer from them, but you can still have fun and use the opportunity to grow exotic vegetables, such as artichokes, or unusual salad greens, such as arugula and ruby Swiss chard. If space is restricted to hanging planters, try a vegetable hanging basket. As long as you water the basket faithfully once or twice a day and feed it once a week, you can harvest a surprisingly large number of vegetables to delight dinner guests.

Whatever the vegetables you decide to grow, do make sure they will do well in your area. Good garden centers are usually very helpful with advice about this and will carry seeds from a reputable local company, as well as from the larger seed houses. If you are growing vegetables for the first time, you may want to start with some of the basics, such as carrots, lettuce, beans, zucchini, and beets, with separate containers for sun-hungry tomatoes, peppers, and eggplants. Climbing vegetables, such as scarlet runner beans, will grow very quickly up a wall or trellis and can be used to hide an ugly neighboring structure or soften the edges of the patio.

Generally, vegetables will mature earlier when beds are raised, since the beds drain better and warm up more quickly in the spring. They will also be productive until later in the fall, especially if the plants can be protected at night with a cold frame (see "Practical Details: Winterizing"). Thus gardening in small spaces is ideal for extending the growing season and increasing the overall yield. Many cool-weather vegetables can be grown well into the winter months in milder areas, including Oriental vegetables, such as Chinese broccoli, choy, and cabbage, as well as European winter vegetables, such as kale, celery, mustard greens, and Swiss chard. Check with garden centers to see which vegetables can grow into the winter months in your area, and experiment.

Most vegetables need abundant sunshine to reach maturity at the right time, although you do have to be careful not to bake them if you have an all-concrete patio or balcony that gets full sun all day. You may need some trellising or light screening against the noonday heat. Adequate watering is also an important consideration. If at all possible, you may want to put in a timed sprinkling system to make your job easier.

Soil and nutrient requirements for vegetables

As a general rule, most vegetables need a nutrient-rich, loamy soil, with lots of good organic matter and a healthy population of earthworms for constant soil aeration. Some vegetables, such as carrots and asparagus, prefer a lighter, more sandy soil; add some sand to your basic mix to grow these vegetables successfully. Likewise, vegetables such as zucchini and Swiss chard are very heavy feeders and need much more nourishment than others.

It is best to start with a general soil mix and amend it for the needs of each vegetable. Garden soil should not be used in containers. It has a tendency to compact like concrete, becoming very heavy and clogging the plants' roots. A good-quality container soil mix, available from most garden centers, is fine. Since these mixes do not have the same nutrient value as enriched garden soil, it is a good idea to add some organic fertilizer to it before planting. For more information see "Practical Details: Soil and amendments."

Leafy vegetables, like lettuce, spinach, cabbage, and Swiss chard, will benefit from a little extra nitrogen (manure, decaying organic matter) so that the leaves will grow faster and be more tender. Too much nitrogen will cause the plants to be higher in carbohydrates and lower in vitamins. Fruiting vegetables, such as tomatoes, eggplants, peas, and beans, need a little extra phosphorus (bone meal, rock phosphate, shells) as well as nitrogen. Root vegetables need a bit more potassium (manure, compost, wood ash), but again not too much. The right balance of nutrients will help your vegetables to grow healthy and strong. If you are in doubt about the composition of your soil mix, it is worth sending a sample to your nearest soil analysis laboratory. They will be able to tell you what nutrients are lacking in the soil. A good garden center should be able to help you with this.

The soil should be replenished with compost or well-rotted manure at the beginning of every season, or replaced if necessary, and it is a good idea to rotate your crops annually to prevent the spread of pests and diseases. There is an easy rule to follow for this: do not grow vegetables that belong to the same family in the same spot two years in a row (see list of common vegetables and their families below).

Container crops need to be watered as often as two to three times a day, depending upon the temperature and size of the containers. Since frequent watering will leach out many soil nutrients, it is necessary to use a soluble fertilizer every two weeks throughout the growing season. Mulching the soil surface with 2 inches (5 cm) of organic matter will help to conserve moisture.

Setting the scene

The following checklist will help you start creating a vegetable garden on your balcony or patio.
- Six to eight hours of sunshine a day.
- Separate 5-gallon (23-L) containers for sun-loving vegetables, such as tomatoes, green peppers, and eggplant.
- Wooden planter boxes to fit your space.
- Appropriate soil mix and fertilizer for various vegetables.
- Vegetable seeds and plants of your choice, as suggested below.
- Basic gardening tools and storage; you may want to store tools on hooks on the wall (under an overhang so they don't get wet).
- Floating row cover material to keep pests from tender young vegetables, and to provide some insulation and protection.
- Watering system. Vegetables need constant watering, so an automated watering system is a real bonus. If this is not possible, keep a water bucket or barrel filled all the time, and have a watering can handy.
- If there is space, a table and chairs.
- If there is space, a cold frame to extend the growing season.

If neat, orderly rows of vegetables take your mind back to the farm, you may want to add some props, such as a garden scarecrow, some farmyard animals made out of concrete, old farm implements, or even a child's model tractor. If you can buy farm-fresh eggs where you live, so much the better.

A starter selection of vegetables

Once you have chosen vegetables you like, do check that they can be grown where you live, with your exposure and climate. Cultivars that work well on the coast may not do well in hot, dry interior conditions, and vice versa, so buy seeds and plants that are selected for your climate. Many vegetables can be grown from seed and planted directly into the ground. Others need to be started indoors and transferred outside as soon as all danger of frost is past. However, remember that vegetables in containers are more vulnerable to late spring frosts than they would be if they were planted in the garden, and they may need extra protection. If you follow the general guidelines and planting dates for growing vegetables in your area and use cultivars suitable for your climate, your vegetable garden will be a great success.

Below are listed some commonly grown vegetables, and the families to which they belong.

The cabbage family (Brassicaceae or Cruciferae)

Most of these vegetables are heavy feeders, especially broccoli and cabbage, and will need a good rich soil to do well, with plenty of manure or other nitrogen-rich fertilizer added. They should be fertilized with a balanced fertilizer once a month. All are susceptible to damage by the cabbage moth, and should be protected for as long as possible by covering them with a floating row cover.

Broccoli can be sown from April to mid-July for harvesting from August onwards. You can start plants directly in the container by sowing three or four seeds in a spot and thinning to the strongest plant when the seedlings are about 1 inch (2.5 cm) tall.

Cabbage. Green, red, and Savoy cabbages can all be grown in containers. Different cultivars will mature at different times, either early, midseason, or late; sow seeds from mid-April to early July, depending on the harvest time. Protect the seedlings from cutworm injury by placing collars made out of paper or cardboard around them. Alternatively, sometimes it works to sprinkle a handful of wood ash or dolomite lime around the base of the plant.

Chinese cabbage. Two types of cabbage are referred to as Chinese cabbage; those that form a head, and those that don't. The best known are the ones that don't, such as bok choy and Chinese mustard cabbage. Sow the seeds in late spring for a summer crop and early summer for a fall harvest.

Collard is grown for its green leaves. Sow the seeds mid-July, and harvest from mid-September onwards. Collard will survive cooler temperatures than will other members of the family, and it can be grown as a winter vegetable in some climates. When harvesting, leave the lower six to eight leaves to sustain growth and pick young leaves as the plant continues to grow.

Kale is easy to grow. It can be sown directly into the ground from mid-June to mid-

July and harvested from late fall to spring in some climates. Frost sweetens the taste and it is a particularly good dietary source of iron. The tender, young leaves are excellent in salads. Little growth occurs during the winter months, but when the weather warms it will continue to grow and should be fertilized again.

Kohlrabi produces a turnip-sized, edible, swollen stem that grows above ground and looks similar to a turnip. It can be eaten raw, stir-fried, or steamed. Begin sowing two weeks after the last frost, and continue every two weeks from spring onwards for a continuous crop. Harvest when less than 2 inches (5 cm) in diameter.

Radish. Sow radish seeds in empty spaces between other vegetables in early spring, as soon as the ground can be worked. They mature quickly and can be harvested in as little as three weeks. Seeds planted in spring will require full sun, but seeds sown later will grow well in part shade.

Arugula is also easy to grow and germinates quickly. Its leaves have a sharp, nutty, peppery flavor, making it increasingly popular as a salad green. Arugula is expensive to buy in the stores, but one packet of seeds will supply you all summer long. Sow every few weeks starting in early spring for a continuous supply.

The tomato family (Solanaceae)

The most important things to remember about eggplants, peppers, and tomatoes are: they need lots of sun; any frost damages them; and they should never be watered from above, since this encourages rot and other fungal diseases. They like rich soil, and are well suited to growing in pots. All of them can be grown from seed; started indoors in late March or early April they can be planted outside in June, as soon as the weather is reliably warm (above 55°F/13°C). They require at least six hours of sunshine a day and daytime temperatures between 65 to 85°F (16 and 25°C) for four months if their fruits are to mature and ripen. If your climate is not usually this warm, try growing them in a cold frame for protection and added warmth, or choose cool-weather cultivars.

Eggplant is very attractive grown on its own, or combined with flowers. It takes three weeks for the seeds to germinate, and another eight weeks before the seedlings are ready to plant outdoors. Eggplants grow best in a slightly acidic soil, and the fruits mature about two and a half months after planting. They are ready to pick when the skin is a very shiny purple color, and are overripe when the skin becomes dull.

Pepper. Any kind of pepper is worth growing for its ornamental value alone. They grow best in a neutral or slightly acidic soil, and are especially suited to hot, dry climates. There are many excellent cultivars, in various shades of green, red, orange, yellow, and purple. Some are very hot; others are mild and sweet.

Tomato. Tomatoes are available in a wide range of shapes and sizes; many have been specifically cultivated for growing in containers and for different climatic conditions. Some of the larger tomatoes will require their own five-gallon (23-L) containers, while others are small enough to do well in 8-inch (20 cm) pots or hanging baskets.

Potato. Potatoes are quite different from eggplants, tomatoes, and peppers, since they are a root crop. They can be grown in containers, although they do take up a lot of room for the size of the crop. However, it is well worth trying to grow some, even if you only have one five-gallon (23-L) container. They need an acid, light, sandy soil, and should never be planted in heavily manured soil. Plant two seed pieces in the container in early spring, and make sure the soil stays moist and drains very well. With any luck you will have a harvest about three months later.

The beet family (Chenopodiaceae)

Beets and their close relatives, Swiss chard and spinach, are easy to grow from seed or nursery-grown plants and are high in vitamins and minerals.

Beet. Beets are one of the most economical vegetables of all, since you can eat both roots and tops. Sow every two weeks from April to mid-July for a continuous harvest. They need a fertile, well-drained soil that has been sweetened with a sprinkling of lime.

Spinach. Spinach is fast-growing but can't take long days or hot temperatures. Sow seeds in early spring and again in early fall in rich, organic soil and full sun. Add nitrogen to the soil.

Swiss chard. Swiss chard, a beet without the root, is grown for its green leaves, which are ornamental as well as nutritious. Chard is an excellent substitute if it is too warm to grow spinach. Sow the seeds directly into the ground every two weeks from April through mid-July.

The pea family (Fabaceae or Leguminosae)

All the legumes like organically rich, alkaline soil, but they do not need a lot of nitrogen; they are able to convert nitrogen gas from the air into usable nitrates, enriching the soil. The best fertilizer for them is one that is high in bone meal. Beans and peas grow rapidly, produce a bountiful harvest, and need little attention.

Bush bean. Snap, wax, purple, and green beans are all known as bush beans and are well worth growing yourself since tasty ones are often hard to find in the grocery store. There are some excellent compact cultivars that grow well in containers. They need warm soil to germinate and can be sown from mid-May to the beginning of July outdoors, or start seeds indoors in April for planting out in May.

Pole bean. Beans that grow to a height of 6 feet (1.8 m) and more are called pole beans and they need the same growing conditions as bush beans. They must be staked on a trellis or wooden posts—thus providing an instant privacy screen, as well as a nutritious vegetable. To make a trellis framework for beans, stretch two wires, one at ground level and the other at about 6 feet (1.8 m), between two stout posts.

Connect the wires with twine, wrapping it every 8 inches (20 cm) or so along the wire. The beans will twine onto the trellis as they grow.

Scarlet runner bean. These beans resemble pole beans but have orange-colored flowers and fleshier pods and will continue to produce prolifically as long as the beans are picked regularly. They are best picked when small and tender—do not wait until they are nearly a foot (30 cm) long and tough and stringy.

The sunflower family (Asteraceae or Compositae)

Lettuce, dandelions, endive, and sunflowers are members of this family. All are easy to grow from seed, and they do even better with a weekly feed of liquid fertilizer.

Dandelion. The greens are delicious to eat, especially when young, and they are high in vitamins and minerals. If a few dandelions decide to volunteer in your pots, throw the leaves into the salad rather than the compost. The roots can be used in vegetable stews.

Endive. The plant resembles lettuce and has slender leaves with wavy, deeply cut edges. Sow seeds mid-April for a late spring harvest, and midsummer for a fall harvest. Endive tolerates frost, and can be harvested throughout the winter where weather permits.

Lettuce. With the aid of a cold frame, lettuce can be grown all year round in many areas. Sow at two-week intervals, in small amounts, starting in April, and continue to mid-August with frost-resistant, winter-hardy cultivars. There are many interesting lettuce seed mixes that are worth trying for more exciting salads.

The onion family (Alliaceae)

Onions, garlic, green onions, leeks, scallions, and shallots are easy enough to grow with a minimum of care, and there are cultivars suitable to most climates. They need fairly deep, well-fertilized soil.

Leek. Leeks are an interesting cool-season vegetable that can be harvested throughout the winter where weather permits. They require a long growing period, and should be fertilized monthly with a granular organic fertilizer for best results. Sow seeds or plant seedlings into a trench and gradually fill the trench with soil as the leeks develop; this blanches them.

The pumpkin family (Cucurbitaceae)

Given the right conditions, these vegetables will trail everywhere, and their vines will grow visibly each day. They like lots of good, organic matter in the soil, and will need constant fertilizing in a pot, but will certainly brighten up a dull, uninteresting corner. The family includes cucumbers, melons, pumpkins, squash, and zucchini.

Cucumber. Cucumbers need warm, dry, growing conditions to do well, and in some areas this may mean waiting until June to sow the seeds. To avoid a bitter taste, ensure the plants are well watered. Cucumber plants can easily be trained up a trellis.

Muskmelon or cantaloupe. Melons should be started indoors in April and planted outdoors in a container in early June. They require full sun and well-drained soil. One five-gallon (23-L) container per plant is ideal.

Squash, pumpkin, and marrow. This large group includes all the plants we know as squash, including spaghetti, acorn, butternut, patty-pan, crookneck, winter, zucchini, vegetable marrow, and pumpkins. They are usually divided into two categories, winter or summer. Summer squash are eaten when they are small, and the skin is thin. They include zucchini, patty-pan, and crooknecks. Winter squash, such as butternut and acorn squash, marrow, and pumpkin, are not harvested until the frost hardens the skin. Then they can be stored for the winter. One plant of both a summer and winter squash will be more than enough for a small family, one five-gallon (23-L) container per plant. Squashes require a fertile, well-drained, rich soil, and plenty of sunshine.

The carrot family (Apiaceae or Umbelliferae)

The two best-known members of this family are carrots and parsley, both of which are slow to germinate and prefer a well-drained, light, sandy soil. To protect them against the carrot rust fly, use a floating row cover until the plants are a good size.

Carrot. Carrots are most tasty when they are young, so it is a good idea to sow successive crops at three-week intervals from mid-April to July, which will ensure a continuous harvest. Fertilize them twice during the growing season.

Other vegetables

Asparagus. Most vegetables are annuals, which means they have a life span of one growing season and must be replanted every year. Asparagus is an exception. It is a perennial vegetable that may produce asparagus spears for twenty to thirty years from one plant. If the container is large enough, (at least 12 inches /30 cm deep and 2 feet /60 cm across) with good drainage and a sandy soil amended with compost or manure, asparagus will grow happily on a sunny or partly shady rooftop or balcony. Prepare the container by digging a wide, flat hole 10 inches (25 cm) deep. Plant one- or two-year-old crowns, cover them with 2 inches (5 cm) of soil, and add more soil on top as the plants grow. Mulch the beds every spring with aged manure and fertilize with granular organic fertilizer in July. Keep the plants well watered, and wait until their second year before harvesting.

Corn. If you have lots of room and sunshine, corn will grow well in containers in a rich soil amended with compost. Choose a small hybrid, and grow it in clusters of four plants spaced about 6 inches (15 cm) apart. Fertilize once a month.

A vegetable hanging basket

Many vegetables are quite happy growing in a lovely moss basket in a sunny location. This recipe is a guide to get you started on your own interesting hanging vegetable basket. Be imaginative and creative in your selection of vegetables, and add some edible flowers, such as nasturtiums and marigolds, for use in salads.

Materials

- Container: a wire basket, 16 inches (40 cm) in diameter and 10 inches (25 cm) deep, with wire hangers for suspending the basket.
- Potting mixture: basic soil mix enriched with bone meal and organic fertilizer.
- Moss for lining the sides of the basket.
- Plant materials: you will need about twenty young plants, either grown from seed or bought from a garden center. The plants below are a guideline; others can be substituted if you like. For example, you can use beets or carrots on top instead of tomatoes.
  — For the top: one or two bush tomato plants, patio cultivars that do not need staking; and five chive plants.
  — For the sides: four leaf lettuce plants, same or different kinds; three spinach plants; three basil plants; and three parsley plants.

Method

Line the basket with a generous layer of moss, starting at the base and working up the sides. Press the moss firmly into the sides and bottom of the basket. Form a collar of moss above the rim of the basket at the top. Place a circle of plastic sheeting in the bottom of the basket to act as a water reservoir and fill the basket three-quarters full with the soil mixture.

There are thirteen side plants. Plan roughly where they will go before beginning to plant. Make sure to distribute them evenly around the basket. Start planting at the lower end. Pass the roots of the young plants through the wire sides and moss lining, making sure the plants are pushed well into the soil and planted firmly. Add more soil and continue planting up the sides (Fig. 1).

Finish with the plants at the top. Start by placing one or two

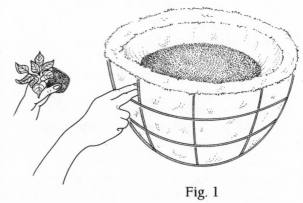

Fig. 1

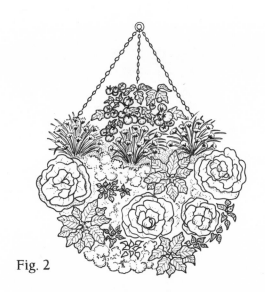

Fig. 2

small stakes into the center, and plant the tomatoes next to them. Arrange the chives around the top rim. Hang the basket on a secure support (it can weigh up to 70 pounds / 32 kg when wet) in a sunny location (Fig. 2).

Aftercare

Water the basket every day, twice a day during dry weather. Fertilize with fish or seaweed fertilizer once or twice a week. After you have harvested your vegetables, dismantle the basket and store, ready for use next year. As long as they are not diseased, tomato foliage and stems can go into a compost. Note: tomato late blight is an increasingly common problem. To protect your plants, never water them from above. If it is a problem in your area, check with your garden center or local experts for pest and disease information. You may need to use a copper spray on young plants.

Santa Fe style

About adobe, fiery food, and the colorful American Southwest

AT THE HEART OF THE NORTHERN NEW MEXICO PLAIN, NESTLED IN THE foothills of the Sangre de Cristo mountains, is the town of Santa Fe, a mecca for artists and shoppers alike. For its size, Santa Fe has more art galleries than any other city in the world. Here you can buy a wide selection of locally crafted goods, including native American pottery, jewelry and blankets; Hispanic metalwork, country furniture, and religious icons; paintings and sculpture; and even award-winning local wines and New Mexican hot chili peppers.

For generations Santa Fe has attracted artists, photographers, and writers, as well as those in search of spiritual growth. Even first-time visitors to the town are smitten by its old-world charm and relaxed pace as they wander its crooked streets and nearby hills. The narrow streets are lined with rustic adobe houses, squatting behind hand-carved wooden gates and half-hidden by gnarled cottonwoods and softly hued holly-hocks. Much of the character of the town comes from the distinctive architecture of the sandy-colored houses, set among rolling hills dotted with piñon pines and juniper trees. Brightly colored pink and turquoise windows and doorways, funky mailboxes, bleached cattle skulls, and braided strings, or *ristras,* of chili peppers decorate the houses, under an expanse of bright blue sky.

In summertime the tourists and locals mingle under the warm high-desert sun, eating more fiery food than in any other part of the country. In late summer the air is full of the smell of roasting peppers, ready to be made into large vats of red and green chili sauce, and local restaurants are justly famous for their marvelous spicy cooking. Chili peppers hang everywhere, an emblem and prime industry for the state.

Santa Fe is a seductive, intoxicating city of magic that entices visitors to come back again and again. If you are among those people who have fallen in love with this part of the world, why not turn your patio or balcony into a little bit of New Mexico, wherever you live? You may not have endless blue skies, but it is easy to re-create the vibrant colors and soft adobe look of the American Southwest, the warm, sandy tones of the desert, and the vibrant reds, yellows, and oranges of heat-loving flowers and chilis. A Mexican wood and leather chair and small table set in one corner of your patio or balcony makes an ideal setting for reading the latest Tony Hillerman thriller, while you're eating nachos and sipping on a marguerita.

The Santa Fe look is an easy one to copy, even if you have limited gardening experience, since its effect is created more by the simple arrangement of furniture, objects, rocks, and pots than by elaborate planting. If your patio is enclosed, so much the better. This will allow you to paint walls or fencing in desert tones, cover the ground with a layer of sand-colored pea gravel or with sandstone or tile pavers, and decorate the garden area with simple Mexican patio furniture, earthenware pots, and wooden artifacts.

Tall, urn-shaped earthen pots look very attractive in this plan, especially when filled with geraniums, coneflowers, bougainvillea, sneezeweed, and other bold flowers that combine the hot hues and tones of summer. You can also use an old wheelbarrow or hollowed-out log filled with the same hot colors, reminiscent of the burnt-dry heat and parched desert hillsides of the high plains, or fill your pots with various kinds of chili peppers that will add color to your garden and zip to your cooking. For a green and softening effect, plant some of your pots or containers with small pines or junipers.

This can be quite striking on a small balcony, especially if you choose your earthenware pots with care. You may not be able to paint your balcony railing and wall, but you might be able to get away with a bright Navajo-style blanket or rug draped over the balcony for a bold backdrop, pots set on a bed of pea gravel, a casual chair and table for relaxation, and white or colored lights for decoration and ambiance in the evening. Even if you only have one pot, you can still echo the heat and sizzle of the desert with your choice of colors and plant materials.

A winter scene can be effective on any patio or balcony when the snow covers pots and small evergreens, especially if the trees are decorated with small, twinkling white lights. In Santa Fe the snow blankets lawns and benches in city parks and softens the already-mellow adobe. It falls heavily on the nearby mountains, making the area a haven for winter sports enthusiasts. The tops of walls and flat roofs of houses and hotels are decorated with transparent, square-shaped containers with little bright lights inside, known as lumières. They cast soft, warm shadows over the tranquil city. Sound is muffled and time seems to stand still.

The shops are filled with offbeat strings of novelty Christmas lights, everything from red and green chilis to spotted cows, pink rabbits, colored fish, and rows of underwear. Many stores outside New Mexico carry these lights, and you can use them to add some fun and humor to your outdoor space. If you prefer the more classic and traditional Santa Fe winter lighting, you may want to make some paper lumières. They cast a lovely, gentle light and are especially effective if you are looking out at them from inside a warm room (see "How to make lumières," below).

Setting the scene

The following checklist will help you start creating a little corner of New Mexico on your balcony or patio.

- Six to eight hours of sunshine a day.
- Lathe or wood fencing for edging the patio or balcony.
- Sand-colored outdoor paint for walls and fencing.
- Sand-colored flooring, pavers, or pea gravel for an all-over sandy, desert look.
- Simple earthenware pots, preferably large and urn-shaped (at least 18 inches / 45 cm in depth and diameter), to fit the space.
- A selection of hot-colored plants and evergreens, chosen from the plant list below.
- Basic soil mix and fertilizer.
- Basic garden tools and storage.
- A watering system.
- If there is room, a table and chairs, preferably made of Mexican wood and pigskin.
- A brightly colored blanket, Navajo-style.
- Colored strings of novelty lights and/or lumières.

For a real Southwest flair, try surprising friends with a meal of beans, posole, and Indian corn bread. Decorate the walls with Hispanic tinwork and woven rugs, relax, and listen for the coyote's howl.

Hot-colored plants and evergreen trees

This theme is a great one for those who love the warm and hot colors—the reds, oranges, and yellows of summer heat. There are so many plants that fall into this color range, especially the easy-care members of the aster, or sunflower, family, that you should have no trouble filling your pots quickly and inexpensively with plants from your local garden center. The following list of plants should get you started; they will all do best with at least six hours of sunshine a day. Water them every day and feed every other week during the growing season.

Climbers

Bougainvillea spp. Vigorous, shrubby climbers that can grow up to 22 feet (6.6 m) depending upon the species. They will not grow as tall in a pot, and can be lightly staked and pruned to maintain a desired height. Bougainvillea are grown mainly for the showy clusters of floral bracts they bear in the summer. Unless your outside temperature stays above 45°F (7°C) all year, you will have to bring the plant in during the colder months. Good cultivars are 'Tahitian Maid', blush pink; 'Barbara Karst', brilliant crimson red; and 'California Gold', gold. Zone 10.

Lonicera spp. (honeysuckle). Honeysuckle can be used instead of bougainvillea and it is much more hardy. Most honeysuckles are deciduous, with oval leaves and trumpetlike flowers. They are twining climbers and will need some kind of support. Good forms are *L. sempervirens,* salmon-red to orange flowers with yellow insides; *L.* x *brownii* 'Dropmore Scarlet', red. Both are zones 4–9. The flowers of *L.* x *tellmanniana* are bright yellowish-orange, spotted crimson. Zones 7–9. One excellent evergreen species is *L. henryii,* with small mauve flowers and black berries in the fall. Zones 7–10.

Perennials

Coreopsis grandiflora 'Sunray' (tickseed). A spreading, clump-forming perennial that can also be grown as an annual, it has daisylike, double, bright yellow flower heads in summer. It grows to 18 inches (45 cm). Zones 4–9.

Echinacea purpurea (purple coneflower). Purple coneflower is an upright perennial with lance-shaped, dark green leaves. Its large, daisylike, deep crimson-pink flower heads with conical brown centers are borne singly on strong stems in summer. It grows from 2 to 2 1/2 feet (60 to 75 cm). Zones 3–9.

Gazania hybrids (gazania). These are perennials that are usually grown as annuals. They have dark green lanceolate foliage and large daisylike flowers in shades of pink, red, bronze, and orange, which close in the evening. They grow to a height of about 12 inches (30 cm), and like full sun and a well-drained soil. Zones 8–10.

Helenium autumnale 'Bruno' and 'Moerheim Beauty' (sneezeweed). Strong upright perennials with dark green leaves and long-lasting daisylike flowers in late summer and fall. 'Bruno' grows from 2 to 4 feet (60 cm to 1.2 m) and is crimson-mahogany, and 'Moerheim Beauty' grows to 3 feet (90 cm) and is a rich reddish-orange. Zones 3–9.

Helianthus x *multiflorus* (sunflower). An upright perennial relative of the common sunflower that bears large, double, golden-yellow flower heads in late summer and early fall. The blooms of 'Loddon Gold' are deep yellow, on 5-foot (1.5-m) flower stalks. Zones 4–9.

Heliopsis spp. (false sunflower). This genus closely resembles true sunflowers but has a much smaller growth habit. It is an upright perennial with dark green leaves and bears flowers freely in late summer. 'Ballet Dancer' has double yellow flower heads with frilled petals and grows from 3 to 4 feet (0.9 to 1.2 m). Zones 2–9.

Penstemon campanulatus (beard-tongue). A vigorous, semievergreen, bushy perennial that blooms from midsummer to fall and has narrow, bright green leaves and sprays of tubular pink, dark purple, or violet flowers. It grows to 2 feet (60 cm). Zones 4–9. 'Garnet' is an attractive but less hardy cultivar with deep wine-red flowers. It blooms profusely in the summer and fall and grows to 2 feet (60 cm). Zones 8–9.

Rudbeckia spp. (coneflower). Moderately fast-growing, erect, branching perennial that is often grown as an annual and bears daisylike, golden-orange flowers with brown centers in summer and early fall. *R. laciniata* 'Gold Drop' grows to 2 to 3 feet (60 to 90 cm); *R. fulgida* 'Goldsturm' to 2 feet (60 cm); and *R. nitida* 'Herbstsonne', one of the finest coneflowers available, to 5 to 6 feet (1.5 to 1.8 m). Zones 3–9.

Tanacetum coccineum 'Robinson's Rose' (painted daisy, pyrethrum). Attractive upright perennial that blooms in late spring and early summer. It has aromatic, feathery leaves and daisylike, single, magenta-pink flower heads with yellow centers. It grows to 2 feet (60 cm). Zones 5–9.

Annuals

Capsicum spp. (chili peppers). Chili peppers are easy to grow in well-drained soil but do need lots of sun, just like their relatives, tomato and eggplant. Do not water them from above, and fertilize regularly during the growing season. For visual appeal, put three different cultivars of chili pepper in one pot; even better if they ripen at different times.

Helianthus annuus 'Teddy Bear' (annual sunflower). Dwarf cultivar of the popular sunflower that grows to 2 feet (60 cm) and is a fully-double deep yellow.

Pelargonium spp. (geranium). Commonly called geraniums, these plants hardly need an introduction. Although they are perennials they are usually grown as annuals and are available in a wide range of forms and colors. For this theme, try to stick to the hot pinks, reds, and magentas.

Dwarf conifers

There are several conifers that tolerate the confines of a container quite well and are available in dwarf forms suitable for a small space. The following would work well for this theme.

Juniperus spp. (juniper). There is a wide selection of dwarf juniper species and hybrids suitable for growing in containers. They range in height and spread from 6 inches to 6 feet (15 cm to 1.8 m). Dwarf cultivars include *J. communis* 'Compressa', and 'Hornibrookii'; and *J.* x *media* 'Blaauw', 'Blue and Gold', and 'Plumosa'. Cultivars are available for zones 3–9.

Picea abies (Norway spruce). Its usual height of 50 feet (17 m) makes it too big for the patio, but look for attractive dwarf forms such as 'Clanbrassiliana', 'Nidiformis', 'Pumila', and 'Will's Zwerg'. Zones 3–8.

Pinus spp. (pines). A genus of small to large conifers with needles in bundles of two, three, or five. Excellent dwarf forms, varying from 2 1/2 to 6 feet (75 cm to 1.8 m) in height and spread, are the cultivars of mountain pine, *P. mugo*, 'Gnom' and 'Mops', zones 3–7; the Japanese white pine, *P. parviflora* 'Adcock's Dwarf', zones 6–9; the dwarf Siberian pine, *P. pumila,* zones 4–7; the Scots pine, *P. sylvestris* 'Beuvronensis', zones 3–7; the white pine, *P. strobus* 'Nana', zones 4–9; and the beach pine, *P. contorta* 'Spaan's Dwarf', zones 6–8. For a truly Southwest look, try *P. aristata,* the bristle-cone pine, a native of Arizona and New Mexico: specimens of this species are among the oldest-known living plants (over 4,000 years old). It is a slow-growing, bushy conifer, hardy in zones 4–8.

How to make lumières

At Christmas time, the walls and flat roof edges of adobe houses and hotels in Santa Fe are decorated with lumières, which cast a soft glow over the city and its white blanket of snow. Paper lumières are very easy to make.

Materials

- Waxed brown or colored paper bags (lunch-bag size).
- Scissors.
- Wet sand.
- Small flat candles, the kind that are used underneath chafing dishes to keep food warm; one for each bag.

Method

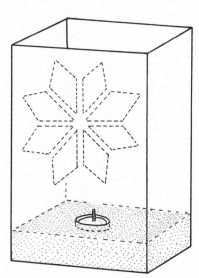

Draw a design, such as a star or a snowflake, on the outside of each paper bag, and cut the design into the bag; sometimes you can buy the bags with designs already cut into them. Put at least two inches (5 cm) of wet sand inside each bag. Set the candles into the sand so that the top of the metal container that holds the wax and the wick is flush with the top of the sand—this is important for safety reasons.

Place the bags on your patio or balcony in protected locations so that they will not fill with water if it rains; under the overhang of a building is a good place. Light the candles, and enjoy!

A colorful Southwest pot

The following combination of plants and materials will give you a hot and sunny pot from spring to late fall.

Materials

- Container: one large, preferably unglazed, urn-shaped terracotta pot, at least 18 inches (45 cm) in diameter and depth.
- Potting mixture: basic soil mix with a handful of bone meal and dolomite lime to sweeten the soil, and fertilizer.

- Plants: one pink or purple *Bougainvillea* spp.(bougainvillea); one *Tanacetum coccineum* 'Robinson's Rose' (painted daisy); one *Coreopsis grandiflora* 'Sunray' (tickseed); one *Rudbeckia nitida* 'Herbstsonne' (coneflower); and two *Pelargonium* spp. (geraniums).

Method

Half-fill the pot with the soil mix and arrange the plants so that the bougainvillea is at the back and the painted daisy, tickseed, and coneflower are in front. The geraniums should hang over the side of the pot. Make sure that the tops of the rootballs are about 1 inch (2.5 cm) below the rim of the pot, and fill in with soil to this level. Add a half-inch (1.2-cm) layer of fine gravel or sand to improve the drainage.

Water well, and place in a warm and sunny spot.

Aftercare

Water every day and fertilize every other week with liquid fertilizer during the growing season. Deadhead the flowers when they are spent.

The urban apple orchard

Dwarf root stock is the key to growing new and heritage fruits in small spaces

EVER SINCE EUROPEAN SETTLERS BROUGHT CUTTINGS OF FAVORITE APPLE trees with them from the old world, the apple has been the most popularly cultivated tree in North America. Wherever the climate made it possible, different apple cultivars for eating and baking were grown in orchards and home gardens, and growers shipped them as far afield as Europe and South America. Only one hundred years ago, North American apple growers harvested over eight hundred different kinds of apples in a range of flavors, colors, and textures we can only dream about today. Some that used to be commercially grown, such as the crisp, lemon-yellow Grimes Golden and the pineapple-flavored Ananas Reinettes can still be found in heritage collections, but many more fine old apples and other fruits have disappeared forever. They have been replaced in commerce by a mere few dozen cultivars, apples such as McIntosh, Spartan, and Red Delicious, pears like Anjou and Bartlett, and cherries such as Bing, that meet the exacting standards of modern agriculture.

Fortunately, a growing band of dedicated people is working to preserve what remains of the older cultivars and to encourage others to grow and enjoy a much wider selection of excellent fruit trees. Most of these growers are amateur horticulturists, and they form part of a worldwide network of people who are concerned about the future of all food crops if we continue to lose genetic diversity at the present rate. Thanks to their efforts, about 200 apple cultivars and 150 cultivars of other fruit trees have been preserved and cultivated, and a wide selection of heirloom apple trees and new, interesting cultivars is becoming more readily available in garden centers and stores. These special trees are, however, quite a different size from the trees of fifty years ago.

As towns and cities developed during the early part of the twentieth century, most town dwellers shared their backyards with an apple tree. The standard old apple tree often reached 30 feet (10 m) or more in height and width, and because it took up so much space, it often served as an extra clothesline, a place to hang a swing or to tie up the dog, and a climbing apparatus for children. When apples ripened in the fall, many a youngster risked life and limb to try and pick those most tantalizing, luscious apples that always seem to hang just out of reach.

Today, as land becomes more scarce, the old, familiar standard apple tree has been replaced by smaller, more compact models, better suited to town gardens, balconies, and patios. These compact trees are produced by grafting favorite cultivars of apples onto dwarf or semidwarf rootstock so that the tree is small, even though the apples are as big and tasty as ever. Dwarf trees are said to make better use of their nutrients than standard-sized trees do, and they will also start bearing fruit two to four years earlier. They are easier to prune, harvest, and care for, and they will live just as long as the larger trees.

The art of grafting apples onto rootstock was first practiced by the early Romans, and successive generations of gardeners have experimented with the technique. By the mid-nineteenth century, many different standards were used to rate rootstock material. The system was very confusing and needed to be simplified and standardized. In 1912 a standardization system was developed at the East Malling Research Station in England, and this is the one in use today.

Under the system, apple rootstocks are labeled with an "M" (for East Malling), followed by a number (indicating its dwarfing qualities). M9 and M27 are considered the most dwarfing; M9 produces a tree that is about 6 to 10 feet (1.8 to 3 m) tall, and M27 produces the smallest tree of all, at about half the size of M9. Another popular semidwarfing rootstock is M26, which produces trees that are 8 to 12 feet (2.4 to 4 m) in height and spread.

Providing the climate is favorable for growing apples, dwarfing rootstock makes it possible for apartment dwellers with a sunny balcony to grow their favorite cultivars of apples in containers. A wooden half-barrel is the ideal size, one for each tree. If you have a sunny wall you can train a tree to grow flat against the wall, a technique known as espaliering (see below). By careful pruning you can train your trees into any number of forms, giving an interesting year-round decorative effect, and there are many shapes from which to choose.

If you are interested in experimenting with espalier methods other than the ones described here, it is a good idea to consult one of the many books devoted to the subject. Most botanical gardens also have examples of espaliered fruit trees. Although espaliering can be labor-intensive for the first few years, it is relatively simple as long as you follow the basic rules, and the apple trees will yield a bigger crop because there is more leaf surface to capture light and more heat radiating from a sunny wall. If you don't have a wall, you can use bamboo stakes to train a young tree into shape.

Since many apples cannot self-pollinate, or are only partially successful at self-pollination, it is important to grow two or more cultivars that can cross-pollinate. Even if the tree can self-pollinate, the fruit set and yield is usually much greater if it is cross-pollinated. Thus, if you have room for several trees, be sure to grow cultivars that can cross-pollinate. If you are limited to growing just one tree, search for one that has three or four different cultivars grafted onto the same rootstock. A tree like this may be hard to find in your local garden center, but many of the specialty apple growers, such as Tsolum River Nurseries on Salt Spring Island, British Columbia; Bear Creek Nursery in Northport, Washington State; and Henry Leuthardt Nurseries of Long Island, New York, will graft cultivars to order and ship directly to you.

Fruits other than apples can also be grown in containers, although apples and pears are the best suited for espaliering. Pears, plums, peaches, nectarines, apricots, and cherries are all available in dwarf forms and many heritage and new hybrids are worth looking for. The list given below details some of these cultivars. There is no need to hurry; be sure to choose your trees carefully, because they could be with you for many, many years.

A patio or balcony orchard in half-barrels can be most effective, and is so simple to create. Paint the half-barrels white, with a black stripe around the middle for added contrast. Plant the trees in good, rich soil that has been amended with a couple of handfuls of organic fertilizer and some dolomite lime. Mulch every year in the very early spring with compost or well-rotted manure. Underplant the trees with small spring bulbs, such as crocuses, grape hyacinths, and snowdrops, for spring color, and with a ground cover such as alpine strawberries for summer. A checkered tablecloth draped generously over a table and a comfortable wooden chair covered with cushions will complete the picture.

Setting the scene

The following checklist will help you start creating an urban apple orchard on your patio or balcony.
- Six to eight hours of sunshine a day.
- One half-barrel, or equivalent-sized container, per tree.
- Fruit trees of your choice, preferably already partially trained.
- White and black outdoor paints and paint brush for painting the outside of the barrel.
- Bamboo or wooden stakes and raffia for training young trees.
- Basic soil mix, with added compost or well-rotted manure, organic fertilizer, and dolomite lime to sweeten the soil.
- A watering system, preferably a drip irrigation system so that the tree roots can be kept moist all the time.
- Basic gardening tools, including pruning shears, and storage.
- If space permits, a table and chairs.

When we think of apples we think of pollination, and bees, and honey. A nice idea would be to add some artificial bees to your patio or balcony. Place an old beehive in one corner, and stencil designs of bees on tables, chairs, cloths, barrels, or wherever they seem appropriate. On the table you could put a basket of fresh apples and a pot of honey to have with tea, and even some beeswax candles.

Fruit trees suitable for containers

Choose apple trees grown on rootstock suitable to your climate and be sure they can cross-pollinate. If you are unsure about either of these factors, consult with your local garden center or fruit-tree expert. As a rule of thumb, apples with the same parentage do not cross-pollinate well, so choose your cultivars with this in mind. The trees that grow best in containers are those that will stay the smallest, so for apples the root-stock should be either M9 or M27.

Apple trees generally grow well in most areas of North America. A few hardy kinds will grow in regions with very cool winters, and a few with low winter chilling requirements will even fruit in the warmer parts of the continent. Hardiness zones for apples are generally given as 4–8, but there are some that grow in 3 and 9. Pears, plums, apricots, peaches, cherries, and nectarines do not have quite the range of apples, and cannot tolerate very cold winters: zones are generally given as 5–8. If you are in doubt, be sure to consult your local garden center or botanical garden for information on the fruits that will grow well in your area, before you send away for a specially grafted tree.

Apples

Of the many cultivars available, here are a few excellent apples that grow well in containers.

'Akane'. A superior apple for the Pacific Northwest, 'Akane' is resistant to scab and powdery mildew, and lends itself well to espaliering. It was developed in Japan in the 1970s from a 'Jonathan' and a 'Worcester Pearmain' and is a bright cherry red when ripe, with white, crisp, juicy flesh. It stores quite well and should be picked in late August.

'Cox's Orange Pippin' and 'Fiesta'. 'Cox's Orange Pippin' is one of the most popular of the old English apples that have made it to North America. It is medium-sized, with orange-red markings on a deep yellow skin and a rich taste. It can be a bit hard to grow, depending upon the climate; however, its offspring 'Fiesta' (a cross between 'Cox's Orange Pippin' and 'Idared') has all the delicious flavor of a Cox's but keeps better. It is well worth a try.

'Fameuse' or 'Snow Apple'. One of Canada's oldest heritage apples, the 'Fameuse' or 'Snow Apple' is said to have come from France as a seed over three hundred years ago. It has crisp white flesh, streaked with red, and is a cold-country apple that ripens in October. Although it doesn't keep that well, it is still a good choice. Its most famous offspring is 'McIntosh', which originated as a seedling of 'Fameuse' about two hundred years ago and is now one of the most widely grown apples.

'Golden Russet'. Like 'Cox's Orange Pippin', the 'Golden Russet' is a really good old English apple that is also grown in North America. It is an exceptionally fine dessert apple, tart, sweet, and very flavorful. It keeps well all winter long.

'Grimes Golden'. This lovely and ever popular apple, tart, spicy, large, and golden-yellow in color, is best eaten straight from the tree. It has been around since about 1800 and is thought to be the male parent of the superb 'Golden Delicious', one of the best apples of this century. Both these apples originated in West Virginia.

'Jonagold'. This large, firm, juicy apple has red stripes over yellow flesh. Its fine flavor makes 'Jonagold' one of the best eating apples on the market today, and it stores well, ripening mid-September to early October. It needs a pollinator, and will not pollinate other varieties.

'Liberty'. An excellent apple for the Pacific Northwest, 'Liberty' is resistant to scab and powdery mildew, and lends itself well to espaliering. It originated in New York in 1980 and is a tart, crisp, juicy apple, red blush over a yellow background. It keeps well, is early-bearing and is ready for picking in mid-September.

'Newtown Pippin'. This succulent green apple has been growing in North America for over two hundred years and was a favorite of Thomas Jefferson. It needs good soil, full sun, and a long warm summer. It is a great apple that keeps well for months, and its flavor is at its best towards the end of winter.

'Northern Spy'. One of the best late apples, 'Northern Spy' bears a lovely red fruit with crisp, juicy white flesh. It grew from a seed planted by an experimenter in New Jersey about 1800 and became a great favorite, even though it takes many years to start bearing fruit. As a dwarf tree it will fruit in four years and is well worth the wait.

Other fruits

If your heart is set on a pear tree, and you can only have one, your best bet is 'Duchess', which is self-fruitful, with large fruits. For peaches and nectarines, try one of the genetically small cultivars such as 'Bonanza' or 'Starlet' (peaches) or 'Nectarina' (nectarines). Even when fully grown, 'Bonanza' only reaches a height of 6 feet (1.8 m). Most dwarf plums adapt to container planting. Dwarf damsons make particularly attractive patio trees, and can usually self-pollinate. 'North Star' cherry is a pretty tree and it will make a good container plant, even though container-grown cherries are unlikely to yield a large crop. Any dwarf apricot tree can be grown in a container; two good choices are 'Hungarian' and 'Golden Giant'.

How to plant, train, and espalier fruit trees

Planting

It is important to know that when you are planting trees on dwarf rootstock such as M9 and M27 you must ensure that the bud union remains 2 to 3 inches (5 to 7.5 cm) above the permanent soil surface, otherwise the grafted tree may root, and you will lose the advantage of the dwarfing rootstock.

Apple trees grown in containers need plenty of water. A drip irrigation hose left permanently on top of the soil surface is best. If you are using a watering can, always water until the water runs out of the bottom of the container and water often. Fertilize in the spring with granular fertilizer, and repeat every month to six weeks until August.

Pruning to control the shape of your young tree can be done during the growing season, as well as in the latter part of winter. As the tree gets older, pruning is done only in the dormant months of winter. Correct pruning is essential to the productivity and health of the tree. Check with your local library or bookstore for books on different pruning methods for various trees.

Training

There are several different methods used to train trees to grow flat against a support. The simplest and one of the most efficient is the cordon, where side shoots are pruned back severely, leaving straight stems loaded with fruiting spurs. Vertical cordons can be single, double, or triple forms. They can even be trained at an angle to the ground, forming an oblique cordon. Oblique cordons grow more slowly than vertical ones, but their fruits tend to be bigger, since more energy is forced into the fruiting buds.

Perhaps the two most useful cordons for a patio or balcony are the triple cordon and the horizontal T espalier. The triple cordon allows for maximum fruit production in a minimal space, and the horizontal T espalier is ideal for training the tree against a wall. In both cases, plants are pruned to force branches to form buds at desired locations. The lead shoots are cut back just above these buds, which stimulates buds to produce several new shoots. These are then trained to the pattern.

Cordons and espaliers need support and close attention for at least three years. After the desired pattern is formed, maintenance consists of checking and retying supports and cutting out unwanted buds before they develop into extra branches. When the espaliered tree has matured sufficiently, the supports may be removed.

How to make a triple cordon

The aim of the triple cordon is to allow the tree to develop three vertical shoots only, and to prune back all other side shoots so that leaves and fruit are borne directly on the three vertical branches. To train the tree in the position you want, it must be supported by substantial stakes of wood or thick bamboo, which can be attached directly to the barrel.

First, plant a bare-root whip (a one-year-old unbranched tree) in the half-barrel. Cut off the top of the tree: the cut should be made 1/4 inch (0.6 cm) above a bud and sloping away from it so that it will activate the buds just below it. The cut should be about 18 inches (45 cm) above the soil surface (Fig. 1). (It may be easier to buy a two-

Fig. 1

Fig. 2

year-old branched tree: if this is the case, you will be starting with a slightly larger plant, but the method is the same.)

Make a framework of wood or bamboo and attach it directly to the half-barrel, just behind the tree. In spring, as side shoots sprout from the buds, encourage three that are evenly spaced and coming from just below the cut. Train one of them straight up, and train the other two to grow horizontally to either side of the central shoot. Allow them to grow upright once they are separated from the central shoot. Prune back any other side shoots that appear (Fig. 2).

In summer prune back the side shoots on the three stems to 3 inches (7.5 cm) so that leaf and fruit production is confined to the three vertical shoots.

Once the tree has reached its desired height, prune back the tops of the three main stems. Continue to prune and support the tree until it is mature and able to support itself (Fig. 3).

Fig. 3

How to make a horizontal T espalier

In order to make a horizontal T espalier you will need a wall or fence behind your potted tree. If you are unable to attach anything to the wall, it would be better to train the tree as a triple cordon, as discussed above. But if you have the place and the space, the horizontal T formation is most attractive and takes up very little room.

First, run horizontal wires at intervals of 18 inches (45 cm) across the wall or fence, the lowest being 18 inches (45 cm) above the surface of the barrel. Plastic-covered clothesline wire works well.

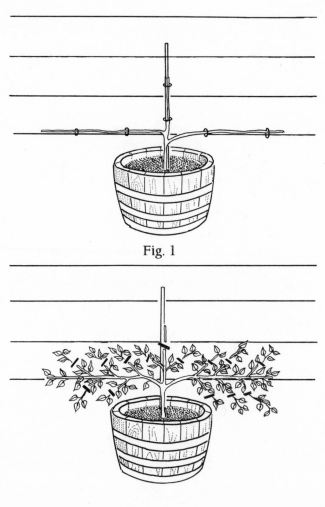

Fig. 1

Fig. 2

Plant a bare-root whip (a one-year-old unbranched tree) in the half-barrel and cut off the top of the tree so that it is 18 inches (45 cm) above the soil surface, using the same procedure as for a triple cordon tree.

As side shoots sprout from the buds, bend them down and train them along the wire. Rub off all the growth from the trunk (Fig. 1).

When the main leader shoot reaches the second wire, prune it to 1/4 inch (0.6 cm) above a set of buds, a little below the wire. This will activate these buds (Fig. 2). Repeat the procedure with the side shoots, as above.

Cut the laterals of the branches on the first wire back to three buds. These will develop into fruiting spurs.

Continue training until the four wires, or as many as you wish, are covered with branches. On the top wire there will be no trunk extension, just the two side branches (Fig. 3).

Fig. 3

$\mathcal{L}$akeside nostalgia

Re-creating the lakeside in the city

THIS NOSTALGIC IDEA IS DEDICATED TO ALL THOSE PEOPLE WHO DREAM of childhood summers by the lake or the ocean: that magical time of endless freedom and no responsibilities, a time when fishing, relaxing, and exploring the world around you, with all its possibilities, was the only important thing on your mind. If you close your eyes and lie back you can almost feel the hot sun on your back, hear the dry grasses rustling in the wind and the softly lapping water, taste bacon and pancakes from breakfast and marshmallows roasting over the evening fire, and see the fireflies flit back and forth in the clear, starry, moonlit sky.

Although this kind of romantic imagining looks even more appealing in hindsight, there is a warm glow that comes with re-creating the possible, and in rekindling, or experiencing for the first time, the joy and magic of another time. With a sense of humor and imagination you can create a lakeside setting in a very small urban area, miles from water. It will be easy-care and low maintenance, leaving you with lots of time to relax in a wicker chair or a comfortable beach chair made from faded, striped canvas.

To re-create the feeling of the lakeside, it is really important to shut out the rest of the world. On a patio, it is easiest to do this by making a fence of some kind; perhaps a picket fence, painted white, pale-gray or sea-blue, or maybe a rustic fence made from long, rounded pieces of wood tied together with wire and bleached in the sun. On a balcony, a screen could be made from bamboo matting tied onto balcony railings or to an existing structure. Look for any artifacts that remind you of the lake to use as props—old wooden canoe paddles, fly-fishing baskets, rods and reels, fish nets and netting, decoy ducks—anything that will enhance the overall effect. These can be attached to the fencing or propped up into corners and, if necessary, protected from the rain. The fly-fishing basket, for instance, could be planted with flowers or a clump of grass.

Sun-bleached wooden planks can be used to re-create the dock or wharf, with a railing of twisted rope along one side, and the top rungs of a nonexistent ladder at one end. The boards should be tongue-and-groove, and can be cut to measure at the lumber store. If you have a ground-floor patio with plenty of space you may want to simulate the lake by making a small water garden beside the dock and stocking it with bog plants, reeds, and water rushes. On a balcony you can use a half-barrel for your water garden, filled with a tall clump of reeds. If you have room, keep a bucket filled with sand nearby and plant tall, outdoor torches in it that can be lit at night, as long as they are a safe distance away from any flammable materials.

Even if you only have space for a single wooden planter, it can be simply and attractively planted with various perennial grasses that will rustle in the wind and provide a refuge for birds and dragonflies. If possible, make your planter from sun-bleached, recycled wood, or paint it pale gray to complement the grasses you plant in it—the simpler the better.

The selection of ornamental grasses available in garden centers today is excellent, with an astonishing range of heights, sizes, colors, and flowering times. They range in size from delicate grasses only a hand-span in height to majestic, towering, plume-crested sheaths that grow to more than 10 feet (3 m). They can be found in a wide range of colors such as blood red, variegated greens and yellows, cream, white, brown, and black. Some are attractively striped or banded. Others have showy flower plumes, spikes or seed heads, and several provide dramatic and lasting interest throughout the winter months.

The most effective way to use grasses in a small space is to choose just one or two that are tall and fluid enough to sway in the breeze, and mass-plant them. In coastal areas and mild climates, grasses will provide color throughout the year and there are even grasses that grow well in the shade. The grasses listed below are reasonably easily available from nurseries and mail-order suppliers. Your local garden center may also stock many interesting and unusual grass species and hybrids.

If you are able to include a lakeside bog garden, the bog plants, reeds, and water rushes suggested in "Water, water everywhere" will help create the right effect. In some areas you will have to find a place to keep your plants during winter so that they do not freeze—perhaps in an underground garage or cool storage area.

The biggest advantage of the lakeside garden may be its easy care and low maintenance; you will be able to go away for weeks at a time and know that your garden can take care of itself, as long as the plants receive a little water now and again.

Setting the scene

The following checklist will help you start creating a lakeside garden on your patio or balcony.

- Six to eight hours of sunshine a day.
- Several wooden planters made, if possible, from bleached, recycled wood and at least 8 to 10 inches (20 to 25 cm) deep, to fit your patio or balcony.

- Basic soil mix and fertilizer.
- Basic gardening tools and storage for them.
- Grasses, bog, and water plants.
- Wooden boards for flooring and patio fencing.
- Bamboo matting for balcony screening.
- Outdoor paint in white, soft gray, or blue for painting fencing, if possible.
- A half-barrel of oak or cedar for the water garden.
- If there is room, a small table made from bleached wood and a comfortable wicker or canvas chair.

To conjure up the mood and feeling of the lakeside, add some lakeside props. As mentioned above, these could include tall garden torches set into a bucket of sand to provide light in the evening, used canoe or rowboat paddles, fishing rods and reels, fly-fishing baskets, fish netting, and decoy ducks. Musty copies of old paperback books and *National Geographics* add an authentic touch.

Grasses for the lakeside

The following grasses are widely available and highly recommended for various exposures and locations. There are many other grasses that can be used to create an effective waterside planting scheme, and the ones given below are meant to get you started. On your next trip to the lake or seaside, take a look at how grasses grow naturally. This will help you to design and plant your containers.

Calamagrostis arundinacea 'Karl Foerster' (Foerster's feather reed grass). One of the best grasses for a strong vertical effect, with stiffly upright clumps of green foliage and narrow white flower spikes that fade to a pinkish-brown and last well into winter. It blooms from June to September and grows to a height of 4 to 5 feet (1.2 to 1.5 m) and a width of 18 inches to 2 feet (45 to 60 cm). It looks interesting planted in long, narrow, wooden planters and needs sun. Zones 5–9.

Carex morrowii 'Aureo-variegata' (variegated Japanese sedge). Although the sedges are not true grasses, they are similar in appearance. They form compact tufts of foliage with usually insignificant flowers. 'Aureo-variegata' is an extremely useful, short-growing, evergreen plant that really likes shade but will tolerate sunshine. Its green leaves have a central stripe of creamy yellow, and it bears pale green flowering spikes in spring. It's excellent for brightening up shady areas. It grows to a height and spread of 12 inches (30 cm). Zones 6–9.

Chasmanthium latifolium (northern sea oats). This is one of the best grasses for shady sites. It is native to North America and hardy to Zone 3. It forms upright clumps of dark green foliage that resemble dwarf bamboo, and its dangling, decorative flower spikes look like flattened oats. It grows happily in the shade and is drought-tolerant, making it well worth tracking down for an easy-maintenance lakeside setting.

It reaches a height of 2 1/2 to 3 feet (75 to 90 cm) and width of 12 inches (30 cm). Zones 3–9.

Festuca cinerea (**blue fescue**). The fescues are low, tufted, clump grasses with fine-textured foliage that ranges in color from silver-blue to green. They are excellent grasses for windy, dry, hot conditions and are at their best in spring and early summer. A good example is *F. cinerea* 'Elijah Blue', a low-growing grass with bright, silvery-blue, very stiff foliage that maintains its color right through the season. It forms a compact 8- to 10-inch (20- to 25-cm) mound and grows in sun or part shade. Zones 4–9.

Hakonechloa macra (**hakone grass**). This attractive, cascading plant has delicate, bamboolike, bright green foliage that turns pinkish-red in the fall. It is an elegant ornamental grass, especially good for a shady spot, and looks beautiful on its own in a medium-sized pot. It grows to 18 inches (45 cm), and combines well with more upright grasses, such as *Imperata cylindrica* 'Red Baron' (Japanese blood grass). It dies back in winter. Zones 5–9.

Helictotrichon sempervirens (**blue oat grass**). This evergreen forms perfectly rounded clumps of intensely blue leaves and is the best blue grass for general purpose use. It does not spread, but always stays in a clump. Tan-colored flower spikes rise 3 feet (90 cm) above the foliage on graceful arching stems from May to July. It grows to a height and spread of 12 to 18 inches (30 to 45 cm). This grass grows best in the sun and it blends well with gray and silver foliage plants and pink and purple flowers. Zones 4–9.

Imperata cylindrica '**Red Baron**' (**Japanese blood grass**). The bright green vertical leaves of this strikingly attractive grass emerge in the spring with wine-red tips, and the foliage becomes more and more red as the seasons progress, turning blood red in the fall. It grows up to 18 inches (45 cm) and prefers moist soil in full sun, although it tolerates light shade. Zones 6–9.

Miscanthus sinensis (**Japanese silver grass**). At least 40 different cultivars have been selected from this superb species grass, and they make excellent specimen plants. All bloom in the late summer or fall, and hold their shape well into the winter, fading to shades of tan or cream. Cultivars vary in leaf color, height, and form. A particularly attractive and readily available cultivar is 'Silberfeder', an architecturally striking, refined, and erect plant that has long leaves arching down from stout stems. Its silvery-white flower heads appear in August and last well into winter. It grows to a height of 5 to 6 feet (1.5 to 1.8 m) and spread of 18 to 24 inches (45 to 60 cm). It likes sun. Zones 5–9.

Pennisetum setaceum '**Rubrum**' (**purple-leafed fountain grass**). This is a medium-sized clump grass with excellent fall and winter color and outstanding burgundy-red foliage throughout the season. The foliage grows to a height and spread of 3 to 4 feet (90 cm to 1.2 m) and showy, rosy-red, bottlebrush plumes arch from the clump in late summer and fall. Zones 8 –10. Its close relative, *P. alopecuroides*, is hardy from zones 5–10. It forms clumps of cascading bright green leaves in spring that change to gold, red-tipped, as the seasons progress, and finally to white, before they die back for the winter. It grows to a height and spread of 2 to 3 feet (60 to 90 cm) and bears buff-colored feathery spikes from August to October. Both prefer sun.

A lakeside pot of grasses

This container will provide color and interest in a sunny spot from spring right through the winter months. It can easily be adapted by adding other plants for a completely different look.

Materials

- Container: a 3-foot-square (90-cm) 18-inch-deep (45-cm) wooden planter made from old, bleached-out wood or new wood painted a light gray.
- Potting mixture: basic soil mix and fertilizer.
- Plants: one *Calamagrostis arundinacea* 'Karl Foerster' (Foerster's feather reed grass); one *Pennisetum setaceum* 'Rubrum' or *P. alopecuroides* (purple-leafed fountain grass); and one *Helictotrichon sempervirens* (blue oat grass).
- Other: a paint brush and light gray paint.

Method

Fill the planter with soil to within about 6 inches (15 cm) of the top. Remove the plants from their pots and set them in place, making holes in the soil for them where necessary, so that the soil level for the plants is about 2 inches (5 cm) below the top of the container. Fill around the plants with soil until the level of the soil is uniform, and firm the soil around the plants. Add a 1/2-inch (1.2-cm) layer of fine gravel or sand to the top to improve drainage. Water well.

Aftercare

Water as necessary and fertilize every couple of weeks with liquid fertilizer.

$\mathcal{G}$oing native
Making a garden with your own native plants

FOR CENTURIES PEOPLE AROUND THE WORLD HAVE RELIED ON THE native plants of their region for food, medicines, ornaments, and cultural symbols. Today we use and grow plants from areas of the world very different from our own, and yet wherever we live we have our own native plants; that is, the plants that naturally grow wild in our region and climate. Happily, gardening with native plants is increasingly popular as more people realize how important it is to preserve and protect biological diversity, and it provides an excellent opportunity to learn more about the natural ecosystem within which you live.

Of all the themes in this book, this one is the broadest in scope, since the native plants of one area differ dramatically from those in another, ranging in North America alone from the bleak Arctic tundra to the sultry Mississippi basin, from the rain forests of the Pacific Northwest to the deciduous woodlands of the East, with thousands of inland lakes, prairie grasslands, deserts, and high mountain ranges in between. Your native garden, therefore, will depend entirely upon the natural landscape surrounding your home.

Where to begin? Fortunately, today there is a much greater consciousness and awareness of the need to preserve what little remains of the natural landscape, and there are more and more specialty nurseries and seed companies that supply native plants. Some of the best companies for this are the ones that specialize in North American native herbs, and they will ship seeds and plants all over the country. Botanical gardens and local gardening magazines are good sources of information about suppliers in your area.

"Going native" opens up a multitude of options and possibilities for container gardeners. For instance, if you live in prairie regions of the American heartland, what could be simpler and more attractive than a container filled with grasses, sagebrush, and some of the many wildflowers that blossom in the grasslands? In many parts of the country, wild roses bloom in profusion, and these lovely untamed plants are usually much more resistant to pests and diseases than the hybrids. They can be grown quite easily in pots, underplanted with native spring bulbs, wild onions, and wild-flowers for spring and summer color and interest. Their rose hips can be harvested in the fall and made into tea.

If there is a particular native tree you like that is small enough to grow happily in a pot, make it the central feature of your patio or balcony, and underplant it with a selection of the many plants that are found growing near it in the wild. Since native plants can be invasive, gangly, hard to cultivate or even downright ugly, it is important to choose your plants carefully from nursery-grown stock. Many growers and botanical gardens are making the selection of plants easier by searching for superior specimens that will adapt well to the garden environment. The goal of such programs is to increase the numbers of local species plants in commercial horticulture, and ensure the continuance of these native species. Your local botanical garden should be able to give you information about any such "plant introduction" schemes that exist in your region.

There are so many lovely native plants that will grow happily in the garden, and it is well worth the time and effort to find them. Do not harvest them from the wild, unless you are saving them from destruction by encroaching civilization. By using native plants you can have a low-maintenance garden that re-creates, as much as possible, the natural habitat of the plants. Although you will probably choose most of your plants for their visual appeal, many of them will attract birds, bees, and butterflies, an added bonus.

In order to illustrate how to make a native garden, I have taken as an example the plants of my own region, the Pacific Northwest. This vast area has a wide diversity of climates, terrain, and natural vegetation, including towering coastal rain forests, semi-arid islands and coastal regions, alpine mountains, yellow-pine forests, sagebrush and bunch grass hills and plains, and dry semidesert interior regions.

Thus, even within the Pacific Northwest, there is no one kind of native garden. It depends upon where you live, and the prevailing climate, terrain, and natural vegetation of your immediate surroundings. A coastal garden, for instance, may include a wide selection of temperate rain forest plants, such as ferns, shade-tolerant shrubs, ground covers, and spring bulbs, or it may resemble some of the drier regions close to the ocean, where arbutus trees, garry oaks, spring bulbs, and even cactus grow. A temperate rain forest garden can be adapted to many areas that also have limited sunshine, a mild climate, and abundant rainfall.

Where possible, choose local materials for your containers, since this will reinforce the natural feel of the garden. In the Pacific Northwest, native cedar is one of the best and most versatile woods for making simple, inexpensive containers. A large patio can accommodate several planters of various sizes and depths; fit them together in as natural an arrangement as possible. You should have enough room for a couple of trees, several shrubs, perennials, bulbs, and ground covers. Your selection might include a vine maple, with evergreen salal, a high-bush cranberry or snowberry, native ferns, kinnikinnick, columbines, clematis, native lilies, and erythroniums.

On a balcony you may only have room for one large cedar box, or you may have the room to group cedar boxes of various depths and sizes together. For this theme it is best that the boxes sit on the ground, rather than being raised up, since some of the plants will be tall. Make sure that one of the boxes is deep enough and large enough to contain a tree, and underplant it with ferns, native bulbs, and ground covers. Add small shrubs, such as a flowering currant, if you have the room. River rocks and moss-covered larger rocks can be carefully placed between the planters, and even used to edge them, to enhance the natural look of the garden. Large rocks or wooden rounds from a large tree can be used for seating.

If all you have is one container, try to make it as big as possible; a half-barrel would be fine. Plant a small tree or shrub in the center and underplant it with ferns and erythroniums, with moss tucked into the corners.

Setting the scene

The following checklist will help you start creating a Pacific Northwest garden on your patio or balcony.

- A semishady location.
- An assortment of square or rectangular, informal wooden planters, preferably made from cedar, and ideally at least 2 feet (60 cm) in diameter and 18 inches (45 cm) deep, to fit the space. If your planters are more than 2 feet (60 cm) across, they do not need to be quite so deep.
- A selection of Pacific Northwest native plants chosen from the ones recommended below.
- River rock or moss-covered rocks for making a path between the planters.
- Basic soil mix, enriched with good compost or leaf mold and fertilizer.
- Basic gardening tools; a storage box made from native cedar is a nice touch.
- A good watering system, preferably a drip system, since these plants will need lots of water.
- Spot lighting to highlight trees and shrubs in the evening would be ideal.
- Large pieces of wood or rocks for seating, or maybe a "twiggy" chair made from alder branches, and a simple wooden table.

You may want to add a selection of objects and artifacts that come from the Pacific Northwest to enhance the theme, possibly including some pieces of carved wood, hollowed-out pieces of log filled with mosses and native plants, wooden Canada geese, and pieces of native art or folk art. There are many artisans making furniture out of pliable wood branches, such as alder, and they make very attractive arbors, benches, and chairs.

Native plants from the Pacific Northwest

To make a Pacific Northwest native garden you will need short, medium, and tall plants to simulate the layered look of the west coast rain forest. The following selection of plants will help you get started. Visit your local garden center and botanical garden to see what native plants are readily available in your area, and consult local gardening books and magazines.

Trees

Acer circinatum (vine maple). A large, many-trunked deciduous shrub or small tree, it grows up to 20 feet (6 m) in the garden, but will remain smaller when confined in a container. It is quite dramatic in April when the wine-colored sepals and white petals emerge before the leaves, and the leaves turn brilliant shades of orange and red in the fall. It grows well in deep shade. Zones 6–9.

Shrubs

Amelanchier alnifolia (serviceberry, Saskatoon berry). An attractive deciduous shrub with oval leaves that turn red or yellow in the fall. The spring flowers form compact, pure white clusters, followed by purplish-black fruits in the fall. Serviceberry grows to about 6 feet (1.8 m) and likes partial to full sun. Zones 5–9.

Leucothöe davisiae (western leucöthoe). An attractive evergreen with dark green ovate leaves and lovely clusters of white gobletlike flowers in June. It grows from 1 to 3 feet (30 to 90 cm) high and prefers a damp spot in semishade. Zones 6–9.

Pachistima myrsinites 'Emerald Cascade' (Oregon boxwood, myrtle boxwood).* An evergreen shrub with shiny, serrated leaves and arching upright branches to 3 feet (90 cm) in length that cascade back to the ground, creating a unique fountain appearance. It looks like a cross between holly and boxwood. Not all growers have had success propagating this cultivar, but if you can find a healthy specimen for sale it is a good choice. Zones 4–9.

Philadelphus lewisii (mock orange). This mock orange is a wild ancestor of the prized garden hybrids, and deserves to be better known. It was introduced to European gardeners by the nineteenth-century botanist-explorer David Douglas. It is a medium to large, many-stemmed and -branched shrub with a height and spread of 6 to 9 feet (1.8 to 2.7 m) and broadly ovate leaves. It bears large, snow-white, fragrant flowers in late June. Zones 4–9. A smaller, more compact shrub is *P. microphyllus,* which is native to the southwest United States and has a height and spread of 2 to 3 feet (60 to 90 cm). Zones 6–9. Both like sun and fertile soil.

Potentilla fruticosa 'Yellow Gem' (shrubby cinquefoil).* This is a low, mounded, deciduous shrub with a distinctive horizontal growth habit. The young twigs are red, contrasting with the hairy, gray, lobed leaves. Flowers are bright yellow and roselike, with five ruffled petals. It works well planted underneath taller shrubs or trees. Zones 2–9.

Ribes sanguineum 'White Icicle' (white-flowering currant).* A deciduous flowering currant shrub with drooping, pure white clusters of flowers in the spring. It grows to a height and spread of 6 feet (1.8 m) and tolerates both sun and shade. Lovely in a layered planting, as a specimen plant, or for massed plantings. Zones 5–9.

Vaccinium ovatum 'Thunderbird' (evergreen huckleberry).* An upright evergreen shrub with intense red-bronze spring foliage, it produces clusters of pink flowers from March to May and shiny, black, edible berries in fall that the birds love. It grows to a height of 6 feet (1.8 m), with half that spread, tolerates sun or part-shade, and likes moist, well-drained, acid soil. Zones 6–9.

Subshrubs, perennials, bulbs, and ground covers

Adiantum pedatum (maidenhair fern). One of the loveliest and most delicate of the native ferns, maidenhair has bright green toothed leaflets on black stems. It is deciduous and prefers partial shade and a rich, dense soil. Grows from 1 to 2 feet (30 to 60 cm). Zones 3–8.

Anemone oregana, A. piperi, and *A. lyallii* (wood anemones). Delicate, shade-loving, deciduous perennials that come up year after year and resemble the anemones you can buy for flower-arranging, only smaller and more fragile. They grow well from seed to a height of 6 inches (15 cm), and come in soft shades of pink, white, and mauve. Zones 4–8.

Aquilegia formosa (wild columbine). This lovely wild relative of the garden columbine is the most common of its genus in the Pacific Northwest. Its nodding red flowers with short spurs are easy to spot in the wild. Hummingbirds love it. It thrives in moist spots, prefers some sun, and grows to a height of 8 to 12 inches (20 to 30 cm). Zones 3–9.

Arctostaphylos uva-ursi 'Vancouver Jade' (bearberry or kinnikinnik).* A vigorous, low-growing evergreen ground cover that has rich green leaves and fragrant clusters of pink flowers in spring. Ideal for trailing over the edges of containers and covering awkward spots, it is best in the sun and is drought tolerant. Zones 4–9. Some species will survive in zone 2, depending upon where they were collected.

Asarum caudatum (wild ginger). This lovely perennial evergreen has deep green, heart-shaped, scented leaves and funny little brownish-purple, thimblelike flowers that hide in the leafy rosette. It is easily grown from seed or rhizome pieces and likes moist, shady places. Zones 5–8.

Blechnum spicant (deer fern). A distinctive and lovely compact fern with finely toothed fronds, some spreading as a basal rosette and others standing straight up. It grows from 1 to 3 feet (30 to 90 cm) and likes partial shade and moist soil. Zones 4–8.

Campanula rotundifolia (Scotch bellflower or lady's thimble). One of the many lovely harebells that grow in this area, its nodding blue bells are each about the size of a thimble and hang down from strong but slender stalks. Likes some sun. Grows to 6 to 8 inches (15 to 20 cm). Zones 2–9.

Cornus canadensis (**bunchberry, dwarf dogwood**). With flowers just like those of the dogwood tree, these tiny plants are just 6 inches (15 cm) high and grow underneath woodland trees and shrubs in moist, shady conditions. In the fall their seeds mature into a bunch of red berries. Zones 2–7.

Dicentra formosa (**bleeding heart**). This charming little plant grows 6 to 8 inches (15 to 20 cm) tall, with heartlike pink or deep rose flowers that hang from drooping stems. It likes moist, shady places. Zones 4–9.

Dodecatheon spp. (**shooting star**). Shooting stars belong to the primrose family and there are several that are native to the Pacific Northwest. They have a rosette of basal leaves and fascinating rose-purple flowers that look like tiny jet-propelled missiles, complete with nose cone. *D. meadia* likes moist, shady places in spring and drier conditions during the summer months. It grows to a height of 8 inches (20 cm) and width of 6 inches (15 cm). Zones 4–9.

Erythronium spp. (**glacier and fawn lilies, dog's-tooth violet**). Looking a bit like small lilies, the nodding, open, trumpetlike flowers of these bulbs are yellow, white, or pink, depending upon the species. Truly a lovely sight when in bloom, they like moist, shady places and come up happily year after year, growing to a height and spread of 5 to 8 inches (12.5 to 20 cm). Zones 3, 4, or 5–9, depending on the species.

Fragaria vesca (**wild strawberry**). Wild strawberry is easy to cultivate and forms a carpet of interconnected plants very quickly. It produces delicately perfumed little berries throughout the summer and prefers a sunnier, drier location. Zones 4–8.

Lilium columbianum (**tiger lily**). This is the most common of the many native lilies in the area. Its smallish flowers are orange and spotted red, their petals furled backwards, and they hang down from 2- to 4-foot (60-cm to 1.2-m) stems. They usually grow best in an open, sunny position but will take some shade. Zones 4–8.

Penstemon fruticosus 'Purple Haze'.* An evergreen or partially evergreen sub-shrub with dark green toothed leaves, its tubular mauve-purple flowers form a solid mound of color for several weeks in late spring. It's superb for trailing over the edges of containers and covering corners. It needs excellent drainage and resents overhead watering. Zones 4–9.

* *Signifies native plants that have been selected for gardeners through the University of British Columbia Botanical Gardens' Plant Introduction Scheme.*

Planting them naturally in a woodland cedar box

This planter will give you a small but lovely native garden for the shade, well suited to a patio, balcony, or shady doorway, such as the entrance to a basement suite. Ideally the container should be of native west coast cedar and as big as possible. The following selection will provide interest and color from early spring to late fall.

Materials

- Container: one large wooden planter, preferably made from cedar, 3 feet (90 cm) square and 18 inches (45 cm) deep.
- Potting mixture: basic soil mix enriched with a generous amount of leaf mold or compost and fertilizer.
- Plants: one *Amelanchier alnifolia* (serviceberry); one *Pachistima myrsinites* 'Emerald Cascade' (Oregon boxwood); two *Adiantum pedatum* (maidenhair fern); three *Lilium columbianum* (tiger lily); three *Arctostaphylos uva-ursi* 'Vancouver Jade' (bearberry); two *Dodecatheon meadia* or *D. jeffreyi* (shooting star); and three *Erythronium* spp. (glacier and fawn lily).

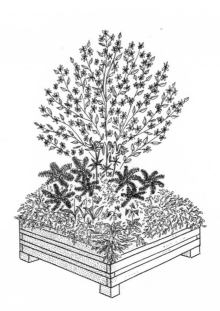

Method

Fill the planter to within 6 inches (15 cm) of the rim and place the serviceberry and Oregon boxwood in appropriate spots, the serviceberry at the back. Add a little more soil and place the lily bulbs in two clumps, so that the tiger lilies are near the back and the glacier or fawn lilies are near the front. Mark the position of the bulbs, add some more soil, and plant the maidenhair ferns, shooting stars, and bearberry, making sure that they are not planted over the bulbs. Bring the soil level to within an inch (2.5 cm) of the rim of the container and add a half-inch (1.2-cm) layer of fine gravel or sand to the top to improve drainage. The bearberry should be at the edge of the planter so it can trail over the side. Water well.

Aftercare

Be sure to water regularly and well, and feed every other week during the growing season with a liquid fertilizer, or every month with a granular fertilizer. Add a generous layer of leaf mold or compost to the planter in the fall.

Old-fashioned fragrance

Lilies, stocks, sweet peas, and other old-fashioned scents are back in style

A LOVE OF FRAGRANCE IS BACK IN FASHION. AN IMPORTANT PART OF THE perennial garden years ago, fragrant flowers were pushed to the back of the border for many years while nurseries proudly displayed the latest prize-winning hybrids. But today there is a resurgence of interest in old-fashioned fragrance, and a wide range of plants are available through nurseries, garden centers, and mail-order catalogs, making it relatively easy for modern gardeners to fill their gardens with scents again.

Our sense of smell is possibly the most evocative and primordial of all the senses. Any smell, whether it is the rich scent of a lily in bloom, the sweetness of newly mown grass, or the refreshing aroma of crushed peppermint leaves, can trigger a flood of memories from deep within the recesses of the brain. The fragrance of some plants will make us feel good, while we may react negatively, or have no reaction at all, to the fragrance of others.

A sense of smell is a very personal thing because each person's brain interprets smells, good and bad, slightly differently. For millions of years we have relied on our sense of smell to keep us safe from danger, and to enhance the joys and pleasures of life. Through the centuries, we have learned to use the volatile oils from plants for their specific beneficial healing properties, forming the basis for the ancient art of aromatherapy.

The essential oils in lavender, for instance, lift the spirits, help to cure headaches and promote a feeling of tranquillity and calm, and the oils in rosemary stimulate the memory, rekindle lost energy, and are tonic to the nervous system. This may help to explain why both these essential oils were so popular in Victorian times, when ladies kept little bottles of smelling salts scented with lavender in their purses, ready to treat anyone who had a fit of the vapors.

While it is nice to know a little bit about aromatherapy when planning your old-fashioned fragrance garden, the most important thing to know is what scents you like, and how they make you feel. You can't go far wrong if you rely on your own intuition: if a plant grows well, smells nice, and makes you feel good, then it's the right plant for you! One person's idea of a fragrant garden may be to fill the space with honeysuckle and sweet peas, while another will want roses and lilies, or lavender and pinks.

Anyone who has lived on the prairies, or in a hot, dry climate, will know how the intense fragrances of lilacs, honeysuckle, and roses fill the air in early summer, making up for the harshness of winter. By contrast, those who live in cooler, more temperate climates may find these fragrances are less intense and often dampened, literally, by rain. Here the gentle delicacy of shade and woodland plants can be enticing, mingling with the soft, damp smell of wet moss and dripping greenery.

Wherever we live, some of our favorite scents are likely to be those of our childhood, or of a special time in our lives. A fragrance garden is a chance to re-create those memories, moods, and feelings. In addition to the old favorites, there are attractive new selections of plants such as roses and sweet peas that still retain a good scent, although it is often the older, less showy ones that have the most powerful scent.

When planning a fragrance garden, the small-space gardener has a huge advantage over those with a larger garden because smells concentrate and intensify when they are confined, and they are more likely to be noticed and appreciated. One medium-sized shrub of daphne, for instance, can fill a small patio or balcony with fragrance, all on its own. The same is true of strongly scented roses, honeysuckle, lilies, Chinese witch hazel, sweet box, and many other plants.

Whether you have a patio or a balcony, try to enclose it so the scents are held within the space. This might be a fence of wood, or bamboo matting tied to balcony railings, or latticework, which will let the light and air through. Fragrant climbers, such as honeysuckle, sweet peas, and climbing roses, can be trained up the fence and through the trellis. You can even screen one side of a patio with a row of potted lilacs, which will provide complete privacy in summer and filtered privacy in winter.

When creating an old-fashioned fragrance garden, it really pays to plan the selection and location of plants carefully, before you buy them. Then the blooms will complement, not fight, each other and can be appreciated for their fragrance when they flower. In some parts of the country it is possible to have fragrance almost all year; in other areas the season is not so long. Wherever you live, try to plan your plant selection so that you can enjoy fragrance as much of the year as possible. The following list of plants should help you plan your garden with these points in mind. You may also want to consider forcing bulbs in the fall for a succession of fragrant blooms indoors during the winter.

Many fragrant plants, such as most roses, need a lot of sun to do well, but others, such as sweet box, sweet violets, and Chinese witch hazel, will bloom happily in sun or part shade. For example, a container in a sunny spot might have a lilac in the center, underplanted with white hyacinths for spring, dwarf lavender and pink carnations for summer, and evergreen sweet box for winter fragrance in milder regions. In the shade, try a Chinese witch hazel or Korean spice viburnum in the center, underplanted with bulbs and sweet violets for the spring, fragrant hostas and sweet woodruff for the summer, and sweet box for winter fragrance.

Whatever the size of your patio or balcony, do try to make room for a seating area, or place the plants close to a door or window, so that you can enjoy their fragrance to the full. If you have room you may want to add some plants that release their scent into the evening air, such as night-scented stock and nicotiana, so you can enjoy their heady perfumes at the end of the day.

Setting the scene

The following checklist will help you start creating an old-fashioned fragrance garden on your patio or balcony.

- Sunshine or part shade, depending upon the choice of plants.
- Fencing, bamboo matting, or latticework, painted white, to enclose the space.
- Many different containers and planters can be used for a fragrance garden. Since the feeling is somewhat old-fashioned and romantic, you might want to use Versailles tubs, or ornate terracotta pots, or even decorated cement containers. If they are to hold trees and shrubs they will need to be at least 2 feet (60 cm) square and 12 inches (30 cm) or more deep. In order to appreciate the fragrance fully, some containers should be raised.
- Basic soil mix and fertilizer.
- A selection of fragrant plants chosen from the ones given below.
- Lattice or trellis at one end or more of the patio or balcony that can act as a frame for fragrant climbers and provide privacy.
- A watering system.
- A lighting system.
- Basic garden tools and storage.
- If there is room, a table and chairs, perhaps a white wrought-iron table and chairs to match or maybe an easy chair.

Since the emphasis is on old-fashioned fragrance, you may want to add props, such as old-fashioned cushions for the chairs, straw hats hanging on the wall, an ice-cream maker on the table, and croquet mallets in the corner.

Plants for fragrance

The following list of plants should help you plan a fragrant garden for as much of the year as your climate allows.

Shrubs and climbers

Daphne mezereum (daphne). This upright, fragrant, deciduous shrub bears sweetly scented mauve-pink flowers in early spring before its leaves open. It needs a well-drained, alkaline soil and will take sun or shade. It grows from 3 to 5 feet (0.9 to 1.5 m). Zones 5–8. Less hardy but very attractive and evergreen is *D. odora,* with deep purplish-pink and white flowers. Zones 7–9.

Hamamelis mollis 'Pallida' (Chinese witch hazel). This deciduous, upright, open shrub will do well in a large container in sun or shade and thrives in acid soil. It can grow to 12 feet (4 m) or more in the garden, but can be kept pruned to about 8 to 10 feet (2.4 to 3 m) in a container. It produces extremely fragrant yellow flowers on bare branches in midwinter, followed by broadly oval, green leaves that turn yellow in the fall. Zones 5–9.

Lavandula spp. (lavender). See "A taste of Provence."

Lonicera spp. (honeysuckle or woodbine). These mostly deciduous, twining climbers are not all fragrant, but many are. All species have oval leaves and trumpetlike flowers, and will grow in any fertile, well-drained soil in sun or semishade, reaching a height of 15 to 20 feet (4.5 to 6 m). Two attractive, fragrant cultivars are *L. periclymenum* 'Belgica' (early Dutch honeysuckle) and 'Serotina' (late Dutch honeysuckle). Both have sweetly scented blooms in yellow, flushed with purple and red. Zones 5–9.

Philadelphus spp. (mock orange). These upright, leggy shrubs bear intensely fragrant white flowers in summer and quickly make a good foliage screen for a patio or balcony. They need sun and good, well-drained soil. There are many attractive cultivars available, such as *P. coronarius* 'Aureus'. It has bright yellow young leaves that turn greenish-yellow with age. It grows from 8 to 10 feet (2.4 to 3 m) and bears clusters of very fragrant, creamy-white flowers in late spring and early summer. Zones 5–9.

Rosa spp. (roses). There are many fragrant rose hybrids suitable for container growing (see "Romance in the Garden"), but if you have your heart set on one of the old garden roses, try one of the vigorous Alba group. These beautifully scented roses are both disease- and pest-resistant. Special favorites include the White Rose of York (*Rosa x alba*), and the pink hybrids 'Celestial', 'Félicité Parmentier', and 'Köningin von Dänemark'. They grow to a height of 5 feet (1.5 m) and will bloom only once, in midsummer, but are lovely when in flower. Zones 4–9.

Sarcococca spp. (sweet box). This attractive evergreen shrub has glossy, dark green leaves and tiny, fragrant white flowers in early spring. It is happy in sun or shade and prefers a rich, fertile soil. *S. hookeriana* var. *humilis* has black berries in the fall and grows to 2 feet (60 cm). Zones 6–9. The less hardy *S. ruscifolia* has red berries in the fall and grows from 3 to 4 feet (0.9 to 1.2 m). Zones 8–9.

Syringa patula (dwarf lilac). This lovely, hardy little lilac is perfect for containers. It grows from 4 to 5 feet (1.2 to 1.5 m) and has small leaves, a compact growing habit, and fragrant, lilac-colored blooms that appear in erect clusters in the late spring and often again in the fall. It needs sun and a well-drained, lime-rich soil. Zones 5–8.

Viburnum carlesii (**Korean spice viburnum**). This excellent container shrub grows slowly to a compact bush of 4 to 5 feet (1.2 to 1.5 m). It is deciduous, will grow in sun or shade, and is happy in any soil. It has downy, oval leaves, and large, rounded, intensely fragrant clusters of tiny white flowers that open in late spring from porcelainlike buds of deep rosy-pink. It even has good fall color. Zones 6–9.

Perennials

Convallaria majalis (**lily-of-the-valley**). Lily-of-the-valley bears white, very fragrant, bell-shaped hanging flowers on 6-inch (15-cm) stems in late spring. It spreads easily from rhizomes, so it is best grown in its own container. It prefers partial shade and rich, moist soil. Zones 4–8.

Dianthus spp. (**pinks and carnations**). Pinks have been popular since Shakespeare's time, with their neat mounds of silver or green foliage and deliciously fragrant flowers, excellent for cutting. All require a sunny position in full sun and well-drained, sandy soil. Good pinks to grow in containers are the so-called modern pinks, the Allwoodii hybrids, made by crossing an old-fashioned pink with a perpetual-flowering carnation. They produce more blooms than the old-fashioned pinks, and are usually double, blooming in June and July and sometimes again during the fall. Good cultivars are 'Daphne', single pink with crimson eye; 'Doris', semidouble salmon-pink, very fragrant; 'Lilian', white, fragrant; and 'Robin', double red. They grow to 10 inches (25 cm). Zones 4–8.

Galium odoratum syn. *Asperula odorata* (**sweet woodruff**). This is a good filler plant that likes shade and will spread into a sweetly aromatic carpet about 6 inches (15 cm) high. Its neatly whorled leaves are topped with star-shaped, white flowers in late spring and early summer. Zones 4–8.

Hosta 'Royal Standard' or 'So Sweet' (**fragrant plantain lily**). These lovely cultivars are very attractive for flower arranging, survive happily in containers, and bear superbly fragrant white flowers on 24-inch-tall (60-cm) scapes in midsummer. For more information on hostas see "In the shade."

Paeonia spp. (**peony**). These are some of the loveliest of the hardy perennials, and some of the most rewarding to grow. Dependable and resistant to most pests, peonies prefer a rich, well-drained soil and sun, although they will grow in light shade. They grow to 3 feet (0.9 m), are extremely long-lived, and should not be disturbed if they are growing and flowering well. They are heavy feeders, and flowering is improved by a fall application of well-rotted manure or compost, and a spring application of bone meal. *P. lactiflora,* the Chinese peony, is the parent of most of today's hybrids and has some lovely fragrant forms; it is well worth the search. Some good fragrant cultivars are 'Sarah Bernhardt', apple blossom pink, ruffled and double; 'Globe of Light', pure rose-pink outer petals, clear golden-yellow petaloids, and anemonelike flowers; and 'Kelway's Supreme', soft blush pink, fading to milk white, double. Zones 3–9.

Viola odorata (**sweet violet**). This lovely little spreading perennial has been used for centuries for its scent, and self-seeds prolifically. It has heart-shaped leaves and fragrant violet or white flowers in early spring. In summer the plants form a dense carpet of green leaves. It prefers to grow in the shade. Zones 6–9.

Annuals and tender perennials

Heliotropium arborescens (**common heliotrope**). Heliotrope is a tender perennial that will only overwinter outdoors in Zone 10, but it can be propagated from cuttings, grows easily from seed (although it may not be as fragrant), and is widely available in the spring as a bedding plant. It likes full sun and a fertile, well-drained soil and grows to a height of 8 to 10 inches (20 to 25 cm). Heliotrope has attractive dark green leaves, and dense, flat clusters of purple to lavender blooms that flower from late spring until frost. It's often grown in hanging baskets and in containers.

Lathyrus odoratus (**sweet pea**). These lovely, fast-growing annuals are so easy to grow and so rewarding that they are a great bonus for container gardeners. They come in a wide range of colors with attractive blossoms that resemble little sunbonnets. They have a delightful fragrance and bloom profusely the more you pick them. It is worth searching for the non-climbing cultivars that grow to about 8 inches (20 cm). They make excellent cut flowers and container plants and can also be used in hanging baskets. They need sun and a good, organically rich soil to bloom well. For extra fragrance, pick seeds selected for their scent, even though their flowers may not be as large.

Lobularia maritima (**sweet alyssum**). This fast-growing annual has lance-shaped, grayish-green leaves and bears rounded heads of tiny, scented, white flowers from summer into the fall. It is widely available at garden centers and is useful for edging containers and filling in gaps. It grows to a height of 3 to 6 inches (8 to 15 cm) and prefers sun.

Matthiola longipetala ssp. *bicornis* (**night-scented stock**) and *M. incana* (**common stock**). Highly scented and great for cutting, stocks were one of the staples of the Victorian flower garden. They grow well in sun or semishade, and like rich, well-drained soil with some lime added. Night-scented stocks grow to 12 inches (30 cm) with spires of lilac-colored flowers that close during the day and open at night, releasing fragrance into the evening air. They are often not readily available as plants, but both are easy to grow from seed. Cultivars of common stock vary in height from 1 to 3 feet (30 to 90 cm) and bear flowers in all colors.

Nicotiana alata (**flowering tobacco plant**). Nicotiana is a perennial, usually grown as an annual, that bears clusters of tubular, trumpet-shaped flowers in a wide range of colors in summer and fall. 'Sensation Series' grow to 2 1/2 to 3 feet (75 to 90 cm); 'Domino Series' grow to 12 inches (30 cm). The colored cultivars are not always fragrant—for fragrance look for the ones labeled "Old Fashioned," or

N. sylvestris; the latter grows to 5 feet (1.5 m). All are excellent container plants, need sun, and a rich, well-drained soil.

Pelargonium **spp. (scented geranium).** Some geraniums have strongly scented leaves. Their flowers tend to be insignificant compared with their more showy ornamental cousins, but their richly scented foliage, from lemony and spicy to rose-scented, makes them a welcome addition to a fragrant garden. They are tender perennials but you can keep them from year to year by overwintering the plants indoors, or taking cuttings from them. Zones 9–10.

Bulbs

Hyacinthus orientalis **(hyacinth).** Hyacinths are well known as indoor plants. Their dense spikes of strongly fragrant white, pink, or blue flowers also look attractive in outside containers. The bulbs will continue to come up year after year as long as the container is protected from intense cold in winter. Plant hyacinth bulbs in rich, well-drained soil with a little bone meal added, in partial shade or sun. Zones 3–9.

Lilium candidum **(Madonna lily).** Probably the best known and most beloved of all the lilies, the Madonna lily has been cultivated for over thirty-five hundred years. It is a symbol of purity, and was prized for its beauty in medieval gardens. It has pure white flowers in summer that face outwards from 3- to 4-foot (0.9- to 1.2-m) stems. The flowers have bright yellow pollen and a heavy fragrance reminiscent of honeysuckle. Unlike the other lilies, the Madonna lily likes lime in the soil, and should only be covered to a depth of 1 inch (2.5 cm). It needs a sunny position to bloom well. Zones 4–9.

Lilium **spp. (lily).** Of all the summer-flowering bulbs, lilies are the most dramatic. They thrive in slightly acidic soil and prefer a well-drained, rich earth with some bone meal added, good air circulation, and at least six hours of sun a day. Lilies should be planted as soon as you get them in the fall, with the bulb tip 3 to 4 inches (8 to 10 cm) below the soil surface. The Asiatic hybrids are unscented, but the trumpet and aurelian lilies (July blooming) and the Oriental hybrids (August) are all richly scented. There are many lovely ones to choose from, such as the glorious white Oriental 'Casablanca'. Lilies vary in height from 2 to 6 feet (60 cm to 1.8 m), depending on the hybrid. Zones 4–9.

Narcissus **spp. (daffodil and narcissus).** All the daffodils and narcissi have some scent, although some are more strongly scented than others. One to look for is 'Thalia', a lovely pale cream that bears two or three delicate blooms on one stalk and has a hauntingly lovely fragrance. Daffodils and narcissi prefer sun or light shade and a well-drained soil. Their cheerful, nodding heads are always a welcome sight in spring and they grow well in containers, as long as the container is protected from very cold winter weather. Zones 3–9.

An elegant container of fragrance

If you have room for only one container, try to make it as large as you can so that you can have something in bloom from early spring to late fall. This plant combination will be fine in sun or semishade, as long as the sun is filtered for some of the day.

Materials

- Container: one Versailles planter (see "Practical Details: Planters") at least 2 feet (60 cm) square and 18 inches (45 cm) deep, painted white. You can also use another wooden planter, or terracotta or concrete container, as long as they are large.
- Potting mixture: basic soil mix enriched with a few handfuls of bone meal, some compost or well-rotted manure, a handful of dolomite lime, and some controlled-release fertilizer.
- Plants: One 5-foot (1.5-m) *Syringa patula* (dwarf lilac); three white *Matthiola longipetala* ssp. *bicornis* (night-scented stock); one *Hosta* 'So Sweet'; six white cultivars of *Hyacinthus orientalis* (hyacinths); three *Dianthus* 'Doris' (modern pinks); and six *Lobularia maritima* (sweet alyssum).

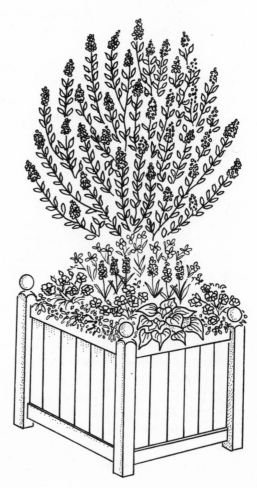

Method

Prepare the container and put enough of the soil mix into it for the lilac to be positioned near the back of the container, with the soil surface about 2 inches (5 cm) below the rim of the container.

Fill in around the lilac, positioning the hyacinth bulbs in two clumps of three in the middle of the pot, at a depth of about 10 inches (25 cm) below the rim of the container, leaving room for the hosta between the two clumps.

Fill the container with soil. Position the hosta between the clumps of hyacinths, in front of the lilac, and plant the three night-scented stocks in the gaps between the hosta and the lilac. Position the three pinks around and to the front of the hosta.

Fill in the gaps around the side with the sweet alyssum. Add a 1/2-inch (1.2-cm) layer of fine gravel or sand to the top to improve drainage, and water well.

Aftercare

Water frequently to ensure the pot does not dry out and feed with liquid fertilizer every other week or granular fertilizer once a month during the growing season. In the fall remove the sweet alyssum and night-scented stocks and prepare the pot for the winter.

In the shade

Shady spots are full of life

SO OFTEN WE HEAR SOMEONE SAY THAT HIS OR HER GARDEN IS FAR TOO shady to grow anything interesting. These skeptics are always astonished to see the abundance of lovely plants that grow best in the shade, bringing interest and life to the dullest corner. Shade brings out the subtleties of delicate whites, creams, greens, and pastels, and vibrant colors are intensified, rather than being washed out by the sun's strong rays.

For container gardeners there are distinct advantages to having a shady spot. In the middle of a hot and dusty summer it provides a tranquil, restful haven from mid-day heat. Plants will not need to be watered quite so often as they would in the sun, since their containers are not exposed to direct sunlight. And the plants are not vul-nerable to the kind of environmental damage, such as scorched leaves, that can hap-pen when an enclosed space surrounded by concrete bakes in the hot sun.

A shade garden conjures up many different images: a moss garden in Japan, where carpets of soft, lime-green mosses drip moisture steadily into the still dark waters of a pool surrounded by maples and azaleas; a Hawaiian paradise of palm trees, tropical fruit trees, birds of paradise, and native silverswords and tarweeds; or the temperate rain forest of the North American west coast, with huge evergreen trees, lush green foliage, moss-draped branches, sword ferns, huckleberries, salal, Oregon grape, bleeding hearts, wild ginger, and foxgloves.

And there are the vast deciduous forests of eastern North America, where hun-dreds of different trees and shrubs, such as viburnum, honey locust, and witch hazel, cover a dense greenery of Solomon's seal, day lilies, columbines, delphiniums, and other native plants. Or the oak woods and beech groves of England, where the fre-quent mild rains create mossy banks carpeted with cowslips, primroses, and sweet violets.

Shade gardens such as these may not be practical to re-create in a small space, but they are useful to imagine since they can give you a good idea of the kinds of plants you like and want to use. It is also important to make the distinction between types of shade. Even if a plant has no direct sunlight, that does not mean it is in total shade. All-year-round, total shade, such as that underneath a tall stand of Douglas firs, is very dense, and few plants can survive these conditions. Most plants that do well in shade actually exist in partial shade conditions, where light filters through taller trees or shrubs. This protects a plant from direct sunlight but still allows it to receive some light. Lilies, foxgloves, and bluebells, for instance, will all grow well in partial shade. Similarly, if your garden area is on the north side of your building, or hemmed in by taller buildings, it may not receive any direct sun during the day, but may still have plenty of light for growing shade-loving plants.

Most shade plants grow best in humus-rich soil with lots of moisture and nourishment. Shallow-rooted trees and shrubs will use soil nutrients quickly, so the container must be fertilized regularly throughout the growing season if smaller plants are to thrive. It helps to make the containers as large as possible. Wood containers are appropriate for a shade garden, especially if you are constructing planters to fit a balcony or patio.

If there is only room for a small window box, hanging basket, or small pot, it can still be a very successful shade container, as long as you water and feed it properly. For small spaces it is still hard to beat the old favorites, such as impatiens, available in many different shades of red, orange, pink, purple and white, with double and single flowers; big orange, white, and red begonias; and fuchsias, with their lovely hanging tubular flowers in an amazing array of color combinations.

Whatever its size, a shade garden can be one of the simplest, easiest gardens of all. Plants can be arranged in layers, just as they are in a native plant garden, so that the dying foliage of early-flowering bulbs will be hidden by the emerging leaves of hardy perennials. For height and structure you may want to feature a small tree or shrub that is attractive throughout the year. A Japanese maple, large rhododendron, or azalea is ideal, especially if the plant has an interesting shape.

There are many very attractive Japanese maples on the market today, and it is worth looking for a form that really appeals to you. Some maples grow in an upright way, opening outwards like an upturned funnel, while others tend to form a solid umbrella of leaves and branches, cascading downwards. Leaf shapes vary from quite plain to deeply dissected and variegated. Many have leaves that turn bright red or purple in the fall (see "The Art of Zen" for more information on maples).

Choose rhododendrons and azaleas carefully. Many are native to the high mountains, such as the Himalayas, and these hardy plants are able to withstand low winter and nighttime temperatures. However, many are not hardy in colder climates and few, if any, can tolerate dry summer heat. They need a well-drained, well-watered acid soil (pH range of 4.5 to 6.0), and their roots need to be kept cool and moist year-round.

Most rhododendrons and azaleas bloom in the spring, within a few weeks of each other, so be sure their colors harmonize and blend well. Pink and white blooms are easier on the eye in a small space than the stronger reds and purples. Other attractive shrubs include the willowleaf cotoneaster, leucothöe, pieris, dwarf pines, Chinese witch hazel, heavenly bamboo, mock orange, and weigela.

If you have room for several shrubs, try to choose plants that are especially attractive at different times throughout the year. These can be underplanted with bulbs and shade-loving perennials. If you only have room for one container, plant a small tree or shrub in the center and underplant it with spring-flowering bulbs for successive blooming: first white crocus and blue *Iris reticulata,* next blue grape hyacinths and pale yellow narcissus, and finally white Parrot tulips. As the bulbs die back, fill in the gaps with variegated hostas and white impatiens. If you have room, plant a selection of Asiatic, trumpet, and Oriental lilies for successive blooming through June, July, and August. In the fall, decorate the tree with strings of cranberries or nuts for the birds, and add little twinkling white lights as midwinter approaches.

Setting the scene

The following checklist will help you start creating a shade garden on your patio or balcony.

- Shade, or partial shade.
- Containers for the plants, as appropriate for your space. Simple wooden planters are best, as large as possible. If you are growing trees and shrubs, and the planter is at least 3 feet (90 cm) or more in diameter, you can get away with a 12-inch (30-cm) depth of soil. If the planter is less than 2 feet (60 cm) in diameter, you will need a 16- to 18-inch (40- to 45-cm) soil depth.
- Basic soil mix enriched with compost and fertilizer.
- Basic gardening tools and storage.
- A good watering system, preferably drip irrigation.
- A lighting system.
- If there is room, rustic chairs and table, such as twiggy furniture, an Adirondack chair, or a chair made from narrow, peeled logs.
- A selection of shade plants, chosen from the ones given below.

Since shady spots can be cool ones too, especially in the evening, you may want to include an outdoor propane heater (see "Practical Details: Patio heaters"), and a propane lamp for evening light. This could be a lovely place to sit and read in the evening, wrapped in a warm blanket, drinking hot chocolate. Add some wind chimes for their soft, soothing sounds.

Plants that grow in the shade

These shade-loving plants are, for the most part, readily available. You may need to make substitutions, depending upon where you live.

Trees and shrubs

Acer palmatum (Japanese maple). See "The art of Zen" for extensive listing.

Buxus sempervirens (boxwood). See "Clipped for style."

Camellia spp. (camellias). There are over 200 cultivars of this glossy-leafed evergreen shrub. They will grow well in containers, but need winter protection in zones 7 and 8. Camellias bloom from October to April, depending on the species, and the flowers range in color from red through pink to white, with variegated forms. They like a lime-free soil mixture enriched with organic matter. They don't like strong sun and windy locations but do very well on a north-facing wall. *C. sasanqua* is winter-flowering and has many good cultivars, including 'Yuletide', single red flowers with yellow stamens; 'Showa-no-Sakae', semidouble ice-pink flowers; and 'White Doves', semidouble white flowers, all to 10 feet (3 m). *C.* x. *williamsii* cultivars tend to be smaller and bloom between November and April, depending on the cultivar: good ones are 'Donation', a compact plant with semidouble silver-pink flowers; and 'J.C. Williams', a pendulous plant with single pale-pink blooms. Zones 7–9.

Choisya ternata (Mexican orange). It is hard to believe that this evergreen shrub, which is related to the citrus family, will thrive in a shady area. Its white, sweetly scented flowers produced in April and May and its glossy, attractive, evergreen foliage make it a must for a spacious patio or balcony in milder climates. It needs winter protection in zone 8. It grows to a height of 6 feet (1.8 m) and prefers fertile, well-drained soil. It requires very little pruning; cut out frost-affected shoots at the base in spring, and trim to shape after flowering. This shrub looks great planted in a terracotta pot. Zones 8–10.

Cotoneaster salicifolius var. *floccosus* (willowleaf cotoneaster). This evergreen shrub grows up to 12 feet (3.6 m). Its willowlike leaves and arching branches will perk up any basement stairwell. It produces white flowers in the spring and red berries in the fall and will grow in any well-drained soil. Zones 7–8.

Euonymus japonicus 'Silver King' (Japanese spindle bush). This is a dense, upright, evergreen shrub with glossy, dark green leaves edged with silvery-white. It lights up a shady corner, and will grow in any well-drained soil. It grows slowly to a height of 4 to 5 feet (1.2 to 1.5 m) and may need winter protection. Zones 7–9.

Hydrangea spp. In mild maritime climates and farther south, these deciduous shrubs are always dependable and ideal for containers. They can grow to a height of 6 feet (1.8 m) and prefer moist but well-drained soil and a top-dressing of aged manure in April. *H. macrophylla* is perhaps the best known for its mophead and lacecap flowers. Flowers are usually blue or purple in acid soil and pink in alkaline soil. Good lacecap cultivars are 'Bluebird', and 'Mariesii'. Zones 6–9.

Ilex crenata 'Convexa' (dwarf Japanese holly). A compact, thornless shrub with tiny, glossy, mid-green leaves and large quantities of tiny black berries in the fall. It grows to a height of 3 to 4 feet (0.9 to 1.2 m) and spread of 2 to 3 feet (60 to 90 m), will grow in sun or shade and prefers a moist, rich soil. Zones 6–9.

Leucothöe fontanesiana 'Rainbow'. This arching evergreen shrub grows to a height of 5 feet (1.5 m) and grows best in moist, peaty, acid soil. It has toothed, leathery, evergreen leaves variegated with cream, yellow, and pink, and bears racemes of white flowers opening below the shoots in spring. An attractive specimen plant, especially underplanted with spring bulbs and summer hostas. Zones 5–9.

Nandina domestica (**heavenly bamboo**). This attractive semievergreen shrub has narrow, lance-shaped, dark green leaflets that are purplish-red when young and in the winter. It bears large panicles of small, star-shaped white flowers in midsummer and makes an excellent screening plant, growing to a height of 6 feet (1.8 m). The dwarf cultivar 'Nana' grows to 2 feet (60 cm). It prefers fertile, well-drained soil and may need winter protection. Zones 7–9.

Pieris spp. (**lily-of-the-valley bush**). These evergreen flowering shrubs are acid-loving and prefer a peaty soil. They can reach a height of about 6 feet (1.8 m) in containers and hardiness varies greatly, depending upon the species. Two good cultivars are 'Valley Rose', low-growing and compact with sprays of waxy pink flowers at the branch tips and bronzy-red new foliage; and 'Variegata', a slow-growing cultivar with small leaves edged with white and fragrant white flowers in early spring. They look most attractive when underplanted with early bulbs. Zones 7–9.

Rhododendron spp. This large family of plants contains rhododendron and azalea species and hybrids that range in size from tiny alpine shrubs to large, spreading treelike forms. Many, especially smaller-growing ones, will thrive in good-sized containers where the climate is suitable. They provide color for many weeks, and beautiful foliage year round. Their growing habits vary widely, and some of the more leggy ones can even be used as informal espaliers along walls. Rhododendrons need acid soil and plenty of moisture. They cannot be allowed to dry out, even in winter, and benefit from an annual top-dressing of aged manure, compost, or leaf mold. One of the most reliable for containers is the hardy little 'P.J.M.', an excellent plant that tolerates summer heat as well as winter cold, will survive to –25°F (–31°C), reaches a height of 4 feet (1.2 m), and produces small trusses of light pinkish-lavender blooms in mid- to late spring. Its round, evergreen leaves turn an attractive mahogany shade in winter. Zones 5–8.

Two good compact species for containers are the *R. williamsianum* and *R. yakushimanum* hybrids which reach a mature height of 3 to 4 feet (0.9 to 1.2 m). *R. williamsianum* hybrids are easily recognized by their small, oval, smooth foliage. In the spring their new leaves are a bronze color, and they bear bell-shaped flowers on loose trusses. Good hybrids include: 'Bow Bells', clear pink; 'Linda', rose-pink; 'Maureen', pink; and 'Willbritt', deep pink with light edges. Zones 7–8. *R. yakushimanum* hybrids are tightly compact, with large leaves covered with a brown fuzz, known as indumentum, on their undersides. They bear neat trusses of large bell-shaped flowers. Those suitable for containers include 'Coral Velvet', coral-pink opening to salmon; 'Ken Janeck', deepest pink opening to white; and 'Yaku Princess', apple blossom pink. Zones 5–8.

Sarcococca **spp. (Christmas or sweet box).** See "Old-fashioned fragrance."

Thamnocalamus spathaceus **syn.** *Arundinaria murielae* **(umbrella bamboo).** See "A touch of the Orient."

Perennials

Most perennials die back to the ground in winter, leaving your pots and planters bare and forlorn. It is a good idea to combine a few of your favorite perennials with evergreen shrubs, small trees, and early-flowering spring bulbs for year-round interest and color. The following perennials will grow well in shady areas of a balcony or patio.

Aconitum **spp. (monkshood).** Full or partial shade. Reminiscent of delphiniums, monkshood is found mainly in shades of blue, some purple, yellow, or white. A good species plant is *A. carmichaelii,* which bears violet-blue flowers in August. Hybrids of *A. henryii, A. napellus,* and *A. pyrimindale* bloom slightly earlier and do not need staking. Good cultivars include 'Bressingham Spire', violet-blue; and 'Spark's Variety', deep violet-blue. All grow to 4 feet (1.2 m). Zones 2–9.

Alchemilla mollis **(lady's mantle) and** *A. alpina* **(alpine lady's mantle).** Lady's mantle grows in almost any soil, sun or shade, and forms very attractive mounds of fresh green, pleated leaves topped with delicate yellowish-green flower sprays in early summer. *A. mollis* grows to 12 inches (30 cm), and *A. alpina* to 6 inches (15 cm). Zones 4–8.

Aquilegia **spp. (columbine).** These lovely cottage garden favorites bloom in early summer, with delicate foliage and complicated flowers with prominent spurs, commonly called granny's bonnets or dovetails. The flowers bloom for several weeks in a wide range of colors and sizes, in sun or shade. They prefer a rich, moist soil, and grow to a height of 18 inches (45 cm). Zones 2–9.

Astilbe **spp.** See "The flower arranger's garden."

Bergenia **spp. (elephant's ear).** This plant's common name comes from the appearance of its thick, oval, leathery leaves, which vary in color from green to purple, depending on the cultivar. They bear open, cup-shaped flowers in various shades of lilac, pink, red, and white in spring or early summer, and reach a height of 9 to 15 inches (23 to 38 cm) depending upon the species. Zones 3–8.

Brunnera macrophylla **(perennial forget-me-not).** Large, branching sprays of pale blue star-shaped flowers give this plant its common name. It has large, heart-shaped leaves and flowers from April to June, growing to a height of 18 inches (45 cm). Zones 2–9.

Convallaria majalis **(lily-of-the-valley).** See "Old-fashioned fragrance."

Cryptogramma crispa **(parsley fern).** This is an ideal small fern for containers. It is deciduous, with parsleylike fronds that grow from 6 to 9 inches (15 to 23 cm) tall. It will tolerate drier conditions than many ferns and prefers shade. Zones 5–8.

Dicentra spectabilis (**bleeding heart**). This is a delicate-looking plant, with pale green, deeply dissected leaves and arching stems rising above the leaves, bearing rosy-red, heart-shaped flowers in late spring and early summer. There is also an attractive white form, 'Alba', that grows to 2 feet (60 cm) or more, and prefers rich, moist soil. Zones 2–9.

Geranium **spp.** (**true geraniums, crane's bill**). Not to be confused with the popular bedding plants, these geraniums are perennial. There are numerous species and cultivars, varying in growing habits and colors, and they grow in sun or shade, depending on the species. For shade look for *G. phaeum*, dark purple; *G. p.* 'Album', white, zones 5–9; and *G. macrorrhizum*, pink, zones 3–8. Saucer-shaped flowers are produced over a long period in summer. They make an interesting ground cover under shrubs and trees, with a height and spread of up to 18 inches (45 cm).

Hedera helix (**common English ivy**). See "Design by color."

Helleborus **spp.** (**Christmas and Lenten roses and other hellebores**). These lovely perennials will take partial or full shade, and their attractive winter and early spring blooms hold their form for weeks. All like a moist, rich soil. *H. niger*, the Christmas rose, forms a foot-high (30-cm) mound of evergreen leaves and delicate white-tinged-with-pink blooms in early January and February. Zones 3–8. *H. orientalis*, the Lenten rose, blooms slightly later in various shades of pink and is taller. Zones 4–9. *H. foetidus*, the stinking hellebore, and *H. argutifolius* syn. *H. corsicus*, Corsican hellebore, both have green flowers from February through April and are up to 2 feet (60 cm) in height. Zones 7–9.

Hosta **spp.** (**hostas**). Hostas like full or partial shade. They are usually grown for their wonderful foliage, ranging in color from narrow, light green leaves edged with white, to round, deeply veined, green-blue leaves more than 6 inches (15 cm) across. Removing the flowers before they bloom increases the life of the leaves. Hostas are some of the best perennials of all for shade. They grow from 6 to 24 inches (15 to 60 cm) depending on the species or cultivar. The following hostas are all good in containers: all *H. fortunei*, especially 'Francee', 'Gloriosa', and 'Gold Standard'; *H. sieboldiana* 'Frances Williams'; all forms of *H. kikutii*, especially 'Green Fountain'; all forms of *H. lancifolia* and *H. minor*; all forms of *H. nakaiana*, especially 'Duchess' and 'Golden Tiara'; all forms of *H. sieboldii* and *H. undulata*; and many other cultivars including 'August Moon', 'Brim Cup', 'Carrie Ann', 'Golden Prayers', 'Hydon Sunset', 'Invincible', 'Krossa Regal', 'Royal Standard', 'So Sweet', and 'Summer Fragrance'. Zones 2–9, depending on the cultivar.

Lamium maculatum (**dead nettle**). Heart-shaped leaves and trailing stems make dead nettle a good ground cover, useful to fill corners. It has white, pink, or yellow flowers, depending upon the cultivar, in summer. It grows from 6 to 24 inches (15 to 60 cm). Zones 3–8.

Omphalodes cappadocica (**navelwort**) **and** *O. verna* (**blue-eyed mary**). These are lovely little plants with bright blue flowers in spring that look a bit like forget-me-nots, only a much brighter and more vibrant blue. They tolerate full shade and grow to 6 inches (15 cm). Navelwort spreads quickly; blue-eyed mary is clump-forming. Zones 5–8.

Primula spp. (primrose and relatives). Most primulas will grow well in full sun or partial shade and moist but well-drained soil, so check the growing conditions they need when you buy them. The primulas most commonly grown are the hybrids, and they can be most attractive as a massed planting, interspersed with spring bulbs. Zones 5–8.

Pulmonaria officinalis (lungwort, Jerusalem cowslip). This hardy perennial has narrow green leaves covered with white spots and attractive, funnel-shaped, purple-blue flowers in late spring. It grows well with a minimum of care, to 12 inches (30 cm). Zones 3–9.

Viola spp. (violet). The old-fashioned violets produce small blooms and are often fragrant. They can be better appreciated growing in containers than in gardens where they are often overlooked. Cultivars such as *V. odorata* 'Christmas' and 'White Czar' are fragrant and have a long blooming season. Zones 6–8.

Climbers

Clematis spp. Many clematis will do well in a container as long as they are planted in a rich soil mix (two-thirds basic soil mix and one-third well-rotted manure or compost) in a container at least 18 inches (45 cm) deep and 12 to 18 inches (30 to 45 cm) in diameter. Not all clematis will grow in the shade but many will, especially the early-flowering species and hybrids. *C. alpina* blooms in April and grows 8 to 10 feet (2.4 to 3 m). Good cultivars are 'Columbine', pale blue; 'Pamela Jackman', mid-blue; 'Ruby', purple-pink; 'Willy', pink; and 'Albiflora', white. *C. macropetala* has blue blooms in May and grows to 8 feet (2.4 m). A good cultivar is 'Markhams Pink', pink. Large-flowered hybrids for shade include 'Alice Fisk', wisteria-blue; 'Barbara Dibley', petunia-red; 'Bee's Jubilee', deep pink, carmine bar; 'Capitan Thuilleaux', rosy-mauve, carmine bar; 'Comtesse de Bouchaud', mauve-pink; 'Dr. Ruppel', rose, carmine bar; 'Hagley Hybrid', rosy-mauve; 'Miss Bateman', creamy white; 'Nelly Moser', pale pink, carmine bar; 'Silver Moon', mother of pearl; 'Vyvyan Pennell', violet-blue; and 'William Kennett', deep lavender-blue. Zones 4–9.

Hydrangea petiolaris (climbing hydrangea). This tough and vigorous deciduous climber clings to support by means of aerial roots. It bears clusters of lacecap-type flowers in June. It takes time for this climber to become established, but when it does it can climb 35 feet (12.5 m) or more. To maintain shape and size, prune in February. Zones 5–9.

Annuals

A shady patio or balcony can be made as colorful as you like by adding annuals and tender perennials to your planters. Bedding plants, such as tuberous and fibrous begonias, fuchsias, impatiens, lobelia, geraniums, and winter pansies, all grow well in the shade. I have not provided details on them here since they are all well known, easy to grow, and fill garden centers in the spring. Just be sure to deadhead regularly, fertilize every week with a liquid fertilizer, and water every day.

Three-tiered terracotta pots for the shade

This planting arrangement will work well for any corner where space is limited. It consists of one large, one medium, and one small terracotta pot stacked one on top of the other so that there is enough space around the rim of the lower pots for plants. The top pot is fully planted. The arrangement makes a strong architectural statement, especially when it is filled with various plants that give shape, color, and interest for many months of the year. The size of the pots will determine the number and sizes of plants that can be used, but otherwise the idea can be applied to almost any theme, whether shade or sun. Even vegetables could be grown in this way. In the sample below the containers are best planted in the fall in mild climates, and kept in dappled shade.

Materials

- Containers: three terracotta pots, identical in appearance but different in size, as follows.
  — Bottom pot is 18 inches (45 cm) high and 30 inches (75 cm) in diameter.
  — Middle pot is 12 inches (30 cm) high and 18 inches (45 cm) in diameter.
  — Top pot is 11 inches (28 cm) high and 12 inches (30 cm) in diameter.
- Two sturdy plastic pots or buckets to sit inside the two lower terracotta pots. One should be about 18 inches (45 cm) high and 18 inches (45 cm) wide, and the other should be about 12 inches (30 cm) high and nine inches (22.5 cm) wide.
- Potting mixture: half basic soil mix and half compost, leaf mold, or aged manure, and fertilizer.
- Plants:
  — For the bottom container: three *Hedera helix* (ivy); twenty-five *Crocus* spp. (crocus); twenty-five *Galanthus nivalis* (snowdrop); five *Convallaria majalis* (lily-of-the-valley); five *Viola odorata* (sweet violets); five white *Impatiens* spp. (impatiens); and three small *Hosta* spp. (hosta), with white margins, such as 'Carrie Ann', 'Brim Cup', or 'Duchess'.
  — For the middle container: fifteen *Crocus* spp. (crocus); five *Narcissus* 'Minnow' (dwarf daffodils); three *Viola odorata* (sweet violets); one *Hedera helix* (ivy); three medium-sized *Hosta* spp. (hosta) with white margins, such as. *H. undulata* 'Albo-marginata'; and four white *Impatiens* spp. (impatiens).
  — For the top container: four winter pansies; one large *Hosta* spp. (hosta) with white margins, such as 'Gloriosa'; and white *Impatiens* spp. (impatiens) if there is room.

Method

Place the larger plastic pot upside-down in the bottom terracotta planter and fill around it with soil to within 3 inches (7.5 cm) of the top of the pot. Place the middle terracotta pot on top and place the smaller plastic pot upside-down in it, filling around it with soil to within 3 inches (7.5 cm) of the top of the pot. Finally, place the third terracotta pot on the top and fill it with soil to within 3 inches (7.5 cm) of the top of the pot. Arrange the plants according to the instructions above and plant them so that their rootballs are properly covered, and the final soil level in each pot is about one inch (2.5 cm) below the rim of the pot, with a 1/2-inch (1.2-cm) layer of fine gravel or sand on the top for improved drainage. Water well.

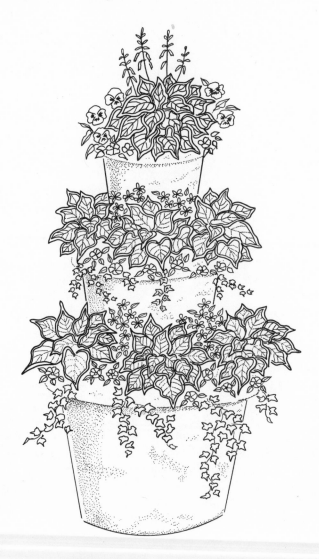

If you are starting this in the fall, plant the crocuses, snowdrops, and lily-of-the-valley, and intersperse them with winter pansies for winter color and interest. In the spring add the ivy, violets, and hostas. Take out the pansies and add the white impatiens in May.

Aftercare

Water well and fertilize every other week with a liquid fertilizer during the growing season. Do not let the pots dry out. In the fall, remove the impatiens. When the perennials have died back for the winter, add fresh winter pansies.

Design by color

Using color themes for mood and effect

COLOR IS ONE OF THE MOST IMPORTANT ELEMENTS IN ANY GARDEN. IT has a direct effect on the way we perceive space, and clever use of color combinations can make an area appear larger or smaller, warmer or cooler. Using the natural light and exposure of a space together with plants of specific colors, sizes, and shapes, we can encourage a particular mood or atmosphere, just as we can inside a house with paints, fabrics, and furnishings. If planting materials are chosen carefully, a sense of harmony and balance will prevail.

In nature, the textures and colors of plants create a harmonious landscape, even though there may be many different colors intermingled. One reason for this is that the colors of flowers have evolved within fairly strict guidelines corresponding to the workings of the natural world. Most insects, for instance, are insensitive to red, but stimulated by and attracted to yellow, green, blue, violet, and ultraviolet. This means there are relatively few insect-pollinated red flowers, but many blue and purple flowers, especially in the spring and summer when insects are most active. Birds, on the other hand, have excellent color vision, particularly for red, which may be why they devour red and orange fruits and berries before we have a chance to harvest, and why hummingbirds love those feeders with big, red, plastic flowers on them.

In the cultivated world of gardening, many plants have been hybridized to produce colors that do not occur in species plants, such as the famous black tulips of the eighteenth century, today's red delphiniums, and the many colors of hybrid roses. Garden centers offer a wide selection of plants with colored foliage and flowers, and there is always the temptation to combine plants that are not found together in the wild. But it makes sense to be careful when making plant selections, since the indiscriminate use of colors in the garden can lead to a feeling of chaos and disharmony.

The artist's color wheel can be a very helpful tool for planning garden color schemes. It helps us see which colors harmonize well and how they can be combined. Basically, all colors are made from a blending of the three primary colors, red, blue, and yellow. Secondary colors are formed when two of the three primaries are combined in exactly equal proportions. Thus blue and yellow combine to form green, yellow and red form orange, and red and blue make violet. Next come the six tertiary colors, formed by mixing a primary with an adjacent secondary so that the color is an intermediary between the two. For example, yellow and orange combine to give a yellow-orange, whereas red and orange make a red-orange. This gives us a natural spectrum of twelve colors that can be arranged in a circle.

According to color theory, there are reasons why some colors work well together and are harmonious, and others do not. As a general rule, two or more colors work well together if they are different hues of the same color, or if they are composed of closely similar chromas (technical jargon for the purity of a color, its intensity, or saturation). Thus a garden in all yellow-toned plants is harmonious (see "Variations on a yellow theme," below), and so, also, is a spring garden where all the flowers are in clear, pure colors, such as bright yellow primroses, violet-colored sweet violets, blue grape hyacinths, yellow daffodils, white snowdrops, and yellow forsythia.

One of the classic combinations is that of the complementary colors, the two colors that are opposite each other on the color wheel. To understand why they are called complementary, try the following experiment: find a solid green object, stare at it for some time, and then shut your eyes. You will be left with a red after-image of the object. Another experiment you can try, when you are next in a tropical paradise and gazing westwards at sunset, is to stare at the blue ocean just at the point where the bright yellow sun is about to drop below the horizon. Depending upon the light, at the instant the sun disappears you should see either a red flash or a green one. The red flash indicates the triangular relationship between blue, yellow, and red, and the green flash is, of course, the combination of yellow and blue.

Rules are made to be broken, or at least stretched, and the color rules are no exception. There are times when color can be used in an off-balance way and it looks terrible, but at other times it will be stimulating and exciting. If you have a flair for dramatic use of color, it's always worth experimenting, but if you are unsure, then begin with simple color combinations and get used to them first before becoming too bold.

If you have felt out of fashion because you prefer bright colors to the cool simplicity of white, take heart! According to color expert Faber Birren in his book *Color and Human Response,* "it is wholly normal for human beings to like any and all colors." He says that our color preferences often change over the years, with extroverts tending towards the warmer colors and introverts preferring the cooler ones. For those of us who garden, perhaps his most reassuring insight concerns the color green, which he says is symbolic of nature and balance. He contends that people who prefer green are almost always socially well adjusted—another good reason to be a gardener.

Although many books have been written about color and personality, surely the most important thing to know is that colors are there to be enjoyed, and if it's your garden then you can do what you like. If you want to add lots of bright colors, do it, and remind any skeptics that it's a sign of normal behavior, as you look at their black tulips with a sad shake of the head.

Just because you are working with a small space does not mean that you should restrict your choices to the cool colors—it all depends upon the effect you want to create. For instance, all the colors used in the Santa Fe theme are warm, and could make the space look smaller if the plants are unwisely chosen. However, the right plants, in hot yellows, reds, and oranges, will create a lively, energetic effect, and will brighten up the space rather than overwhelming it. The other materials, such as sand or pea gravel for the flooring, paint, decorative blankets, and furniture, should be chosen to harmonize with the palette of the plants (or vice versa, just as long as the colors blend).

It can be fun to plan a garden in which one color predominates, but a word of caution about becoming obsessive in this. For instance, a blue garden is a lovely idea, but is likely to be quite boring unless some other color, such as white or yellow, is used to spice up the blue and bring life into the garden. The blues will look more blue if the right complementary color is added, and the garden will be more beautiful. Likewise, a garden that relies on gray foliage plants can be very effective if complemented with flowering plants in shades of pink, purple, and lilac. Gray-foliaged plants tend to be quite drought-resistant, and this scheme feels restful on a hot day.

Ever since Vita Sackville-West created the White Garden at Sissinghurst, England, gardens with a white theme have been popular. It is easy to see why. The coolness of white has a calming effect, and makes a space feel larger than it is. All pale colors, especially white, come into their own after dark, unlike the deeper reds and blues, which will tend to fade into the night. When snow covers the ground in winter it is luminous, even when the moon is new. Under a full moon, the reflected glow from the snow will light up the landscape as if it were daytime. White flowers have the same effect. Few things are as stunning as a fragrant patch of white 'Casablanca' lilies in the moonlight, a white rose in full bloom, or a strongly scented bed of white stocks and tobacco plants. Many perennials have white cultivars but you may have a hard time finding the ones you want. So if you are thinking of doing an all-white garden—or any specific color theme—it pays to find out what is available in your area first.

Variations on a yellow theme

This scheme focuses on the color yellow. Yellow lifts the spirits. It is bright and cheerful, warm and lively. Yellow works especially well in a shady or semishady spot, where its liveliness energizes the space. The lovely gold-centered ivy, *Hedera helix* 'Goldheart', for instance, can be used to cover an ugly wall or drainpipe, underplanted with lilies or daylilies in various shades of yellow and orange.

Many trees and shrubs are tinged with yellow, such as golden euonymus, potentilla, or holly cultivars, and they can be underplanted with hostas and some bright yellow flowers such as coreopsis, chrysanthemums, and marigolds. Lime green can be effective too, and will have a gentle, softening effect. Good lime-green plants are lady's mantle, rue, dill, and green zinnias. Various gray-leafed plants, such as artemisia, senecio, and santolina, can be used to tone down the yellows.

The best way to create a yellow-theme garden, or any color theme, is to choose the most important plants first, the trees and shrubs, and gradually build up the other plants around them. Try to resist the temptation to select plants at random from the garden center in the hope that they will work well together once you get them home. That way lies madness.

Setting the scene

The following checklist will help you start creating a color-theme garden on your patio or balcony.
- Sun or shade, depending upon your location.
- Containers that are part of the color scheme. For example, try to find terracotta containers that are glazed with blue, yellow, or white, so they will either blend with or provide a contrast to the yellow flowers. Or use wooden containers painted yellow, blue, or white.
- Basic soil mix and fertilizer.
- Plants that fit the color theme (for a yellow theme, see the list below).
- Watering and lighting systems.
- Garden tools and storage.
- If there is room, a table and chairs, probably painted white, so that they will not fight with the color scheme. Cushions and cloth could be in yellow, or blue.

One of the cheeriest of all yellow flowers has to be the sunflower, so why not make this a feature of your yellow garden? You could have a bird feeder with sunflower seeds, extra pots in which you are growing just sunflowers, sunflowers stenciled on the tablecloth or chair cushions, and even a copy of a Van Gogh sunflower painting on the wall.

Yellow plants

Trees and shrubs

Elaeagnus pungens 'Maculata'. This evergreen, bushy, slightly spiny shrub has glossy, dark green leaves marked with a large, central, deep yellow patch. It has very fragrant, urn-shaped, creamy white flowers from mid- to late fall, sometimes followed by small fruits. It does equally well in sun or shade in any soil and tolerates heat, wind, and drought. It will grow to 6 feet (1.8 m). Zones 7–9.

Gleditsia triacanthos 'Sunburst' (honey locust). This handsome, medium-sized tree with lovely, ornamental, golden-yellow pinnate leaves is an excellent specimen tree for a container. It needs moist, well-drained soil, and grows to about 20 feet (6 m). Zones 5–9.

Hamamelis mollis 'Pallida' (Chinese witch hazel). See "Old-fashioned fragrance."

Potentilla 'Elizabeth'. This dense, bushy, deciduous shrub has small, deeply divided leaves and large, bright yellow, roselike flowers that appear from late spring to fall. It needs well-drained soil, prefers sun, and grows to a height of 30 inches (75 cm). Zones 3–8.

Senecio x 'Sunshine'. This plant is especially grown for its gray foliage, which contrasts nicely with yellow. It has attractive, silver-gray, wavy-margined leaves, white-felted below and downy above, and bears bright yellow, daisylike flowers in mid- to late summer. It grows to 2 to 3 feet (60 to 90 cm) in height and will tolerate most soils as long as they are well drained. It prefers sun, but will grow in partial shade. Zones 9–10.

Vines and climbers

Clematis tangutica and *C. orientalis*. Two lovely, late-flowering clematis that grow 10 to 12 feet (3 to 3.6 m) with lantern-shaped, single, yellow flowers, followed by fluffy, silvery seed heads. They grow well in sun or partial shade and like their roots cool and moist, in rich, well-drained soil. They need to have a trellis or some kind of support, and belong to the group of clematis that should be pruned back severely in the fall, since flowers come on new growth. Zones 6–9.

Hedera helix (common English ivy). Ivy is a vigorous, evergreen, self-clinging, climbing or trailing perennial. It is widely used in gardens, and in containers and hanging baskets as a filler and for trailing. Most will grow in sun or shade. Common ivy is hardy in zones 5–9. Attractive cultivars are 'Baltica', green with white veins, zones 3–9; 'Glacier', small leafed, with soft gray-green leaves edged with white, and the lovely 'Goldheart' with small, dark green leaves with bright yellow centers, zones 8–9.

Humulus lupulus 'Aureus' (yellow-leafed hop). Not the hops for making beer, but a nice form for the yellow garden with yellowish leaves and greenish flower spikes in the fall. It grows vigorously and will cover a trellis or wall easily during the summer. It likes full sun. Zones 6–9.

Thunbergia alata (black-eyed susan vine, clock vine). This is a lovely annual climber, moderately fast-growing, with toothed oval to heart-shaped leaves and rounded, rather flat, small flowers, orange-yellow with dark brown centers. It blooms profusely from early summer into fall, grows up to 10 feet (3 m), and needs full sun.

Perennials

Achillea 'Moonshine' (yarrow). A particularly attractive yarrow cultivar, 'Moonshine' bears soft yellow flowers in flat heads throughout the summer above a mass of small, feathery, gray-green leaves. It grows to 24 inches (60 cm), likes sun, and will grow in most well-drained soils. Zones 2–9.

Alchemilla mollis (lady's mantle) and *A. alpina* (alpine lady's mantle). See "In the shade."

Carex morrowii 'Gold Band' and *C. elata* 'Bowles Golden' (golden sedges). These are evergreen, tuft-forming perennial sedges with narrow, yellow-striped leaves. They are an excellent addition to a yellow container, especially when you are looking for the soft, feathery appearance of a grass in a shady spot. 'Gold Band' grows to a height of 6 to 8 inches (15 to 20 cm) and 'Bowles Golden' to 16 inches (40 cm). Zones 6–9.

Coreopsis verticillata 'Moonbeam' (threadleaf coreopsis). Its delicate, finely divided foliage and tiny, star-shaped, pale yellow flower heads make this cultivar a good container plant. It is a bushy perennial, needs sun, and grows to a height of 18 to 24 inches (45 to 60 cm). Zones 3–9.

Corydalis lutea (yellow corydalis). This evergreen, clump-forming perennial has fleshy, fibrous roots and much-divided, semierect, basal, gray-green leaves. It bears a profusion of slender yellow flowers with short spurs in late spring and summer, grows to 8 to 12 inches (20 to 30 cm), and likes sun. Zones 5–8.

Doronicum cordatum (leopard's bane). Leopard's bane blooms in the spring; its clear yellow, daisylike flower heads on slender, branching stems rise above heart-shaped, bright green leaves. It takes sun or partial shade and grows to 30 inches (75 cm). Zones 2–9.

Euphorbia polychroma syn. *E. epithymoides* (cushion spurge). Spurge is truly a marvellous splash of yellow in the spring when it bears heads of bright yellow flowers above green leaves. This bushy perennial grows to 20 inches (50 cm) and likes sun and moist soil. Zones 2–9.

Hemerocallis lilio-asphodelus syn. *H. flava* (lemon daylily). Daylilies are robust, clump-forming, spreading perennials with very fragrant, delicate, lemon- to chrome-yellow flowers in spring and early summer. Each flower lasts only a day or two, but new flowers continue to come out over a long period. They grow to 2 feet (60 cm) or more. One clump of daylilies in a blue pot looks stunning. They prefer sun and fertile, moist soil. Zones 2–9.

Hosta fortunei 'Albo-picta' and 'Aurea'; also 'Goldbrook', 'Gold Standard', 'Golden Prayers', 'Golden Tiara', 'Hydon Sunset'. These cultivars are all suitable for a yellow garden. For more information on hostas see "In the shade."

Lysimachia nummularia 'Aurea' (creeping jenny). A creeping, ground-hugging perennial useful for filling in spots in a container or trailing over the edge. It has greenish-yellow leaves and bright yellow flowers in summer. It prefers sun and well-drained soil. Zones 2–9.

Mimulus luteus (yellow monkey flower). This attractive perennial prefers rich, moist soil and a shady spot. Throughout the summer it bears yellow, snapdragonlike flowers with red or brown spots above hairy green foliage. It grows to 12 inches (30 cm). Zones 6–10.

Origanum vulgare '**Aureum**' (**golden marjoram, golden oregano**). An attractive, aromatic herb that forms a dense mat of golden-yellow leaves in spring, turning pale yellow-green in midsummer. A few leaves will add a nice zip to salads. It likes full sun and well-drained soil. Zones 4–8.

Primula spp. (**primroses and primulas**). Primulas will grow well in full sun or partial shade and moist but well-drained soil, so check the growing conditions they need when you buy them. Besides the showy yellow hybrid primulas, consider growing *P. vulgaris*, the true primrose, for its delicate, faintly scented, pale yellow flowers. Zones 5–8.

Ruta graveolens (**common rue**). Rue is a compact, bushy plant with aromatic, finely divided blue foliage and it bears small, mustard-yellow flowers in summer. The blue foliage contrasts well with yellow plants. It grows to about 2 feet (60 cm) and likes sun and well-drained soil. Zones 4–9.

Annuals

Antirrhinum majus (**snapdragon**). Although they are perennials, snapdragons are usually grown as annuals and there are some excellent yellow cultivars, notably 'Rocket Yellow'. They need sun and a rich, well-drained soil; frequent deadheading extends their blooming season. They grow from 8 inches to 3 feet (20 to 90 cm) depending upon the cultivar.

Argemone mexicana (**Mexican prickly-poppy**). With its stiff, prickly leaves and fragrant, poppylike, orange or yellow flowers, this bushy plant adds form, structure, and fragrance to a summer container. It is a half-hardy perennial and thus usually grown as an annual, preferring full sun and a well-drained soil. It grows to 2 feet (60 cm) with half the spread.

Calceolaria '**Sunshine**'. This is another perennial that is usually grown as an annual. It bears crowded clusters of pouchlike, golden-yellow flowers above broadly oval, basal, green leaves in late spring and summer. It grows to 8 inches (20 cm) and likes sun and well-drained soil.

Helianthus annuus (**sunflower**). What could be simpler or more striking than sunflowers in a large, blue ceramic pot? Now we can grow knee-high sunflowers with blooms 8 to 10 inches (20 to 25 cm) across, perfect for growing in pots. Good forms are 'Sunspot', to a height of 18 to 24 inches (45 to 60 cm); and 'Teddy Bear', to 2 feet (60 cm).

Nicotiana alata '**Lime Green**' (**flowering tobacco plant**). See "Old-fashioned fragrance." 'Lime Green' bears greenish-yellow flowers that bloom from summer through to early fall. It grows to a height of 2 feet (60 cm) and needs sun and a fertile, well-drained soil.

Tagetes patula **cultivars** (**French marigold**). These are fast-growing, bushy annuals that have deeply divided, aromatic leaves and bear single or double flower heads in shades of yellow, orange, red, or mahogany in summer and early fall. To make sure you get the colors you want, choose plants when they are in bloom. They grow to 12 inches (30 cm) and like full sun and fertile, well-drained soil.

Zinnia elegans 'Envy'. An attractive annual with pompomlike, green flower heads on 2-foot-long (60-cm) flower stalks. Zinnias also make good cut flowers. Grow in full sun in rich, well-drained soil.

A bright pot of sunlight

It is easy to make a yellow-themed patio or balcony garden for either sun or shade. A wide array of plants is available. The container described here is very simple and makes use of a combination of yellow, blue, and green. Yellow and green come from the plants, and blue from the pot. This is an effective way to combine colors. For instance, blue flowers could be planted in a yellow pot to provide an equally strong contrast.

Materials

- Container: one dark blue glazed pot, about 16 inches (40 cm) across at the mouth, and 18 inches (45 cm) deep.
- Potting mixture: basic soil mix and fertilizer.
- Plants: one *Coreopsis verticillata* 'Moonbeam' (threadleaf coreopsis); two *Origanum vulgare* 'Aureum' (oregano); and three *Hedera helix* 'Goldheart' (ivy).

Method

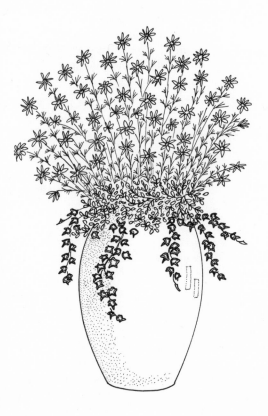

Fill the pot to within 4 inches (10 cm) of the rim with soil mix. Make a hole in the soil in the middle of the pot and plant the coreopsis in it. Fill the soil in around the plant. Put the oregano and ivy plants around the coreopsis and firm the soil around them, topping up with soil to within 1 inch (2.5 cm) of the rim of the pot. Put a 1/2-inch (1.2-cm) layer of fine gravel or sand on the top for improved drainage. Water well and place in a sunny position on your balcony or patio.

Aftercare

Water every day and fertilize every other week with liquid fertilizer during the summer. Once the flowers have finished blooming in the summer you can experiment with other yellow flowers for the following spring—perhaps plant some white snowdrops, yellow crocus, yellow daffodils, white tulips, and blue and yellow primulas. Protect it from freezing during the winter and enjoy when spring comes around. Think of this as your yellow and blue pot and try as many different combinations as you can with the passing of the seasons.

Romance in the garden

Roses bring thoughts of love and romance

FOR THOUSANDS OF YEARS WILD ROSES HAVE INHABITED THE COUNTRY-side in the northern hemisphere, tumbling down steep riverbanks, clinging to eroding cliffs and rocky mountain ledges, clambering through trees and shrubs, and hugging harsh and windswept northern plains. The climates they live in are as diverse as their growing habits, and they can be found growing in northern Canada and Siberia as well as the near-tropical heat of India and North Africa. Twenty-five species of wild roses thrive and flourish throughout North America, but in Asia and Europe there are hundreds more.

Historical records show that wild roses were brought under cultivation by the Chinese about five thousand years ago; three thousand years later rose gardens had become so popular that huge parks were devoted to them. Decorative pottery and jewelry indicates that the Egyptians were using wild roses as art motifs at about this time, and they started a thriving business in rose cultivation, shipping roses to Rome in galleys. Thus began the Romans' love affair with the rose, and large nurseries were set up in the south of Italy to supply the needs of Roman high society.

The Romans introduced many indigenous roses such as *Rosa gallica* and *Rosa alba* into their gardens and many Roman writers included descriptions of them in their correspondence. One of the greatest of these writers was Pliny the Younger, a Roman statesman and orator who was also a keen gardener. The letters he wrote between 97 and 107 A.D. describe the many roses he was growing in sunny areas of his garden. Since then, amateur and professional growers alike have continued this fascination with the rose and experimented with growth and hybridization, while botanists and plant explorers have traveled the world and risked their lives, all in search of the perfect rose.

A big breakthrough happened at the beginning of the eighteenth century when eight species roses were brought to Europe from China. Unlike the European roses that only bloomed once a year, in June or July, the China roses were able to bloom repeatedly throughout the growing season. These roses were not nearly as hardy as the European roses. However, years of crossbreeding has produced hardy, cold-resistant hybrids from these delicate plants and there are attractive hybrids with bigger, better, longer-lasting blooms and lovely colors that can be grown in almost every area of North America. Breeders have also developed thornless plants, miniature forms, and pest- and disease-resistant hybrids—all desirable traits for container gardening.

One of history's most celebrated lovers of roses was the Empress Josephine, wife of Napoleon I. In her magnificent gardens at Chateau Malmaison she attempted to grow every known kind of rose and had collected about 250 different types by the time she died in 1814. Many of them were immortalized as engravings by French artist Pierre Joseph Redouté. One color that we associate with roses today is conspicuously absent from these engravings—a really good yellow. Rose growers had been trying to produce a good yellow rose for some time with no success, and it was not until 1910 that a French rose breeder, Joseph Pernet-Ducher, succeeded in making the first pure yellow garden rose the world had ever seen. His research had taken twenty-five years. After thirteen years of crossbreeding a golden 'Persian Yellow' with hybrid tea roses, he created 'Soleil d'Or', light yellow on the outside but orange-red or pink on the inside. Twelve years later he finally achieved a pure yellow garden rose, and called it 'Rayon d'Or'.

The value of a discovery such as a new color is so great that rose breeding is surrounded by an aura of romance and adventure. Painters, writers, poets, and musicians have claimed the rose as a symbol for love, friendship, and beauty. Politicians and churches have used the rose to gain popularity. There are endless stories about this magical plant, but there is one that stands out from all the rest. This true story has become a symbol of love and friendship, and represents some of the finest qualities of human nature.

In 1939 when Francis Meilland, whose father, grandfather, and great-grandfather before him were also rose growers in France, found a sturdy plant with magnificent pale gold blossoms growing from one seed he had nurtured, he knew he had bred something valuable. He had no idea how valuable, nor did he realize how long it would take him to find out. He showed his new rose, known only as 3-35-40, to other rose growers that year and it caused a sensation. The pointed buds bore petals ranging in color from ivory to pale gold, with edges fringed in a delicate pink. The flower stems were strong and straight, and the foliage was a lush, rich, dark green. Number 3-35-40 was the queen of the rose show and many put in their order for this perfect hybrid tea.

The world was heading into World War II. Francis Meilland hastily sent cuttings from the rose to the United States, Italy, and Germany, and the bundle of stems addressed to Robert Pyle, a Pennsylvania rose grower, was aboard the last American plane to leave France in November 1940, a step ahead of the German invasion. Not until the war ended, five years later, did Francis learn that his exported cuttings had been used to propagate the rose that many experts consider the best ever developed.

Within a decade it was blossoming on more than 30 million rose bushes throughout the world. Meilland had named his rose 'Madame A. Meilland' after his mother. In Germany it had been named to the glory of god, 'Gloria Dei'; in Italy 'Gioia', or joy; and in the United States it received the name by which we know this rose so well today: 'Peace'. Francis Meilland was able to patent his rose, and his name lives on in all the many Meilland rose cultivars available in garden centers today.

Fortunately the crossing, recrossing and back-crossing of roses of the past has produced so many cultivars that there are some suited to every part of the country, and for every use imaginable. The most suitable roses to grow in containers are small in stature; the polyantha hybrids, China rose hybrids, miniature rose hybrids, and some of the smaller climbers.

Polyantha roses produce large clusters of small blooms and grow to a maximum height of 3 feet (0.9 m), making them ideal for massing in planters or large pots. They bloom profusely on both old canes and new ones, ensuring a long blooming period, in colors ranging from deep red to white, with many shades of pink. Old China roses are less hardy than the polyanthas. Their beauty, however, is hard to resist, and most have an exotic tropical fragrance. China roses also flower repeatedly, and often bear their blossoms in clusters. Low-growing cultivars of China roses rarely exceed 3 feet (0.9 m) in height.

Miniature roses are ideal for planting in window boxes or wicker baskets and placed by a doorway or on a table, and some of the climbing roses are especially useful as screening plants. The latter can be attached to pillars, trellises, and wires secured to the walls. If you have room, you may want to try a standard rose tree; many hybrid tea cultivars, including 'Peace', are available on a standard root stock. However, although a standard tree rose will add height and elegance, it is unlikely to be successful over the long term. They tend to perform well in their first year, less so the second, and are definitely unhappy by the third. Perhaps life in a container just isn't for them.

Rose bushes grown in containers will give you much pleasure during the late spring and summer months, but for added color in winter and early spring, underplant them with winter pansies, violets, and bulbs. You may also want to leave room to plant an evergreen shrub, such as a boxwood or camellia, for winter color.

Setting the scene

The following checklist will help you start creating a romantic, rose-filled garden on your patio or balcony.

- Six to eight hours of sunshine a day.
- Planters and containers placed to fit your space. For 3-foot-high (0.9-m) roses the container should be at least 24 inches (60 cm) deep. Wood is the best material to use for growing roses successfully since it tends to hold moisture the best. Drainage holes in the planters are very important.

- Potting mixture: a good-quality container soil mix, plus a handful of bone meal and controlled-release fertilizer for each plant.
- Basic gardening tools, including secateurs, gardening gloves, and storage.
- Watering and lighting systems.
- If there is room, comfortable chairs, a table, and a patio umbrella.

If you are making a romantic, rose-filled garden, it should feel as if love is in the air. Be excessive with the rose motif and design around it, using your favorite rose-patterned fabric to make cushions, tablecloths, and seat covers. Include anything else you can find for your outdoor setting that has roses on it, such as a teapot, tea cups, vases, and plates. Decorate the middle of the table with a basket of miniature roses.

Roses for containers

Most roses will grow in containers for a season or two without too much trouble if they are watered and fertilized adequately. However, for permanent planters it is important to choose roses that do not mind the restrictions of a container, such as the ones given here, and treat them well.

Roses in containers do need special care. They should be spoiled with plenty of organic mulch and watered and fertilized regularly. It is also important to repot roses in fresh soil every two to three years. Make sure the roses are hardy for your area. In cold climates where the winters are severe, choose roses that have been grown on their own rootstock, rather than budded. The advantage is that if your plant should freeze due to extreme winter conditions, new growth that comes from the base is the rose you planted, rather than a wild rose rootstock.

The list of roses given below is meant to be a guideline. All grow successfully in containers and provide continuous bloom throughout the summer and early fall. Use the list to get started, and add your own favorites as you go along.

China roses (*Rosa chinensis*)

The smaller hybrids available today are suitable for growing in containers. Their continual bloom and exotic, heady fragrance make them appealing for patios and balconies. They are not hardy, and should be grown only in mild climates or where they can be protected from cold and wet winters. Zones 8–10.

'Cecile Brunner', the sweetheart rose. This charming rose grows to 3 feet (0.9 m), with small, dark, glossy leaves and clusters of double flowers shaped like miniature hybrid tea roses. The blossoms are delicately fragrant and shell-pink, slightly deeper in color in the center. An excellent rose and good for cutting.

'Hermosa'. A lovely rose that bears fragrant clusters of small, lilac-pink, semidouble flowers with petals that are rolled at the edges, and bluish-green foliage. It makes a good screening hedge and grows to 3 feet (90 cm).

'Irene Watts'. A free-flowering rose with fragrant clusters of pale salmon-pink blossoms and glossy green foliage. It grows to 3 feet (90 cm).

Polyantha roses

These tough, compact, fairly disease-resistant roses make good hedging for balconies or rooftops. They are also ideal planted in groups in a large container or as a specimen underplanted with pinks or other low-growing perennials. Much of their beauty lies in the continuous bloom of small, clustered flowers throughout the summer months and early fall, since most have no fragrance. They are often listed as patio roses in garden centers. Zones 5–9.

The following hybrids all grow to approximately 2 feet (60 cm), although 'The Fairy' can grow to 3 feet (0.9 m), and 'Orange Triumph' to 4 feet (1.2 m). All bear flowers about 1.5 inches (3.7 cm) across, except 'Happy', with flowers half that size.

'Dick Koster', deep pink semidouble flowers.
'Happy', tiny crimson-red semidouble flowers.
'Margo Koster', globular, salmon-pink double flowers, slightly fragrant.
'Mothersday', globular, deep red double flowers and small, glossy foliage.
'Orange Triumph', red-orange semidouble flowers borne in huge trusses; at its best in late fall.
'The Fairy', clusters of buttonlike, pink double flowers and attractive glossy-green foliage.

Miniature roses

These dense, compact plants grow no higher than 2 feet (60 cm) and many hybrids range between 6 and 12 inches (15 to 30 cm). Most miniatures bloom continuously from late spring to fall, producing 1/2- to 2-inch (1.2- to 5-cm) blossoms in every color possible. Miniatures are ideal for planting in sunny window boxes or in smaller pots placed at eye level. Here are a few favorites from the hundreds of cultivars available. Zones 6–10.

'Baby Betsy McCall', 18 to 20 inches (45 to 50 cm), fragrant, light pink double flowers on strong stems. One of the best hybrid tea forms.
'Baby Darling', 12 to 14 inches (30 to 35 cm), salmon-apricot double flowers and a light fragrance.
'Baby Masquerade', 24 inches (60 cm), yellow buds blushed with rose mature into shades of light pink, yellow with red, and blends of these colors. Vigorous and free-flowering from late spring to late fall, with dense glossy foliage.
'Cinderella', 18 to 20 inches (45 to 50 cm), long-lasting double flowers of shell-pink turning to white, with dense glossy foliage. Fragrant and excellent for cutting.
'Lemon Delight', 12 inches (30 cm), semidouble clear yellow flowers opening from a mossy pointed bud.

'Rise 'n' Shine', 18 inches (45 cm), double golden-yellow flowers and nice thick foliage. An excellent hybrid tea form.

'Stacy Sue', 18 inches (45 cm), double soft pink blossoms, dainty and abundant.

Climbers

The following selection includes only those climbers that have a long flowering period and neat growing habit; nearly all of them are fragrant. Zones vary according to hybrid: the most hardy is 'John Cabot'.

'Aloha', 6 feet (1.8 m). A stiff, bushy rose with attractive, leathery, green foliage and pink buds opening into strongly fragrant, cupped, fully double, terracotta-colored blooms. It flowers heavily in June and September with many flowers in between.

'Altissimo', 7 to 10 feet (2.1 to 3 m). The single, velvety, scarlet-red flowers of this rose, with its contrasting golden stamens, make it a lovely choice. It blooms continually from June throughout the summer months and has a light fragrance.

'Compassion', 10 feet (3 m). An excellent climber with attractive, glossy, dark green foliage that bears pink flowers early in the season, but from August onwards they change to a rich shade of salmon-apricot. It flowers heavily in June and September, with many flowers between and after these months, and has a heavy, heady fragrance.

'Crimson Glory', 10 feet (3 m). This rose has large, velvety, semidouble, deep crimson flowers and an overwhelming fragrance. It blooms continuously from late May through to September.

'Golden Showers', 6 feet (1.8 m). One of the most popular short climbing roses, this one is hardly ever without blooms from June to September, and is ideal for containers. It is predominantly upright, with bright lemon-yellow flowers and a sweet, lemon fragrance.

'John Cabot', 8 feet (2.4 m). Specially bred by the Canadian Department of Agriculture to withstand the Canadian winter, this attractive rose has a good fragrance and a profuse display of magenta flowers throughout the season.

'Parade', 10 feet (3 m). Deep pink flowers with a strong fragrance are borne plentifully in June and September, with many flowers between. This rose is hardy and adaptable, copes well with shade, and is a good choice for a north wall.

'White Cockade', 7 feet (2.1 m). This rose bears flowers in profusion from midseason onwards. The semidouble white flowers have hints of pink and cream and a pleasant fragrance.

Planting a wicker basket of miniature roses

Wicker baskets and roses make a charming combination, especially when you choose a nicely shaped basket and plant it to the brim with your favorite miniature roses. Set on a table, placed by a doorway, or perched on a window ledge, it will give you many months of pleasure. There are dozens of roses to choose from, in many different colors, and it is best to buy them in full bloom so that you can be sure to get exactly what you want. Roses need sunshine, but if you cannot provide six hours of sun a day, don't despair: the same basket can be planted with double pink impatiens for a shady table, and it is remarkable how similar the effect can be.

Materials

- Container: wicker basket, any shape or size.
- Potting mixture: a good-quality container soil mix, plus a handful of bone meal and controlled-release fertilizer.
- Plants: two or three miniature roses, depending upon the size of the basket; and one or two containers of blue lobelia or white alyssum (optional).
- Other: plastic sheeting and moss.

Method

Line the basket with plastic and make slits in the plastic at the bottom for drainage. Add 2 inches (5 cm) or more of the potting soil. Plant the roses, bringing the soil level up to within 1 inch (2.5 cm) of the top of the basket and add half an inch (1.2 cm) of fine gravel or sand for improved drainage. If you are adding annuals, such as lobelia and alyssum, separate them into small clumps and plant them around the edge. Cover the surface between the plants with moss and water well.

Aftercare

Water the basket daily. Fertilize with liquid fertilizer every two weeks. Deadhead the flowers as they fade. Remove the roses from their basket at the end of the summer and plant them in a large container or a friend's garden for the winter months, retrieving them the following spring.

Clipped for style

The ancient art of topiary, from teacups to peacocks

THE ART OF CLIPPING TREES AND SHRUBS INTO HEDGES AND FANCIFUL forms is an ancient one that began in the heyday of the Roman Empire. Pliny the Elder, who was one of the greatest observers and collectors of information in Roman times, was the first to give an account of the clipping of the Mediterranean cypress (*Cupressus sempervirens*) and native boxwood (*Buxus sempervirens*), the two plants most commonly used. Unfortunately, he lost his life during the eruption of Vesuvius in 79 A.D., when curiosity took him a little too close to the volcano's toxic fumes.

Luckily his nephew, Pliny the Younger, survived, and he was also a keen gardener and prolific letter writer. He wrote frequently about his garden in Tuscany, and these letters are the best accounts we have of the use of topiary in ancient Rome. Pliny thought of plants as construction materials, and clipped his hedges into animals and letters of the alphabet, even having his own name cut out in boxwood. The art was conceived as a way to illustrate a theme using natural elements. It became so developed that Pliny records whole scenes cut out from boxwood and cypress showing huntsmen and their quarry and even fleets of ships.

Since Roman times the art of topiary has gone in and out of fashion. It reached its high point during the seventeenth century in northern Europe, where grand gardens were clipped, shaped, and formalized, in sharp contrast to the natural surroundings of the landscape. One of the best examples of these gardens to survive almost three hundred years is the topiary garden at Levens Hall in Cumbria, in the United Kingdom, which was designed by Monsieur Beaumont, gardener to James II. The overall plan of the topiary garden is essentially the same today as it was then, and thousands of visitors come each year to admire the many fine specimens that remain.

By the early eighteenth century there was a revolt against all formality in garden design. The art of topiary came under harsh scrutiny, particularly by some of the most influential literary critics of the time, whose remarks effectively destroyed most of the carefully designed formal settings of seventeenth-century houses in Britain. According to Alexander Pope, for instance, "We seem to make it our study to recede from nature, not only in the various tonsure of greens into the most regular and formal shape, but even in monstrous attempts beyond the reach of the art itself: we run into sculpture and are yet better pleased to have our trees in the most awkward figures of men and animals, than in the most regular of their own." (*The Guardian,* 1713).

Maybe they just lost their sense of humor. Whatever the explanation, topiary fell into disfavor for over a century. It was not really revived as an art form until the latter part of the nineteenth century with the work of people like Sir Robert Lorimer, designer of the gardens at Earlshall, Fife (1895), and Major Lawrence Johnstone, who began the gardens at Hidcote Manor in 1907. Their strong and imaginative approach to the use of formal hedging and topiary as an element of design had a powerful influence on many other smaller gardens.

Today there is a great interest in topiary on both sides of the Atlantic, and many public parks and gardens are including clipped trees and shrubs in their designs. One example is the topiary project in Columbus, Ohio, at the Deaf School Park. Here George Seurat's painting *Afternoon on the Island of La Grande Jatte* was brought to life in topiary. Sculpted metal frames were used to shape yew trees into forty-six plant figures: women in long dresses carrying parasols, men wearing top hats, and children and dogs enjoying a nineteenth-century French Sunday afternoon.

Free-standing stuffed animals are a new and popular form of topiary. A North American invention, these unusual ornaments are made from wire and metal frames, sculpted into desired shapes, filled with absorbent moss as a growing medium, and planted with ground covers such as ivy, creeping fig, and periwinkle. A few years ago, the Rockefeller Center was the habitat for a large gathering of stuffed topiary jungle animals, and since then larger-than-life green elephants, giraffes, and lions have found their way into our urban concrete jungles. More recently, stuffed topiaries on a much smaller scale have taken over garden centers and flower shops everywhere, and these little rabbits, frogs, dogs, and teddy bears are frequent inhabitants of steps, doorways, and other non-green spaces.

If you have an appreciation for the unusual, and you are clever with scissors, consider creating a topiary fantasy for yourself. With garden shears, time, and patience, many evergreens can be transformed into a garden of make-believe, giving life and form to teacups, birds, animals, ships, and chairs. Free-standing topiaries, or pots and planters containing trees and shrubs clipped into interesting shapes, can transform your balcony, patio, or concrete parking lot from dreary and dull to whimsical and delightful. One commonly seen and popular form is the poodle topiary, where evergreens are clipped back along their branches and the foliage only allowed to grow at branch ends, into round balls, rather like the haircut given to poodle dogs. Topiaries can also be simple and elegant, especially if you use large terracotta pots containing topiaries classically shaped into spheres, cubes, cones, pyramids, or cloud forms.

Different styles of topiary create different effects. Topiaries in the form of geometric shapes provide strong architectural elements, and give a formal flair to a patio, balcony, or rooftop, whereas oversized living sculptures provide humor and a touch of the bizarre. Imagine Godzilla or King Kong looming over a balcony railing, staring at passersby on the street below; or a peacock displaying its feathers to the sky; or even a large boxwood bush cut into the shape of an easy chair that looks so inviting your guests try to sit in it.

Topiaries can be used on their own, to provide a simple decoration, or they can be used as ornaments within a garden of a different theme, such as a shade garden or a fragrance garden. If you only have room for one pot, consider a simply shaped, formal, evergreen topiary clipped into a precise cone, box, spiral, or ball. If it is near the door, underplant it with annuals in colors that match. For instance, near a purple door, plant matching purple petunias and they will complement it all summer long.

The pot you choose for your topiary is very important. It should be big enough to support the visual size and nutritional needs of the plant, and simple in form. Versaille boxes make excellent containers for topiary, as do Italian terracotta pots and elegant concrete containers. If you want to try your hand at a whole hedge of topiary, you may want to use a long wooden planter. It should be at least 18 inches (45 cm) deep and 24 inches (60 cm) wide for standard-sized boxwood and other topiary plants of comparable size.

Setting the scene

The following checklist will help you start creating a topiary garden on your patio or balcony.

- Sun or shade, depending upon the plants you choose.
- Large wooden or concrete containers, 18 to 24 inches (45 to 60 cm) in diameter and depth, depending upon the size and form of the plants you choose.
- Plants: for evergreen topiary trees and shrubs, choose from the list below; for stuffed topiary sculptures, use moss and ivy (see "How to make a stuffed topiary sculpture," below.)
- Additional plants, if desired, for summer color.
- Basic soil mix, amended as necessary for the individual needs of the plant, and controlled-release fertilizer.
- Basic gardening tools, including a good pair of hand shears and small pruning clippers or secateurs, and storage for the tools.
- Water with a drip irrigation system if at all possible, to supply continuous moisture to tree roots.
- A lighting system.
- If there is room, a table and chairs.

A formal topiary calls for the patio or balcony to have a feeling of elegance, with clipped evergreens, simple furniture, and Versailles tubs or terracotta pots as planters.

If it is more informal, you may want to follow a specific theme, and add to it with props. For example, a wilderness/homesteading theme could include a stuffed topiary animal, such as a moose or bear, together with old boots, planted up with moss and ferns, barn siding, and more trees to give an impression of the forest. Or you could have a whale or shark topiary, and create a beach scene; or Mickey and Minnie Mouse with Disney memorabilia; or . . .

Suitable plants for topiary

Many plants are suitable for clipping into geometric shapes and animal figures. The best are evergreens that have a dense growing habit, are pliable, have small leaves, and tolerate a fair amount of clipping. They must also be winter hardy for your area, otherwise you will have to shelter them from heavy snow and extreme temperatures. Deciduous shrubs can be used, but they lose their appeal in winter and are better as topiary hedges in larger gardens.

Select topiary plants that will like the conditions you can offer them, and provide them with the right soil mix, depending upon their particular needs. Make sure that the pot has proper drainage holes and is large enough to take the rootball of the plant with room left over for extra soil. Once the plant is potted up, the soil level should be about an inch (2.5 cm) below the rim of the pot. Water regularly, making sure that the plant's roots are never allowed to dry out.

Container-grown trees and shrubs may need to be moved to larger pots every five years. Replace as much of their soil as possible every year, and fertilize with a small handful of controlled-release fertilizer in spring. Mulch with a top-dressing of compost, steer manure, or mushroom manure annually. In regions where snowfall is heavy, place netting over the topiary to prevent the branches from separating or breaking under the weight of the snow, and knock the snow off as soon as possible.

The plant list given below should help you get started. These plants have all proved to be successful for topiary as long as they are pruned and shaped on a regular basis.

Buxus sempervirens (common boxwood) and *B. microphylla* (dwarf boxwood). There are about seventy species of boxwood, but these two are the ones usually used for evergreen hedges and small-scale topiary. They have small, ovate, dark green, glossy leaves ideal for forming tight, compact shapes. *B. microphylla* is hardier and lower in stature than *B. sempervirens*, but there are so many cultivars of both that it is often difficult to distinguish between them. Good ones to use for dwarf geometric shapes and small animal or bird figures are 'Compacta' and 'Koreana'; they grow up to 2 feet (60 cm) in height and width. An excellent larger cultivar is 'Suffruticosa', to 3 feet (90 cm).

All grow at a rate of 1 to 4 inches (2.5 to 10 cm) a year, and will live for fifty years or more. They will grow in a basic soil mix and tolerate sun and shade. They should be clipped in the spring; watering the foliage before you cut it will help to prevent it from turning brown. Boxwood propagates easily from softwood cuttings. Zones 6–9.

Cupressus sempervirens (Italian cypress). This is one of the true cypresses and is the evergreen conifer used in Roman times for topiary. Italian cypress grows best in warmer areas, such as California and Arizona. Most hybrids are too large for containers, with the exception of 'Stricta', which grows slowly to a height of 20 feet (6 m) if left unpruned, less in a container, with a diameter of only 3 to 4 feet (0.9 to 1.2 m). This makes it ideal for shaping into a spiral form. Its foliage is deep green with rounded, red-brown cones. It thrives in any ordinary, well-drained soil and prefers sun. Zones 7–10.

Hedera helix (English ivy). Ivy is the plant most commonly used for stuffed topiary sculptures. See "Design by color."

Ilex crenata 'Convexa' (dwarf Japanese holly). See "In the shade."

Lavandula angustifolia (English lavender). See "A taste of Provence."

Ligustrum spp. (privet). The privets used for topiary are evergreen flowering shrubs that bear white flowers in July or August, depending upon the species. They grow well in a basic soil mix, in sun or shade, and will tolerate ocean winds and sea spray. A good species to try is *L. texanum* syn. *Ligustrum japonicum* 'Texanum'. It is a compact and upright shrub and grows to 6 to 8 feet high (1.8 to 2.4 m) and 4 to 6 feet (1.2 to 1.8 m) wide. Zones 7–9.

Rosmarinus officinalis (rosemary). This classic Mediterranean herb is one of the most popular plants for creating small designs such as standards, poodles, hoops, and hollow frame animals. See "A taste of Provence."

Taxus spp. (yew). Several species of yew, notably *Taxus baccata, T. cuspidata,* and *T. x media,* are ideal for sculpting into shapes and figures, and yews have been used as topiary material for centuries in regions where it is too cold for cypress. All yews are narrow-leafed evergreens. They have a good rate of growth, and topiary sculptures formed on a frame will take on the desired shape in three to four years. By using a combination of yews with different growing habits, one can achieve almost any imaginable form of topiary.

Good cultivars include *T. baccata* 'Repandens', a flat-topped, low-growing yew with a height of 2 feet (60 cm) and spread of up to 15 feet (5 m); *T. cuspidata* 'Aurescens', a hardy, spreading plant growing to only 1 foot (30 cm), with a 3-foot (90-cm) spread; and many smaller cultivars of the hardy *T. x media,* including 'Brownii', height 8 feet (2.4 m), width 11 feet (3.3 m), and 'Densiformis', with a height and width of 6 to 10 feet (1.8 to 3 m). 'Densiformis' has a dense, rounded growing habit, the perfect shape for a big bear. There are many yews to choose from, so use your own favorites and experiment. Yews need good-sized containers, ordinary soil, and good drainage, and they thrive in sun or shade. They cannot tolerate their roots drying out. They can be clipped two or three times a year. A good, strong, metal frame placed around the yew will help to establish the form or figure you want (see "Creating an evergreen topiary," below). Zones 5–8.

How to make a stuffed topiary sculpture

Stuffed topiary sculptures are whimsical and fun to make. They do well in a shady spot, tucked in among the pots and planters.

Materials

- A heavy wire frame made into the shape of your choice. You can use a ready-made frame, or make your own with heavy wire, bent and welded into shape.
- Fern pins (wire floral fasteners shaped like hair pins), available from hobby shops or florists' shops. Hair pins can be used if fern pins are unavailable.
- Nylon fishing line.
- Fresh moss, available from florists' shops, garden shops, and hobby shops.
- Pruners and lightweight garden gloves.
- Plants that can grow in fresh moss. Ivy is ideal (see plant list above) and grows quickly once established. Tender ivy cultivars tolerate indoor conditions and the topiary can be brought indoors for the winter. The number of plants you use for your topiary will depend upon how patient you are—the more plants you use, the more quickly the sculpture will be covered with ivy.

Method

Soak the moss in water for a few hours before using and pack a 3-inch (7.5-cm) layer of moss in the bottom of the frame.

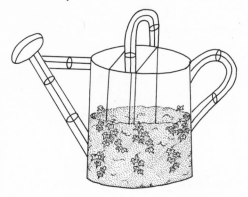

Fig. 1

Set a few plants in place, with their roots placed on top of the moss and their stems and leaves sticking out from the frame. Place plants evenly around the frame. Keep layering moss and plants until you reach the top (Fig. 1).

If a part of the frame is difficult to plant, it will have to be covered rather than planted with ivy. First stuff the form with moss and tie it down with dacron line. Bring ivy runners across and attach them to the moss-covered frame with fern pins. If the area is too narrow to use pins, just tie the ivy down with the dacron line. The ivy will begin to root in the moss if the moss is kept moist.

Mist the finished topiary daily for a week. Water sparingly at first, and then water well when the surface layer of the moss has dried out (Fig. 2).

Fig. 2

Aftercare

Treat your topiary as you do a potted plant. Water when needed. Don't allow it to dry out completely. If it does, soak the whole figure in water, then continue to water normally. Fertilize with a weak solution of liquid fertilizer weekly throughout the growing season. Groom the topiary by cutting out dead leaves and pinning back runners, and bring it indoors before it freezes in winter.

Creating an evergreen topiary

To make living sculptures, the creator has to combine artistic skills with plant knowledge. From the list above, select a plant suitable for the topiary you want—formal or informal, architectural or lifelike. The example below uses a metal wire form as a guide, but you can also sculpt a plant without using any kind of form or guide. When you have decided on a style of topiary, choose a container that will fit it and your space, fill it with basic soil mix and a small handful of granular fertilizer, and you are ready.

Method

First, choose a plant that is happy to be shaped into the form you want. Make a sturdy wire frame and insert it into the soil-filled container to see how its shape and scale will look in relation to the space and size of the container (Fig. 1).

If you are happy with the frame, remove it and plant the shrub in the container. Water the plant well, and replace the frame around it (Fig. 2).

Fig. 1

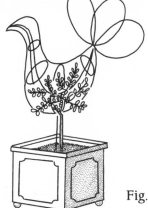

Fig. 2

As the plant grows, its branches can be tied onto the frame and encouraged to fill it. Branches that grow out from the frame should be cut back so that they cover the exterior of the frame and reinforce its shape. When you prune depends on the plant and your climate. Always work from the top of the plant downwards, and clip it twice a year to keep it looking neat (Fig. 3).

Aftercare

Once the topiary sculpture has filled in, it will need very little further attention except for twice-yearly pruning and regular watering.

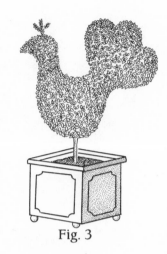

Fig. 3

How to make a standard herbal topiary

Materials

- Container: clay pots are the most attractive for herbal topiaries. Start with an 8-inch (20-cm) size.
- Potting mixture: two-thirds basic soil mix and one-third sand, with a dash of bone meal and organic fertilizer.
- Plants: suitable plants are bay laurel (*Laurus nobilis*), lavender (*Lavandula officinalis*), myrtle (*Myrtus communis*), rosemary (*Rosmarinus officinalis*), and scented geraniums (*Pelargonium* spp.).
- Other: bamboo stakes or skewers; raffia or cloth strips for tying the stem to the bamboo (do not use wire or twist ties, as these will cut into the growing stem); pruning shears.

Method

Choose a small, healthy plant with one good, straight, main stem. Plant it in the clay pot in the fertilized soil mixture and stake it, pushing the stake to the bottom of the pot. Tie the stem to the stake at 2-inch (5-cm) intervals along the length of the stem. Don't tie it too tightly (Fig. 1).

Your standard will begin to grow taller and develop new leaves. The plant will look gangly at first, but allow the stem, which will become a trunk, to grow to 12 or 15 inches (30 or 38 cm) (Fig. 2). When it has reached

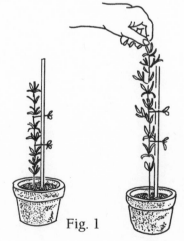

Fig. 1   Fig. 2

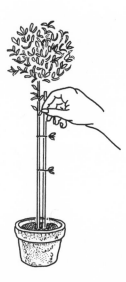

Fig. 3

this height, pinch off the lower leaves, leaving the leaves and branches on the top two inches (5 cm) of the plant. This will become the head of the standard, which will form into a round bush (Fig. 3).

Encourage fullness at the top by pinching off the tips of the branches. Continue to remove any branches that start below the topiary ball.

Aftercare

Water regularly and fertilize weekly during the growing season, and bring the plant indoors into a cool location when the weather gets cold. Repot when the plant has outgrown its container. Prune as necessary to maintain the ball shape.

$\mathcal{A}$ touch of the Orient

Traditional Chinese gardens explore
the relationship between people and nature

THE CHINESE HAVE ONE OF THE OLDEST GARDENING TRADITIONS IN THE world. They have cultivated plants for over five thousand years, and were the first civilization to grow trees and shrubs in containers, using them to decorate their enclosed courtyards, buildings, and walkways. Elaborate glazed ceramic pots were made especially for these treasured plants, and the Chinese became expert in the arts of pruning, wiring, and shaping trees. Potted trees were especially important for the New Year festivals. At this time, a wide range of flowering trees and shrubs, such as peaches, apricots, and forsythia, were potted up and forced into bloom.

The Chinese use rocks, buildings, walkways, water, and plants to express the nature-based Taoist philosophies and concepts that underlie their culture. They have great awe and respect for the natural landscape, and in their gardens they strive to represent it in its entirety. Thus mountains, lakes, and rivers become craggy rocks, ponds, and streams, and the marvelous diversity of natural vegetation in the Chinese countryside is represented by carefully selected plants, chosen for their form and symbolic meaning.

To Western eyes, the rocks are the strangest and most unique forms in a Chinese garden, for they seem out of proportion, dominating their environment. However, the Chinese believe that the rocks contain the energy of the universe, evoking a sense of the remote, the eternal, the all-powerful forces of nature itself. Thus the rocks chosen for each garden play a very prominent role, and the arrangement of them has great significance for the balance and harmony of the garden.

Whether the garden is large or small, all the elements in it are chosen and arranged in such a way that the male and female energies, the yang and the yin, are balanced, and the life energy, or *Qi,* flows freely. This means that Chinese gardens tend to be energetic spaces, in contrast to the contemplative atmosphere that predominates in most Japanese gardens. The creation of a classical Chinese garden is a complicated and time-consuming task, one that often took a lifetime to complete.

The largest of the formal gardens, and the most overwhelming, are the imperial gardens of the former emperors. These massive gardens include hills, mountains, huge manmade lakes, ornate pavilions and corridors, all symbols of the empire in microcosm. They were carefully planned and are on a scale that is hard to comprehend.

On a smaller scale, and therefore perhaps more interesting for gardeners, are the exquisitely crafted gardens of the traditional elite. These small, walled gardens are energetic spaces of great harmony, each intricately constructed from the four key elements of the Chinese landscape: pitted and craggy limestone rocks to represent the mountains; a variety of architectural forms including pavilions, covered walkways, terraces, and lookout platforms; a few well-chosen plants, used symbolically as well as for their natural beauty; and water, to promote a sense of calm and stillness.

At this time there are only two places in North America where you can see a classical Chinese garden. One is the Astor Court Garden in the Metropolitan Museum of Art, New York, a re-creation of a segment of a Suzhou garden. The other is the Dr. Sun-Yat Sen Memorial Garden in Vancouver, British Columbia, a much larger garden and the only full-sized one yet built outside China. Both were made completely authentically, using materials and craftsmen from Suzhou, and are well worth a visit.

In China, many people still make pilgrimages to the nation's famous scenic spots to revel in the majesty of the landscape. One of the most popular is the Huangshan or Yellow Mountain scenic area of Anhui province, a massive parkland of mountain peaks, clouds, and valleys. Here the natural landscape remains essentially the same as it has been for thousands of years, except for carefully placed viewing pavilions, paths, and bridges that blend into the contours of the land. The mountainsides are covered with a wide variety of native plants, including 30-foot-high (9-m) rhododendrons, elegant native pines (*Pinus huangshanensis*) and large groves of 50-foot-high (15-m) bamboo. So popular is this area as a tourist attraction that thousands of people stay in the mountains every night so they can watch the sun rise over the Sea of Clouds. In spite of this, the landscape itself remains natural and unspoiled.

It was because of their love of this natural beauty that the Chinese carried the art of reduction one step further and put plants and whole mountain scenes into containers. They felt that if they miniaturized the landscape they could concentrate all its magical qualities and advance their search for immortality, and they dwarfed and extended the lives of trees by slowing the rise of sap (just as they slowed their own pulse and breathing in their attempts to extend human life).

At least fourteen hundred years ago, Chinese scroll paintings depicted miniature trees and shrubs in ceramic pots. This Chinese art that we know as "bonsai" gradually spread throughout the Orient, and by about the eleventh or twelfth century it was widely practiced in Japan. The Japanese adapted and refined the techniques used by the Chinese and today bonsai is known principally as a Japanese art (see "The art of Zen: Making an informal, upright Japanese-style bonsai").

The Chinese have continued to create their own forms of bonsai, and these potted trees—mainly evergreens in various sizes and shapes of pots, and some flowering plants—can be found throughout China, especially in and around the two "garden cities" of China, Hangzhou and Suzhou. Chinese bonsai tend to be larger than Japanese bonsai, and not quite as refined in shape or as carefully manicured.

The Chinese have also developed a style of gardens-in-a-pot known as "penjing." Penjing are unique to China, for they are the ultimate expression of the Chinese desire to miniaturize the landscape. Thus they consist of rocks, plants, water, small buildings, and figures—representations of the mountains, trees, lakes, rivers, people, animals, and buildings—all contained in one small pot, or placed onto a moist slab of rock or stone.

Penjing and Chinese bonsai are both ideal for a small balcony or patio, and they make interesting conversation pieces. Penjing do not have to re-create Chinese landscapes, but can be made to represent any landscape you like. It might be a west coast landscape with sharp mountain peaks, fallen logs, clear lakes, and trees clinging to the lower rock faces, or it might be a Southwest cactus garden, with desert plants and snake-tracks in the sand. Whatever the landscape, the challenge is to reduce it so that all the elements work together.

The plants below can be used for penjing and Chinese and Japanese bonsai, although many other plants can also be used. If winters are too cold to leave miniatures outside, you may be able to move them into an unheated but protected space, such as a friend's unheated greenhouse; or bury the containers in a thick layer of sawdust, put them in a sheltered spot, and cover the whole thing with breathable landscape fabric. In really cold climates, choose plants that will survive well indoors, such as some of the tender azaleas: protect them from excessive heat and dryness, water frequently to keep the soil moist, and put them outside again in the summer.

If you use light-weight containers you will be able to move them easily, taking advantage of the best light conditions and protecting the plants from the worst of the winter weather. Most of them should be lightly shaded during hot summer months and watered very regularly, sometimes twice a day, so that they do not dry out. If you are careful in your selection of plants and materials, your miniatures will be objects of beauty for many years to come.

To soften the edges on your patio or balcony and add to the theme, plant clump bamboo in large, Oriental pots (with holes drilled in the bottom for drainage). Clump bamboo is much better suited to the confines of a pot than the more robust spreading bamboos. A good species is umbrella bamboo, described below.

Setting the scene

The following checklist will help you start creating a Chinese-style garden on your patio or balcony.

- Sun, filtered shade, or semishade conditions, depending upon the plants you use and your climate.

- For a penjing, see "Making your own penjing forest" below.
- Large, decorated, Chinese egg pots, with holes drilled in the bottom for drainage, basic soil mix, and bamboo.
- Additional stones set into sand and arranged in patterns for the flooring, if possible. If you can't use stones, consider painting a design on the floor—simple geometric shapes and patterns, or the outline of a bird such as the crane—typical of the kind seen in Chinese gardens.
- If there is room, a simple stone bench or glazed ceramic seat decorated with Oriental motifs.

If you feel ambitious, have the space, and your patio or balcony can stand the weight, you can add some larger rocks to represent mountains. If you are able to paint on a wall, try a trompe l'oeil Chinese garden window for an authentic effect. It could be geometric in design, or have a crane or flower image. Paint trees or more bamboo inside the center of the design, to indicate that there is a landscape on the other side of the window.

Bamboo for large pots

Thamnocalamus spathaceus syn. *Arundinaria murielae* (umbrella bamboo). This shade-loving bamboo will grow to a height of about 10 feet (3 m) and forms a clump of arching, slender canes with apple-green leaves. It makes an excellent windscreen and gives privacy to a rooftop, patio, or balcony setting. It must not be allowed to dry out so keep it well watered, but otherwise it is easy to look after and not fussy about soil. Zones 7–10.

Plants to use for Chinese and Japanese bonsai and penjing

The best plants to miniaturize are those that have a long lifespan, are resilient to transplanting, are compact in growth, and have slender branches and small leaves. The best way to get the plants you need is to look in your local garden center for plants with unusual shapes and contortions. Unless otherwise specified, use a potting mixture that is approximately one-third peat moss, one-third sand, and one-third quality topsoil. Avoid an all-purpose commercial potting mixture that has fertilizer added since this will cause the plants to grow too vigorously.

Evergreens

Probably the most popular of all the trees for bonsai and penjing, evergreens are relatively easy-care and are attractive year round.

Buxus spp. (boxwood). Boxwood is highly suitable for bonsai because of its small leaves. It is hardy and can withstand drought well, grows in almost any soil, and it only needs a little watering. For more information see "Clipped for style." *B. sempervirens* and most of its cultivars work very well. Zones 6–9.

***Juniperus* spp. (juniper).** If you only have one tree in a pot, a juniper is a good choice. It is easy to train and shape, likes full sun, and is extremely drought-resistant, although it can tolerate wet conditions if the soil is well drained. It prefers rich, peaty soil mixed with an equal amount of sand. Junipers are extremely long-lived, and there are some bonsai specimens that are over 150 years old. *J. rigida* (Mount Hakone or temple juniper) is one of the best needle junipers to use, and it is available in many beautiful cultivars. Perhaps the most popular species used for bonsai is the prostrate *Juniperus sargentii*. Zones 6–9.

***Pinus* spp. (pines).** Pines are also ideal for bonsai, and prized for their beautiful form, long life, and simple culture. They love full sun, not too much water, and a soil that is half sand and half rich, peaty topsoil. See the plant lists for "Santa Fe style" and "The art of Zen" for further information. Plants available for zones 3–10.

Deciduous plants

Even if you live on the tenth floor, you can mark the passing of the seasons with a deciduous tree or shrub that bursts forth with buds and blossoms in the spring, has rich leaves and ripening fruit in the summer, bright colors in the fall, and an interesting shape and form in the winter. The following are all good choices for bonsai and penjing.

***Acer* spp. (maple).** The maples are the most popular of all the fall-coloring trees used for bonsai, and the genus is discussed at greater length under "The art of Zen." Some good species to try are *Acer palmatum* (Japanese maple), zones 5–8; *A. capillipes* (snake bark maple), zones 6–9; *A. circinatum* (vine maple), zones 6–9; and *A. griseum* (paper bark maple), zones 6–8. They like full sun or partial shade and will grow in almost any soil.

***Larix* spp. (larch).** Larches are very hardy and stand up well to pruning. They look like pines when in leaf but are actually deciduous, with apple-green leaves in the spring, changing to a rich golden-yellow in the fall. Larches like a moist, well-drained soil, full sun in spring and early summer, and partial shade in midsummer. *L. kaempferi* syn. *L. leptolepis* (Japanese larch) is best for bonsai since its branches are much finer than those of other larches. Zones 5–8.

***Prunus mume* (flowering apricot).** The flowering apricot is one of the most loved flowering plants in Japan, and has a long tradition of use as a pot plant in China. These trees are prized for their early bloom, delicate colors, and fragrance. There are about two hundred different forms available, and the ones usually chosen for miniaturizing are those with the simplest white blossoms and the oldest, most weathered trunks. They like full sun, lots of water during the summer, and a soil mix that is 50 percent pasteurized soil, 20 percent leaf mold, and 30 percent sand, with some lime added as a sweetener. Zones 7–9.

Rhododendron spp. (azaleas). Many azaleas, particularly the dwarf species and cultivars, are used for bonsai. Azaleas are acid-loving plants and need plenty of moisture, so add well-moistened peat moss to the soil mix and keep well watered.
Apply micronized iron in early spring. Most prefer dappled shade but some will
tolerate full sun, and all should be shaded from the direct rays of the sun in midsummer. A popular Japanese bonsai specimen, and one of the most stunning when
in flower, is *R.* x *obtusum* (Kurume azalea). Zones 5–8.

Salix spp. (willow). A number of willows are suitable for bonsai. *S. babylonica* (the
weeping willow) makes an attractive weeping tree. Zones 6–9. *S. caprea* (the goat
willow) can be trained into any style. Zones 5–8. Willows need rich soil, so plant
them in 60 percent pasteurized potting soil, 20 percent leaf mold, and 20 percent
sand. They are water-loving plants that should never be allowed to dry out: stand
the pots in water during the summer. They like full sun.

Wisteria spp. A wisteria bonsai is spectacular when it blooms and its highly scented,
pale lilac flowers hang down in long racemes. Generally the species used for bonsai are *W. floribunda* (Japanese wisteria), and *W. sinensis* (Chinese wisteria). Wisteria like full sun as long as they have lots of water, and prefer a rich, well-drained
soil mix with plenty of well-rotted manure added to it. Zones 5–9.

Making your own penjing forest

You can make a traditional penjing forest for your patio and balcony by using rocks
and plants arranged in a shallow container and adding other elements such as people,
animals, and buildings to complete the scene. In order for your penjing to be successful, the plants you use will need to be top- and root-pruned carefully so that they will
grow successfully in their small container. If you are in any doubt about this, be sure
to consult an expert or a detailed book on the topic. It takes experts many years to
become proficient, and it is easy to make mistakes if you have never seen it done. The
best time to plant a penjing is in springtime, just as the plants are beginning to sprout.

Materials

- Container: a flat tray with a shallow lip high enough to hold some water. Look for
  shallow terracotta and glazed ceramic containers that are specially made for bonsai and penjing.
- Rocks or stones: any natural stones can be used; avoid beach stones, which hold
  too much salt. Choose rocks with interesting shapes that remind you of the landscape you want to replicate, and make sure that all the stones in a penjing come
  from the same location and are the same kind of stone.
- Potting mixture: as recommended for the individual plants, or a good commercial
  bonsai soil mix. If you buy commercial potting mixture, make sure it does not
  have any added fertilizer as this will cause the plants to grow too vigorously.

- Plants: five, seven, or nine small trees about 8 to 12 inches (20 to 30 cm) high that are suitable for grouped arrangements, such as the larch *Larix kaempferi* syn. *L. leptolepis*. (Small trees such as these are best found through a bonsai grower or specialty store.)
- Other materials: small gravel chips, moss, and any miniature objects—birds, animals, people, buildings—to complete the scene.

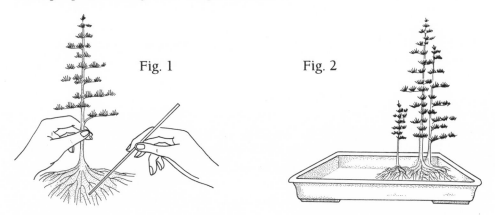

Fig. 1   Fig. 2

Method

Prepare the potting mix.

Take the plants out of their pots and remove most of the soil around the roots of the plant, using a chopstick. Do not tear or cut the roots; if they are a little long, prune them carefully (Fig. 1).

Place the plants in the container in an asymmetrical fashion, taller trees at the front, shorter trees at the back, to increase the sense of perspective. Move them around until they form a pleasing, natural-looking arrangement (Fig. 2).

Place the rocks between the plants to give interest to the arrangement. Make sure all the rocks are the same color; the rocks help to hold the trees steady.

Don't flatten the soil surface but mound it up in places so that you have one or two groupings of trees. Make sure there is more room in the front of the pot so that the forest looks open, and put the trees closer to the edge of the pot at the back.

Press the soil down firmly with your thumb; add extra potting soil mix and firm until the soil fills the pot, is mounded around the plants, and roots are properly covered. Make a gravel path through the "forest" to represent a river through the trees, and add some moss to the soil banks.

Prune the trees so that they are open, with no branches overlapping. It can be a bit tricky to do this pruning correctly, especially if you are a novice, so take it slowly, prune a few branches, stand back and look at your arrangement, and do more if it looks necessary. You can always prune more later.

Immerse the penjing in water to the base of the trees and hold there until air bubbles have stopped coming up from the pot. Drain and put into a semishady place. Now add miniature birds, people, buildings, and any other artifacts needed to complete the landscape. Your penjing is now ready (Fig. 3).

Aftercare

Be sure to water the penjing well by immersing it in water up to the base of the tree trunks at least once or twice a week. Keep it out of

Fig. 3

direct sun. In the winter cover the pot with moss or bark mulch to protect the roots, and keep it in a sheltered spot. If necessary bring it into a more protected location (this will depend upon your winter conditions).

Feed once a month with a weak solution of liquid fertilizer (one-quarter strength) during the spring and early summer months in order to keep it in prime condition. Prune and shape as necessary as the plants grow and mature. The roots will need to be pruned by the second year.

A simple tree-in-a-pot

This pot is elegant on a balcony or patio, and suitable for both Chinese and Japanese themes. It will provide color and interest throughout the growing season and a lovely, upright form in winter.

Materials

- Container: a glazed ceramic container, at least 18 inches (45 cm) wide and deep.
- Potting mixture: basic soil mix with one-third well-soaked peat moss added.
- Plant: *Acer palmatum* (Japanese maple) cultivar.

Method

Make sure the pot is large enough to contain the rootball of the tree, plus about 2 inches (5 cm) to spare around the plant for extra soil. Take the tree out of its container and make sure the roots are loosened and not pot-bound.

Put some soil into the container and plant the tree, adding soil around the base and sides so that the finished soil level covers the rootball and comes to about 1 to 2 inches (2.5 to 5 cm) below the rim of the pot. If the tree is in a burlap bag, put the burlapped rootball into the pot, fill around the burlap with soil, cut the twine and loosen the burlap around the top, and cover with soil as before. (If you can remove the burlap without damaging the rootball then do so, but otherwise it is safer to leave it in place and allow it to rot away over time.)

Water the pot well to ensure that there are no pockets of air trapped below the tree.

Aftercare

Water well and regularly to make sure the tree's roots do not dry out. Follow the general instructions given for care of maples in "The art of Zen."

The art of Zen

Simplicity and tranquillity are the key to Japanese gardens

THE ENTRY TO A JAPANESE TEA GARDEN IS MODEST AND UNASSUMING: A simple path that passes underneath an arched doorway, with a glimpse of water, stone lanterns, and trees beyond. At the threshold is a rounded, weathered stone. As you pass over the stone and enter the garden, you leave the material world behind. You walk along well-marked paths with no distractions. Each rock, tree, shrub, and vista is carefully arranged to soothe the spirit and focus the mind. Finally you arrive at the tea house. Here you take part in the age-old ceremony of tea, a communion between the giver and the receiver that signals a cleansing of the spirit in an atmosphere of harmony, respect, purity, and tranquillity. You leave the garden with a sense of that spirit, and pass back into the outside world with a renewed vision and serenity.

To many people it may seem strange that a stroll through a garden and the simple act of sharing a bowl of tea can be a profoundly spiritual experience, and yet that is the experience offered in a Japanese tea garden. Throughout the centuries there have been some amazing and wonderful garden traditions: the hanging gardens of Babylon, the great gardens of the Mogul Empire, the gardens of the Chinese Emperors, the monastery gardens of Medieval times, and the more recent garden styles of the Italians, the French, and the English. Each of these gardening traditions has its own unique character and history, but it is in the gardens of Japan that attention to detail and respect for nature has been carried to its highest art form.

A Japanese tea garden is deceptively simple. To the untrained eye, it may seem as if it is almost too simple, uninteresting even, with a limited selection of trees and shrubs underplanted with mossy banks, meandering paths, stone lanterns, streams and ponds, tea house and viewing pavilion. However, all these elements are precisely placed, maintained and manicured so that the visitor to the garden is almost unaware of the landscaping, except that the garden is even more beautiful than it would be in nature.

Careful attention is given to the different seasons: the cherry blossoms in spring, iris blooms in summer, maple leaves in the fall, snow on stone lanterns in the winter.

There is something of interest and beauty to see throughout the year, enhancing the sense of harmony. Plants are tended and pruned individually, fences and buildings are carefully maintained, and pathways are sited to allow visitors to feel at ease when they stroll, sure that they will reach their destination even though they cannot see around the corners. Lakes and streams are manmade, but look entirely natural, and the landscape outside the walls is carefully incorporated into the overall plan, making this borrowed scenery an integral part of the whole. The garden is both a part of its environment and apart from it, allowing for an easy transition from one to the other.

There are many Japanese tea gardens in North America, especially in the Pacific Northwest where the climate is so similar to that of Japan and where it is possible to grow most of the same plants. Portland in Oregon, Seattle in Washington, and Vancouver in British Columbia are particularly well known for the quality and integrity of their gardens, and visitors come from around the world to enjoy their serenity.

Underlying the natural beauty of Japanese gardens is the philosophy of Zen Buddhism, a religion based on a deep respect for nature in all its forms. Zen Buddhism and the tea ceremony were brought to Japan from China by Cha'an Buddhist monks in about the eleventh century and were quickly adopted by the aristocracy.

The monks used to drink green tea before they meditated in order to keep their minds alert, and gradually the tea ceremony was incorporated into the philosophy of the tea garden. During the ceremony, guest and host sit and share the giving and receiving of tea. The guest receives the bowl, holds it carefully, and looks into its emerald-colored depths, green with the color of nature. In this quiet moment of reflection, negative thoughts and actions are left behind, and there is a renewed faith in the positive values of the guest's life. These feelings go with the guest as he or she leaves the tea house and reenters the outside world.

The practice of Zen leads to a simplification of art and life in all its forms, and individual objects become filled with symbolic meaning. Zen Buddhists strive to be at one with nature, not to analyze it or distance themselves from it, and we too can learn to listen to the materials and forms we use, and communicate with them. By appreciating the ideas of Zen, we can open up to a whole new world in the garden.

The idea that we can be connected to our environment, whoever we are and wherever we live, is something most gardeners understand instinctively. From it grows the desire to re-create nostalgic memories of our childhood or grow fragrant plants that trigger memories. Most small children have the gift of seeing life in the rocks and trees around them, but many of us lose this facility as we get older. Creating a Japanese-style garden is an opportunity to connect once more with the life-force of nature.

Simplicity is the key. It is better to have one carefully chosen and pruned tree in a simple pot than it is to clutter up your balcony or patio with too many things. You may want to create a screen around your space with a simple fence of bamboo poles, and use rounded pebbles on the floor or ground, interspersed with a path of larger, flat stones, leading to a simple tree in a pot. A water feature is especially soothing in a

Japanese garden, and a good way of making one is to fill a simply shaped, deep ceramic bowl with water and place a pump in the bottom of it. Arrange a large, open piece of bamboo over the surface of the water. The water is pumped from the bowl up to the bamboo tube; then it trickles gently down the bamboo spout and back into the open bowl. The bowl can be raised on a stand or placed on pebbles for added effect.

If your space is very small, you may want to try your hand at bonsai. It seems most likely that the art of bonsai was first introduced into Japan from China in the eleventh century by the same Cha'an Buddhist monks who introduced the tea ceremony. The monks believed that their little trees were holy, a link between the divine and the human. Today the art of bonsai is popular worldwide.

If you have more space, you can create a lovely effect by making large, simple wooden planters as a continuous edging to the patio or balcony, and arranging azaleas, pines, and maples in them. Underplant them with moss, or leave the earth bare. The plants should vary in height so there is a gentle layering of green. Add a flowering cherry, if there is room, and have your own blossom festival when it flowers in the spring. Cover the rest of the ground or floor with smooth pebbles, and add a simple wooden bench so that you have somewhere to sit and reflect.

Setting the scene

The following checklist will help you start creating a Zen-style garden on your patio or balcony.
- Filtered sun or semishade.
- Smooth pebbles and larger rocks, and fine gravel or sand for the flooring.
- Simple earthenware pots suitable for the chosen plants, or wooden planters large enough for trees (at least 12 inches /30 cm deep and 24 inches /60 cm in diameter, or 16 to18 inches /40 to 45 cm deep if the planters are not as big).
- Plants: consult the list below for a suitable selection.
- Basic soil mix, amended with one-third soaked peat moss to make a more loamy, slightly acid soil.
- If you are making a bonsai, you will need containers, soil, and plants (see "Making an informal, upright Japanese-style bonsai" below).
- Basic garden tools, and a good pair of pruning scissors.
- Watering and lighting systems.

To create the mood of a Japanese Zen garden, try to screen your patio or balcony from the outside world at eye level, but do not make your screen so high that it blocks any view of nearby trees: borrowed scenery is an important part of a Japanese garden. Add a water feature if you can, the simpler the better. Use shoji screens across your windows, tatami mats on the floor, and grow bamboo in pots if necessary to increase your privacy.

Maples, azaleas, and pines for a Japanese garden

There are several species of maples, azaleas, and pines that are native to Japan, and these are probably the plants we most associate with Japanese gardens. The following plants all work well in containers and can be used for any garden theme, as well as this one.

Acer palmatum (Japanese maple). Although Japanese maples are native to Japan, they have been grown extensively in many other parts of the world and are remarkably adaptable to differing soil and climatic conditions. They are widely used as specimen plants and are available in an astonishingly wide range of forms, with unusual barks and variegated and colored leaves of many sizes and shapes.

Japanese maples are easy to plant since their root structure is predominantly a fibrous network that stays in the upper level of the soil, and this makes them good container plants too. They will grow well in a basic soil mix with added peat moss, although they are quite forgiving as long as they are watered regularly, the soil is well drained, and they are given a twice-yearly dose of granular fertilizer. The richer the soil the more rapid the growth, so for container growing it is probably wise not to enrich the soil too much. Maples and azaleas both grow best in slightly acid soil. If the temperature drops below 20°F (–7°C), the roots freeze and the plant will die; to protect it, wrap the outside of the containers with styrofoam sheets covered in burlap.

At least 140 different cultivars of Japanese maples grow well in containers, so the list below is just a sampling. You may not be able to find them in your garden center, since most are specialty items that may only be available from specialty growers like Vertrees Nursery in Roseburg, Oregon. Talk to your local garden center to see what they can bring in, and be fussy: with a bit of effort they can probably get some of the more unusual ones. The following cultivars have lobed leaves and an upright growth habit. Zones 5–8.

A. p. 'Kamagata' is a very hardy plant that tolerates winters of 0°F (–18°C), full sun to semishade, and even drought. It has delicately lobed leaves whose edges are strongly tinted with red to rusty-red when they unfurl in the spring, becoming a bright, light green by early summer. In the fall the leaves turn brilliant shades of yellow and orange with an occasional touch of red and they remain well into the late fall. It grows to 3 to 6 feet (0.9 to 1.8 m).

A. p. 'Kotohime' has one of the smallest leaf forms of all the Japanese maples. New leaves often emerge as a bright rose or orange-red, maturing to a bright, light green in the summer, and yellow-orange in the fall. It is a sturdy plant that is well suited for bonsai. 'Goshiki kotohime' is the variegated form, with leaves that are green underneath covered with minute, overlapping white, cream, light yellow, pink, and red markings. It looks quite brilliant in the spring, the leaves becoming a darker green during the summer.

A. p. 'Red Pygmy' is a most unusual plant with thin, maroon-colored, straplike leaf lobes. It is a very slow-growing dwarf hybrid that contrasts well with other maples in shape and color.

A. p. 'Tsuchigumo' is an excellent semidwarf that reaches 6 to 10 feet (1.8 to 3 m) at maturity with interestingly convoluted leaves. The new leaves are rust-red, soon turning to bright green, and they hold this color all summer. In the fall the leaves turn bright gold with crimson edges.

Dissectum Atropurpureum group (red lace-leaf maples). The red tones, delicate lacelike foliage, and cascading branches make these plants among the most popular for landscape plantings, and they are the ones most people think of as Japanese maples. The plant form is pendulous, becoming twiggy and dense as it matures. There are many lovely related cultivars, notably 'Brocade', 'Crimson Queen', 'Ever Red', 'Garnet', 'Inaba shidare', and 'Red Filigree Lace'. Also lovely are the cultivars whose green spring and summer foliage turns various shades of yellow, gold, and orange-yellow in the fall. Particularly attractive are 'Filigree', 'Flavescens', 'Roseo-marginatum', and 'Seiryu'. The latter is one of the only upright lace-leaf maples.

Rhododendron **spp. (rhododendron and azalea).** Like the maples, members of this genus like to grow in moist, loamy, slightly acid, or neutral soil. In their native habitats, many of these plants grow in the filtered shade of taller trees, and you will need to provide semishade for most of them to do well in containers on your deck or patio. For rhododendron species and hybrids see the plant list for "In the shade"; following are some azaleas, which are used more commonly than rhododendrons in Japanese gardens. Many of them, such as the hybrids of *R. molle, R. occidentale,* and the Exbury hybrids, are fragrant, making a lovely addition to the patio or balcony. Most of them are deciduous, but their bare winter forms are most attractive, especially when covered with snow and twinkling white lights.

R. kaempferi. A hardy, free-flowering deciduous species with almost ovate, dark green leaves. Its funnel-shaped flowers in orange, salmon-pink, or brick-red, with darker speckles, appear in clusters of two to four, usually in May but sometimes later. It is the parent of the Kurume azaleas and other related cultivars, such as 'Martine', bright pink. It has a height and spread of up to 5 feet (1.5 m). Zones 6–8.

R. occidentale. A hardy, free-flowering deciduous species with sweetly fragrant, funnel-shaped flowers that are white, sometimes tinged with pink, with a yellow blotch, borne in late spring and early summer. It can grow to a mature height of 10 feet (3 m), less in a container. It is the parent of many excellent hybrids that are well worth asking for in your garden center. They include 'Exquisita', cream flushed with pink, with a ray of orange; 'Graciosa', cream-pink with an orange-yellow basal blotch; and 'Irene Koster', rose-pink with a yellow blotch. Zones 6–8.

R. schlippenbachii (royal azalea). This is my favorite, although it definitely needs semishade and is susceptible to spring frost damage. It has translucent pale pink flowers that usually appear before the rounded mid-green leaves. The leaves turn red and orange in the fall. It usually grows to about 6 to 8 feet (1.8 to 2.4 m), with a spread of 4 to 6 feet (1.2 to 1.8 m). Zones 5–8.

Pinus **spp. (pine).** Pines are an integral part of a Japanese garden, and are widely used for bonsai also. A number of attractive pine forms are listed in the "Santa Fe style" section. All pines love full sun, but they only need a modest amount of water. They like sandy soil, and are best planted in a mix that is about one-third sand, one-third peat moss, and one-third good topsoil, or a commercial equivalent. Of all the pines, the most commonly grown in containers are *P. parviflora* (Japanese white pine) and its cultivars, such as 'Yatsubusa', zones 6–9; *P. thunbergii* (Japanese black pine), an excellent large specimen that is hardier than the white pine, and its cultivars, zones 5–8; and *P. sylvestris* (Scots pine) and its cultivars, such as 'Beuvronensis' and 'Watereri', zones 3–7.

Making an informal, upright Japanese-style bonsai

Hundreds of books have been written on the art of Japanese bonsai. I do not have enough space here to go into much detail, but the suggestions below for making an informal, upright style of bonsai should help you get started. However, the art of bonsai takes time to learn, and is far beyond the scope of this book. Learning how to prune and shape the trees is both a delicate art and an exact science. If you follow these instructions you will be able to make a very pleasing "small plant in a pot," but it is unlikely to win prizes at a bonsai show! If you become enthusiastic and want to pursue this further, there are many bonsai clubs, growers, books, and experts to consult. A list of plants that can be used for Japanese bonsai is given under the theme "A touch of the Orient."

Materials

- Container: a shallow, glazed ceramic pot suitable for bonsai, with a drainage hole in the bottom.
- Potting mixture: as recommended for the individual plants, or a good commercial bonsai soil mix.
- Plants: one young tree suitable for bonsai, such as *Pinus sylvestris* 'Beuvronensis'.
- Other: bonsai pruning tools and chopsticks.

Method

Remove the tree from its pot and tease out the rootball—easiest done with a chopstick. Disentangle the roots and comb them out. Prune out a few of the roots carefully with a pair of sharp scissors so that the rootball will sit comfortably in the pot with a little room to spare around the edge (Fig. 1). (This is a tricky process; if you are in doubt about which roots to prune, don't do it.)

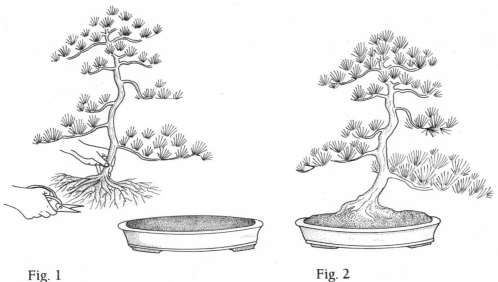

Fig. 1   Fig. 2

Cover the drainage holes with plastic mesh, and fill the base of the pot with a thin layer of the prepared soil. Place the tree in the correct position and fill the pot up with soil, making sure there are no holes. Press the soil down well and soak by immersing pot and plant in a bucket of water up to the base of the tree. Prune the tree carefully into a pleasing shape (Fig. 2).

Aftercare

Keep well watered to prevent the roots from drying out. It is best kept in semishade until it is well established. Feed once a month with a weak solution of liquid fertilizer (one-quarter strength) in order to keep it in prime condition. Be sure to protect it from excess winter cold. Prune, shape, and repot as necessary as the plant grows and matures.

There are fairies at the bottom of the garden

Alpine plants and miniature bulbs delight the child in all of us

AS ANY CHILD KNOWS, THERE ARE FAIRIES AT THE BOTTOM OF THE garden. They live in the trees and flowers, and they talk to the birds and butterflies. At night they come out into the garden and play, and in the daytime they sleep, on the branches of trees, curled up on a leaf, or deep in the hearts of flowers. They like the tiny flowers best, dwarf bulbs and alpine plants that are just the right size to snuggle into . . . or so we might imagine, for no other plants in the garden can bring a sense of magic and enchantment as surely as do the delicate but hardy little plants of the high mountains.

Alpine plants seem to compensate for their tiny size with an amazing array of intricate forms, leaf shapes, and vibrant flowers, beginning with early bulbs, such as white snowdrops, blue iris, and yellow crocus, that push their way up through the snow in early spring. Soon these are followed by coral-pink saxifrages, clear blue campanulas, rich, deep blue gentians, lavender-colored phlox, white pulsatillas, and all the many lovely flowers that inhabit the foothills, slopes, and meadows of mountain ranges, hostile northern climates, rocky outcroppings, and seaside cliffs.

Even though we call them alpines, many plants classified by this name do not come from mountain areas. The term is used today to describe almost any plant or shrub that is dwarf, hardy, and perennial, whatever its geographic origin. Most true alpine perennials are less than six inches (15 cm) in height and tend to bloom in late spring and early summer at low altitudes. Rock plants that grow naturally at lower altitudes tend to be somewhat larger than their alpine relatives, and the ones that bloom in the late summer and early fall are especially useful for extending the flowering season in rock and container gardens.

Perhaps it is because their habitats are so diverse that the growth and cultivation of alpines seems intimidating to many gardeners. Plants that come from the relatively rich soil of lower mountain slopes, such as columbines, delphiniums, and geraniums (now all domesticated and widely grown in perennial garden beds), will need very different handling from plants that survive on the unstable scree farther up the mountain. The more the wind blows, and the more extreme the weather conditions are, the smaller and more compact the plants will be, hugging the ground for their very survival.

As soil becomes scarce it becomes low in nitrogen and other minerals, and the plants have adapted over the years to these lower levels—one reason why rich garden soil is far too strong for most alpines. Mountain soil may be high in potassium if the underlying rock is granite, or high in calcium in limestone areas.

Some plants live in moist places, where their roots are continually supplied with fresh mountain water (very hard to re-create, in any garden), and others, such as campanulas and violets, manage to survive by moving on once they have exhausted nutrients in the immediate area, either by sending out long runners or by spreading their seeds far and wide. Cushion and mat-forming plants are particularly well adapted to mountain living; they use their long roots to attach themselves firmly to the underlying rock and seek out food and water. In this way they are similar to desert plants, but unlike desert plants, they cannot conserve water at all and will die if they dry out, even for a short time.

Many tiny plants are true rock plants that have learned how to survive tucked into crevices and holes in rock faces, cliffs, and mountainsides and can be found all the way from the seashore up into the high mountains. The majority of high mountain plants are found in open ground, especially on north-facing slopes where they are exposed to the sun but are less likely to dry out than they would if they faced south.

The alpine growing season is short and intense. Mountain plants emerge from the snow anywhere from May to July and are usually buried again in October, giving them three or four months to show their full glory before going back into hibernation. By contrast, the same plants will have anywhere from six to eight months to grow in the garden—not necessarily an advantage.

In the garden, alpine plants are faced with a new set of challenges. Low-altitude air is denser and more polluted, and less sunlight and ultraviolet light gets through. Climatic conditions are variable, bringing an earlier, more erratic spring and a later, less consistent fall, confusing the plants' sleep patterns. During the growing season the plants may be attacked by a host of pests and diseases they have never encountered before and are not equipped to repel. The best that any gardener can do is provide the most suitable habitat possible and be prepared for a few failures along the way.

Fortunately for container gardeners, troughs are a very good way to grow alpines, and they offer the balcony and patio gardener a fascinating and rewarding hobby, one that can become the passion of a lifetime. Troughs can be hewn out of stone, made from earthenware, or created by the hypertufa method, out of peat moss, cement, and perlite. They are easy to make yourself by following the instructions given in this section.

The soil used in the trough is very important, since it must meet the needs of the plants you want to grow. Be sure to find out the likes and dislikes of the alpines you buy, before you purchase them. If it rains a lot where you live, you will have to protect your plants from the worst excesses of the rainy season.

While troughs are usually planted with sun-loving species accustomed to mountain soil, if you choose your plants carefully you can make an alpine garden to suit sun or shade, as long as the plants receive the right soil and amounts of light and nutrients to thrive. Alpine plants can also be grown in other types of containers, as long as they are relatively shallow and have good drainage. For instance, you can make interesting and unusual containers from hollowed-out driftwood pieces, rotting tree trunks, old sinks, and fissured rocks.

There are likely to be many resources available to you, besides books and magazines. Your botanical garden may have an alpine garden, separated into different geographical sections, and most garden centers carry an assortment of alpine and rock plants. If you are looking for more help, try an alpine garden club. It will be full of avid alpine gardeners who are always ready to help newcomers with information and plants, and you may become as enthusiastic as they are.

No matter how fond of alpine plants you become, never be tempted to gather them from the wild. Leave them where they belong so that others can enjoy them for centuries to come.

Setting the scene

The following checklist will help you start creating a garden of alpine and miniature plants on your patio or balcony.
- Six to eight hours of sunshine a day.
- Troughs, pieces of driftwood, and other containers for alpines. You can make the troughs yourself, following the instructions given in this chapter.
- Soil mix made from one part peat moss, one part sterilized, well-rotted leaf mold, and one part gritty sand; or buy a commercial mix made for alpines.
- Alpine plants suitable for your containers and climatic conditions.
- A watering system.
- Tiny white fairy lights.
- Basic gardening tools and storage.
- If there is room, a table and chairs.

Children love anything miniature, and an alpine garden is a great place to accentuate all things childlike—which includes fairies. You may want to include a low, children's table, stenciled with fairies, and matching, fold-up wooden chairs painted in soft colors. Paint a trail of rose petals on the ground, leading from your door to the troughs and to pieces of driftwood that are artfully arranged in the corner, moss growing on their sides, tiny gentians and phlox in full bloom. When night comes, white fairy lights can be used to illuminate the scene.

Alpine and rock plants

Some of the most devoted and passionate gardeners are those who grow alpine plants. They will search far and wide for interesting and unusual species, no matter how hard to find and difficult to grow. Most of the plants below, or similar species or cultivars, shouldn't be too hard to find and will grow in a basic alpine plant soil mixture consisting of one-third peat moss, one-third sterilized, well-rotted leaf mold, and one-third gritty sand, unless otherwise noted.

Trees and shrubs

Acer circinatum 'Little Gem' (dwarf vine maple). This dwarf cultivar of the many-trunked vine maple takes ten years to grow to a height and width of 18 inches (45 cm), making it an excellent choice for an alpine garden. It has good fall color and likes moist, well-drained soil in filtered sunlight. Zones 6–9.

Andromeda polifolia (bog rosemary). A plant of bogs and damp places, this evergreen shrub prefers acid, peaty soil and grows well in shade. It produces compact clusters of pink, bell-shaped flowers in May and June. In its typical form it can reach a height of 18 inches (45 cm), but there are some excellent compact forms that only grow to half that size, notably 'Compacta', 'Major', and 'Minima'. Zones 2–7.

Chamaecyparis obtusa 'Nana' and 'Minima'. These are among the best dwarf conifers, with dense, dark green foliage in tight, rounded sprays. They grow to a height and spread of 18 inches (45 cm) in ten years and do well in well-drained soil in full sun or partial shade. Zones 4–8.

Penstemon menziesii (penstemon). A creeping shrub with attractive violet-blue to purple flowers in June, penstemon grows well in full sun or light shade in a moist, well-drained soil. It reaches a height of 8 inches (20 cm) and spread of 2 feet (60 cm) in five years. A smaller, more compact species is *P. davidsonii,* with a height of 3 inches (7.5 cm), rich purple flowers in June and July, and dense, bronzed-green foliage. Zones 4–8.

Pinus densiflora 'Alice Verkade' (Japanese red pine). An attractive miniature conifer that grows to a height of 12 inches (30 cm) and width of 18 inches (45 cm) in ten years. It prefers a sandy, well-drained soil and filtered sunlight. Zones 4–7.

Rhododendron impeditum. This slow-growing, evergreen rhododendron reaches a height of 12 inches (30 cm) and width of 18 inches (45 cm) in ten years. Its tiny, aromatic leaves are gray-green, and it produces small, funnel-shaped purplish-blue flowers in April and May. It does well in full sun and light shade in a well-drained, moist, acidic soil. Another species, *R. keleticum,* reaches a similar size and prefers the same conditions for growth. It has mid-green leaves and bears mauve-red blossoms in June. Zones 6–8.

Tsuga canadensis 'Pendula' and 'Jeddeloh' (weeping Canadian hemlock). Dwarf conifers that grow to a height of 12 inches (30 cm) and width of 2 feet (60 cm) in ten years, they have bright, new, green growth in April and May. They prefer moist, well-drained soil and filtered sunlight. 'Jeddeloh' is the more compact of the two. Zones 4–8.

Perennials

Androsace lactea (rock jasmine). This is a compact, cushion-forming, vigorous evergreen that flowers in April and May with loose umbels of clear white flowers. All members of this family need very well-drained soil and protection from rain in winter. It grows to a height of 4 inches (10 cm) with a wider spread. Other attractive species are *A. alpina,* pale rose flowers to 1 inch (2.5 cm); and *A. cylindrica,* pure white, to 2 inches (5 cm). Zones 4–8.

Astilbe chinensis 'Pumila' (dwarf astilbe). Just like the garden cultivars, but smaller, dwarf astilbe has fernlike leaves and bears spikes of small rose-purple flowers in July and August. It grows well in sun and partial shade, and prefers moist soil conditions. It grows to a height of 10 inches (25 cm) and width of 18 inches (45 cm). Zones 5–8.

Campanula zoysii (bellflower). This is a choice and lovely bellflower that bears compact bunches of pendulous, tubular, lilac-blue flowers in May and June over a mat of small, glossy leaves. It prefers some lime in the soil, grows to a height of 1 inch (2.5 cm) with a wider spread, and is very fond of sun. Zones 4–7.

Dianthus microlepis (dwarf pink). This pretty little plant forms a tight ball of gray-green leaves dotted with small pink flowers in May and June. It grows to 2 inches (5 cm) in height with a wider spread, and likes lots of sun and, if possible, some lime. Zones 5–7.

Gentiana septemfida (gentian). This is one of the easiest gentians to grow and it will flourish in almost any soil or situation. It forms compact tufts of green leaves and deep blue flowers are borne at the end of leafy stems in July and August. It grows to a height of 6 inches (15 cm), with a slightly wider spread. A particularly good variety is *cordifolia.* Zones 3–9.

Gentiana verna (spring gentian). This ever-popular gentian comes in many forms; one even has yellow flowers. The most commonly cultivated form is *G. v. angulosa,* which grows to a height of 3 inches (7.5 cm) and bears fine flowers of a deep azure-blue in April and May. It grows well in full sun but needs continuous moisture and must not be allowed to dry out. Zones 4–7.

Lewisia spp. This genus is increasingly popular in the alpine garden. Lewisias are nearly all evergreens that prefer moist, well-drained soil and full sun. The most commonly grown are cultivars of *L. cotyledon,* a widely distributed and variable species, which bear white, rose-tinted, salmon-pink or deep rose flowers in spring, the color varying with the cultivar. They form a dense rosette of fleshy leaves, to a height of 4 inches (10 cm) and width of 8 inches (20 cm). Zones 3–9.

Phlox nana (Santa Fe phlox). The stems of this little plant are straggly, growing to a length of 8 inches (20 cm), ideal for softening the edge of a trough. The flowers are pastel pink with a white center and they bloom in June and July. It likes a well-drained soil and full sun. Zones 3–9.

Primula farinosa (primula). This is one of many primulas that grow well in an alpine garden. It bears umbels of yellow-eyed rose-lilac flowers in March and April and grows to a height and width of 4 inches (10 cm). It prefers moist, acid soil and full sun or partial shade. Another attractive cultivar, and one of the easiest to cultivate, is *P.* x *forsteri* f. *bilekii,* which grows to 2 inches (5 cm), bearing rose-pink flowers with white centers in April. Zones 5–7.

Saxifraga spp. (saxifrages). There are more than three hundred species of saxifrages and many are alpines, readily available for growing in containers. If you want to collect only one genus of alpines, this is a good choice. Saxifrages range in size from 2 inches (5 cm) to 6 inches (15 cm) and more, with flowers in various shades of white, orange, yellow, and pink, depending upon the species. *S. burseriana* bears white flowers in February and March; *S. flagellaris* has golden flowers in April and May; and *S. aizoides* has star-shaped, bright yellow or orange flowers, sometimes with red spots, in May and June. Zones 4–8.

Bulbs and tubers

Cyclamen coum (cyclamen). Grown from a tuber, this plant requires well-mulched, moist soil and light shade. It produces delicate, silver-marbled foliage, and its magenta-colored flowers with crimson bases bloom in February. It grows to a height of 3 inches (7.5 cm). Zones 5–9.

Iris reticulata (netted iris). This easily grown species iris blooms in February and has deep blue flowers with a yellow blaze. It is one of a wide choice of dwarf iris blooming at this time. Others to watch for are *I. danfordiae,* clear yellow and honey-scented; *I. histrioides,* bright blue; and cultivars of *I. histrioides* and *I. reticulata,* such as 'Cantab', pale blue; 'Harmony', deep royal blue; and 'Pauline', deep dusky violet-pink with a white spot. They require well-drained soil and a sunny or lightly shaded position, and grow to a height and width of 6 inches (15 cm). Some are fragrant. Zones 5–9.

Narcissus cyclamineus (dwarf daffodil). This lovely dwarf species bears rich, golden, trumpet-shaped flowers in February and March and needs moist, well-drained soil and partial shade to grow well. Three bulbs will form a clump of daffodils 6 inches (15 cm) high and wide in five years. Zones 3–9.

Tulipa tarda (tulip). This species tulip flowers in March, with white or cream, yellow-centered flowers. It requires a well-drained soil that is allowed to dry out in the summer. (If that is not possible, lift the bulbs after they have flowered and the leaves have died back, and store in a cool, dry spot, replanting them again in the fall.) In five years this tulip bulb will form a clump 8 inches (20 cm) high and 12 inches (30 cm) wide. Zones 3–9.

How to make a hypertufa trough for alpines

One attractive way to display tiny plants, especially bulbs and alpines, is in a trough, known as a hypertufa trough, made from concrete, perlite, and peat moss. Trough gardens are easy to make and remarkably weatherproof. The following instructions can be used to make a simple rectangular form; you can make square and round troughs using the same method.

Materials

- Polyethylene sheeting.
- Two sturdy cardboard boxes, one 1 1/2 to 2 inches (4 to 5 cm) larger in length and width than the other.
- Strapping tape.
- Portland cement.
- Perlite.
- Peat moss.
- Half-inch (1.2-cm) wire mesh.
- Three pieces of doweling,1/2-inch (1.2-cm) in diameter and 6 inches (15 cm) long.
- A sharp knife or razor blade.
- A large rubber bucket.
- Rubber gloves.
- Measuring cup (such as an empty coffee can).
- Wire cutters.
- An old knife or scraper.

Method

Choose a good working space where a bit of mess won't be a problem (a heated workshop or garage), and where you have access to water.

Prepare the mold out of the cardboard boxes, fitting the smaller box, closed end up, neatly inside the other, so that there is a 1 1/2- to 2-inch (4- to 5-cm) gap between the sides of the boxes when nested. If it is necessary to cut the smaller box to fit, do so and tape it to the required size with strapping tape. The inner box should be 4 to 6 inches (10 to 15 cm) deep, the outer one at least 3 inches (8 cm) higher.

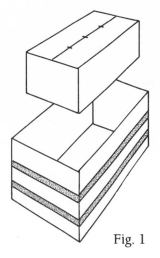

Fig. 1

Wrap a couple of bands of strapping tape near the top and bottom of the outer box to keep the cardboard from buckling under the pressure of the wet mixture (Fig. 1).

Now it is time to mix the hypertufa. Use one part cement to one-and-a-half parts peat moss and one-and-a-half parts perlite. Mix with enough water to reach the con-

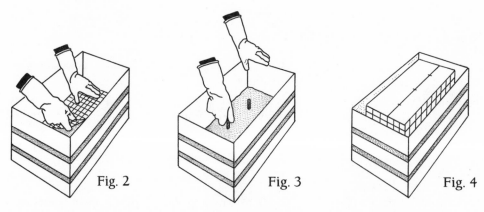

Fig. 2   Fig. 3   Fig. 4

sistency of cream-style cottage cheese, in small enough quantities each time so that it doesn't harden before you can use each batch.

Put a 1-inch (2.5-cm) layer of the mix in the bottom of the box. Place a piece of chicken wire (cut to size and with holes cut in it for the doweling to pass through) on the concrete (Fig. 2). Set the wooden dowels upright in the concrete so that they will make drainage holes and add another 1-inch (2.5-cm) layer of concrete mix to cover the wire completely, packing it down evenly to remove all air bubbles and straightening the dowels (Fig. 3).

Place the smaller box upside-down and centered inside the larger one and push it slightly into the concrete. Cut a strip of chicken wire long enough to fit around the small box, and of a width equal to the height of the small box, pressing it firmly into the concrete at the bottom of the large box.

Wait thirty minutes, then fill the space between the sides of the two boxes with enough concrete to encase the wire and cover its edges (Fig. 4). Pack the mix in by the handful and tap the box gently on the work surface to prevent and remove air bubbles. Leave it to cure, undisturbed and at room temperature, for three days, then remove the outer box. Mist the outside lightly with water and leave it for another seven days. Remove the inner box and dowels and allow at least another week for it to cure completely.

Since concrete is high in lime, which is toxic to many plants, place it outdoors to weather for several weeks so that the lime can be leached by rainfall. If it does not rain, you will need to water the trough thoroughly several times, allowing the water to drain away each time, until you are confident that the excess lime is gone.

Your trough garden is now ready to plant.

Planting a trough garden

This little trough garden measures only 8 by 12 by 18 inches (20 by 30 by 45 cm) yet it provides color and interest throughout the year with its combination of alpine trees, shrubs, bulbs, and perennials.

Materials

- Container: a concrete trough that is 8 inches (20 cm) deep, 12 inches (30 cm) wide, and 18 inches (45 cm) long, with drainage holes in the bottom, covered with a few shards of broken pottery or fine plastic mesh so that the soil won't wash out.
- Potting mixture: equal parts of peat moss; sterilized, well-rotted leaf mold; and gritty sand, or buy a commercial alpine mix.
- Plants: one *Pinus densiflora* 'Alice Verkade' (pine); one *Androsace lactea* (rock jasmine); one *Gentiana septemfida* (gentian); one *Primula farinosa* (primula); three *Narcissus cyclamineus* (miniature daffodils); one *Penstemon davidsonii*; and one *Phlox nana* (Santa Fe phlox).
- Other: three small, decorative rocks and extra gritty sand for the soil surface.

Method

Cover the drainage holes with pieces of broken ceramic pot and cover the pot pieces with a handful each of fine gravel, or cover the drainage holes with fine plastic mesh. Either way, the water can drain easily out of the trough but the soil will stay in. Cover with a layer of soil to within about 4 inches (10 cm) of the rim of the trough.

Arrange the plant materials, leaving spaces for the decorative rocks. Make holes for the plants in the soil mixture if necessary, and fill in with more soil, firming the plants gently into place and leaving a maximum of one inch (2.5 cm) above the level of the soil, just enough room for the top-dressing. This will allow for the inevitable settling of the soil. Place the rocks carefully in position.

Water well and add a one-inch (2.5-cm) layer of sand or fine gravel to the surface of the soil for a top-dressing. Make sure that the trough is placed in a spot that is protected from direct, early morning winter sun, especially when the weather is very cold and the trough is without a snow cover.

Aftercare

Once planted, little care is necessary. The trough should not be allowed to dry out, and during hot, dry weather you may have to water every second day. The top-dressing of sand will allow it to retain moisture as well as protect it from excessive heat. There is no need to fertilize weekly, but you can use a diluted solution of liquid fertilizer once a month during the growing season if you wish.

Water, water everywhere

Lions spout water and half-barrels make good aquatic environments for fish

RUNNING WATER IS ONE OF THE MOST COOLING AND RELAXING SOUNDS in the garden as it gently flows over stones or trickles from the nearest wall or water fountain. Ponds and streams are rewarding additions to any garden, soothing to the mind and calming to the spirit. They encourage dragonflies and birds to visit, and are always interesting to watch, especially if you have fish. It's no wonder that so many gardeners have been installing water features and that nurseries are stocking up on oxygenating plants, bog plants, and water lilies.

Patio and balcony water gardens can be just as successful as larger ponds, and as much fun. Anyone can have a water feature outdoors during the summer months, even if winters are very cold. Once installed they are easy to maintain and need a minimum of attention while they are in use.

There are basically two different types of water gardens or features you can install on a balcony or patio—those at ground level or those that hang on the wall. The type you choose will depend upon your garden space and climate. For instance, outside a basement suite accessed by a stairwell, overhung with trailing green plants, you could fix a water feature onto the wall, half-hidden within the plants, so that the water spurts out between the tendrils of lush undergrowth and falls into a basin below. Where winters are very cold, drain the water out for the winter and start it up again in the spring.

Wall-hanging water features are available in many different forms, shapes, and sizes, although most of them are similarly constructed. They consist of a top piece with a stylized spout that shoots out the water, often from the mouth of a lion or frog, and a bottom piece that is usually half a bowl, so that the flat side will fit flush against the wall. Sometimes the whole thing comes in one piece, rather like a rectangular wall plaque. Usually, though, the two pieces are separate so that they can be installed at the most appropriate distance apart, depending upon the particular location. The water is usually recycled by means of tubing and a pump, which are hidden by overhanging greenery.

Wall fountains can be installed on many patios or balconies, even if you are not able to attach them to the wall. In this case it is easy enough to make a sturdy wooden framework for the water fountain, and grow climbing plants such as sweet peas, ivy, and clematis so that they will trail up and around it. Even old metal bed frames can be used, as long as they have a backing strong enough to bear the weight of the fountain. These plant-and-water frameworks make excellent screens for an exposed space, hiding unsightly views and protecting privacy.

If you want to grow aquatic plants and keep fish, you will need a water garden at ground level. The best containers for this are either a half-barrel or a large ceramic pot. Wooden half-barrels make very good containers for water plants. They should be scrubbed thoroughly first and then filled with tap water. Unless you are sure the wood is leak-proof, you may want to take the precaution of lining the barrel with PVC pond liner or sealing it with a silicone sealant.

Well-glazed ceramic pots need only be filled with water. Once the chlorine has evaporated from the water the pot can be stocked with plants. You will need five or six bunches of submerged oxygenating plants to supply the fish and other plants with oxygen and keep the water healthy. Include a couple of ornamental plants, such as miniature water lilies.

The best time to plant a water garden is in the late spring, just as the plants are beginning to wake up and put on a spurt of growth. Once the plants have been in for a couple of weeks and are established, it is time to add goldfish and water snails, and sit back and watch the fun. The fish will need to be fed occasionally, but not too often since you want them to eat up any insects that happen by.

Water lilies need at least six hours of sun a day to bloom properly. There are many other water plants that do not need as much sun, so even if your patio or balcony is in the shade it is still possible to have a water garden. The only drawback to a lot of sun is container size: even a half-barrel is a very small pond, and the water in it will warm up more quickly than in a larger pond, making it too warm for fish and plants by midsummer. It is important to use the largest container you can and protect it from intense midday heat.

There is a novel way to solve this problem if you have a large space. Make a mounded pile of river rocks with a depression in the center, line the depression with a piece of vinyl pool liner, cover the top of the liner with more rocks, and you have a mini-water garden with partially insulated sides. With a small pump and tubing, water can be recirculated from the pond over some of the rocks to create a small waterfall effect. You will even have room for a few small fish and plants.

Whatever the size or shape of your container, it is easy to submerge a small pump in the water to create a little fountain, or attach the pump tubing to a concrete or terracotta water feature, such as a frog or fish, that will spurt water back into the pond. You can even install a wall fountain above the water garden, pumping the water from the barrel or pot so that it passes up to the spout of the wall fountain, spills over into the catchment basin, and cascades down into the water garden again.

In most parts of the country, water gardens in barrels will not survive the winter months outdoors. However, water plants and fish adapt well to an indoor environment, as long as the water in their container is topped up regularly to account for evaporation. Ceramic pots, such as the many attractive and frost-resistant blue, brown, and green glazed pots that are made in China and Thailand today, are a much better bet than wooden barrels for an inside garden. Barrels are likely to seep with moisture, and the outside of the barrel may crack if it dries out indoors. You may want to keep a barrel outside as a water garden for the summer and have a large pot indoors for the winter. You can maintain a successful water garden this way for years.

Water gardens make good aquatic environments for fish, and small children love to peek into the depths to watch them. They enjoy fishing for them too, so you may have to remind them that the fish should not be disturbed and supervise them when near the pool (for safety reasons, as well as for the health of the water garden). If not, you may find all your water plants on the floor and a four-year-old happily sloshing an arm shoulder-deep in the water, while terrified fish swim madly in circles. Otherwise water gardens, like aquariums, can provide endless hours of entertainment and education for older children, and are well worth the effort to make.

Setting the scene

The following checklist will help you start creating a water garden on your patio or balcony.

- For a ground-level water garden: a wooden half-barrel or large ceramic pot; aquatic plants, including oxygenating plants, floating plants, and other pond plants, such as water lilies; plastic pots for the plants; fine mesh to line the pots; ordinary soil; fine gravel or sand; goldfish and water snails.
- For a water garden on the wall: a concrete or terracotta wall fountain; framework to support it; water pump and tubing; and pots of ivy and clematis to climb or trail around the fountain.
- If there is room, a garden table and chairs.
- A patio umbrella.
- Cement garden ornaments, such as a duck, snail, or frog.

Since water and frogs or ducks seem to go together, why not use one of these for a theme? For example, you could paint the floor with lily pads and place concrete frogs on them and ducks nearby. You could decorate your cloth, chair cushions, or umbrella with frogs or ducks, and paint the table and chairs green. If you collect ducks or frogs this would be an excellent place to display them.

Plants that grow in water

Oxygenating plants

These are the plants that live submerged in the water and release oxygen. They are essential for the life of fish and the other plants and will be your first priority.

Elodea canadensis (**Canadian pondweed**). A semievergreen plant that forms a dense sward of foliage underwater and has dark green leaves. Zones 3–9.

Hottonia palustris (**water violet**). Dense whorls of divided green leaves form a spreading mass of foliage on this deciduous plant. Lilac or whitish flowers appear above the water surface in summer. Zones 8–9.

Vallisneria **spp.** (**eel grass**). An evergreen, submerged water plant, frost tender, eel grass requires sun or semishade and needs thinning out from time to time. It can be propagated by division in spring or summer. Zones 9–10.

Floating plants

These cover the surface of the water, keeping it cooler and helping to reduce algae by lessening light in the water.

Azolla caroliniana (**mosquito fern, water fern**). The fronds of this tiny, deciduous water fern are colored red to purple in full sun and pale green to blue-green in shade. Zones 7–10.

Hydrocharis morsus-ranae (**frogbit**). A deciduous plant with rosettes of kidney-shaped, olive-green leaves and small, white flowers during summer. Zones 7–10.

Pistia stratiotes (**shell flower, water lettuce**). This lovely, evergreen, floating plant must be brought in during the winter, except in tropical climates. It has hairy, soft green foliage that is arranged in lettucelike whorls and produces insignificant greenish flowers. Zones 8–10.

Other pond plants

These plants are grown in pots in either deep or shallow water. Shallow water plants are known as marginal plants and their containers can be quite shallow. A 6-inch (15-cm) depth of water is fine, as long as the water is always kept topped up so that the plants do not dry out. Following is a selection of commonly available plants.

Acorus calamus '**Variegatus**' (**variegated sweet flag**). This semievergreen bog plant has swordlike, tangerine-scented leaves with cream stripes, flushed rose-pink in spring. It prefers sun and grows to a height of 30 inches (75 cm). Zones 4–10. A much smaller relative is *A. gramineus* 'Variegatus', which has grasslike leaves and no scent. It grows to a height of 10 inches (25 cm). Zones 6–9.

Aponogeton distachyos (**water hawthorn, cape pondweed**). This deciduous, deep-water plant has floating, oblong, mid- to dark green leaves and prefers sun. Fragrant white flowers are produced throughout the summer. Zones 9–10.

Butomus umbellatus (**flowering rush**). A deciduous rushlike perennial with narrow twisted leaves and umbels of pink to rose-red flowers in summer. It grows to a height of 3 feet (90 cm) and likes sun. Zones 6–10.

Caltha palustris (**marsh marigold**). A deciduous marginal plant with attractive, rounded, dark green leaves and clusters of buttercup-shaped, bright, golden-yellow flowers in spring. It grows to a height of 24 inches (60 cm) and prefers sun. The cultivar 'Flore Plena' has double flowers. Zones 4–9.

Eichhornia crassipes (**water hyacinth**). A deep-water plant that has glossy evergreen leaves floating on air-filled leaf stalks, it prefers sun and bears spikes of blue-lilac flowers in summer. Zones 8–10.

Iris laevigata (**beardless Japanese iris**). This rhizomatous iris grows to 2 to 3 feet (60 to 90 cm) in height and bears blue, blue-purple, or white flowers in early to midsummer. It grows well in sun or semishade in moist conditions or in shallow water. Zones 5–9.

Menyanthes trifoliata (**bog bean**). A deciduous marginal plant that has tripartate leaves and fringed white flowers in spring. Prefers sun. Zones 5–8.

Nymphaea spp. (**water lilies**). There are many different kinds of water lilies varying in color, growth habits, preferred depth of water, flowering time, and length of flowering season. Your local supplier or garden center should be able to help you make a choice suitable for your situation. For a container, however, you will want to look for a neat, small-leafed plant that is happy to stay contained in a small space. The lily pads provide shelter for fish and help to reduce the spread of algae. Most water lilies need at least six hours of sunshine a day in order to bloom. The following plants are particularly well suited to container-growing. Zones 5–10, depending on the species and cultivar.

N. odorata 'Minor' has white flowers and a strong scent.

N. tetragona 'Alba' syn. *N. pygmaea* is white, and is one of the smallest of all the water lilies.

N. 'Pink Opal' is a small plant with star-shaped pink flowers and a strong scent.

N. laydekeri 'Rosea' is very small and has deep rose-colored flowers that have a strong scent.

N. 'James Brydon' is a rich red with orange stamens. This excellent, small water lily tolerates some shade.

N. 'Ellisiana' is very small and has vivid dark red flowers with dark green leaves.

N. x *helvola* has marbled leaves and soft, sulfur-yellow flowers. It is very small.

Pontederia cordata (**pickerel weed**). A deciduous marginal plant with lance-shaped, glossy dark green leaves, it bears dense spikes of blue flowers in late summer and prefers sun. Zones 4–9.

Saururus cernuus (lizard's tail, swamp lily, water dragon). A deciduous perennial with clumps of heart-shaped leaves and creamy flowers in spring. It is a bog plant, prefers sun and grows to a height of 10 inches (25 cm). Zones 5–9.

Sparganium erectum syn. *S. ramosum*. A vigorous deciduous or semievergreen perennial with narrow leaves, this marginal water plant is one of the few that does best in full shade. It bears small, greenish-brown burrs on flower spikes in the summer and grows to a height of 3 feet (0.9 m). Zones 5–9.

Typha minima (dwarf cattail). A deciduous perennial with grasslike leaves, this cattail bears spikes of rust-brown flowers in late summer, followed by decorative, cylindrical seed heads. It grows to a height of 18 to 24 inches (45 to 60 cm) and likes sun. Zones 6–9.

Making a water barrel for the patio

Materials

- Containers: one sturdy wooden half-barrel, lined with vinyl pool liner or sealed with a silicone sealant so that it does not leak; plastic pots for the pond plants (big enough for the plants, but able to fit beside each other on the bottom of the barrel); fine mesh to line the pots; ordinary soil; and fine gravel or sand.
- Plants: half a dozen bunches of oxygenating plants, such as *Elodea canadensis* (Canadian pondweed) or *Vallisneria* spp. (eel grass); a pond plant such as *Nymphaea x helvola* (water lily); and some floating plants, such as *Hydrocharis morsus-ranae* (frogbit).
- Wildlife: four or five small, ordinary goldfish, available from your local pet shop, and two or three water snails.

Note: Oxygenating water plants and water snails can sometimes be obtained from pet stores that sell fish, but usually you have to get them from a garden store or a supplier who specializes in water plants.

Method

Fill the trough with tap water and leave for at least four days so that any chlorine will evaporate.

Plant the oxygenating plants in ordinary soil without added manure or compost (it will decompose, giving off gases) in a plastic pot that has been lined with plastic mesh to prevent the soil from leaking out. Cover the surface of the soil with sand or gravel to prevent the fish from stirring up the soil, making the water dirty. Plant the water lily or pond plant in the same way in another plastic pot. Lower the two pots gently into the water. Place a few floating plants on top of the water. Leave the plants for at least a week to acclimatize.

When the plants are acclimatized, introduce the goldfish and water snails into the

water. In order not to shock the goldfish, gradually add some of the water from the barrel into their water, and add more over a period of hours until it contains about 50 percent water from the barrel. Gently lower the container into the barrel and release the fish. The snails will keep the sides of the container clean, the fish will eat any insect intruders, and the oxygenators will keep the water healthy, so that the water garden will be self-sustaining.

Aftercare

Keep an eye on the water level and add more water as necessary. Feed the fish every few days, but otherwise leave them to fend for themselves. They will be quite happy eating any flies and other small insects that come their way.

The flower arranger's garden

Cutting flowers and greenery for indoor pleasure

SO MANY LOVELY FLOWERS ARE HARD TO FIND AS CUT FLOWERS AND expensive to buy, and yet they are easy to grow. Even if your patio or balcony is small, you will have room for some of your favorites. Annuals such as snapdragons, cornflowers, sweet peas, and cosmos, as well as less commonly known flowers, like bells-of-Ireland and cup-and-saucer vine, make excellent container plants and thrive when cut. With most annuals, the more you cut them, the more they flower.

With a bit of thought you can grow many kinds of plants for flower arranging, beginning in the spring with early-flowering dwarf narcissus and harvesting right through to the last asters in the fall. There are many attractive dwarf perennial hybrids that grow well in small containers. Several grasses, seed heads, and flowers, such as yarrow, larkspur, and astilbe, will dry well, making them useful for dried flower arrangements in the winter. Many evergreen shrubs are prized by flower arrangers for their good-looking foliage, and regular trimming actually helps to keep the shrubs in shape.

Fragrant flowers are especially valuable in a cutting garden. A leisurely weekend breakfast is all the nicer when the table is decorated with a delicate vase of freshly picked flowers; maybe sweet box in the winter, followed by the first tiny iris and daffodils, white lily-of-the-valley, multicolored sweet peas, or strongly scented carnations. If the climate is just too cold where you live to have flowers in bloom early in the season, it is worth planting bulbs in pots for forcing indoors. Then you can enjoy the fragrance and color of hyacinths, daffodils, tulips, and crocuses, even when snow is still thick on the ground.

A cutting garden should be planted so there will be attractive flowers in bloom throughout the season. This means some careful planning before you start, so you don't end up with everything flowering in May and hardly anything for the rest of the summer.

A rectangular wooden planter makes a practical and convenient cutting garden—the bigger the better. It should be large enough to grow at least one small, broad-leafed, evergreen shrub; three or four medium-to-tall perennials and some smaller ones, all with different blooming times (from late spring to early fall); a selection of spring-flowering bulbs; and a selection of your favorite annuals. If there is space, try to include one or two ornamental grasses, especially those with attractive flowering spikes (see "Lakeside nostalgia"), and some of the many herbs that look good in the cutting garden, such as fennel, dill, and lavender (see "A taste of Provence").

If you have room for a lot of containers, think about adding an eclectic mix of hanging baskets, grow bags, window boxes, and pots of varying shapes and sizes so that each plant can have the growing conditions it needs. Some plants, such as lily-of-the-valley, tend to be very invasive and are best in their own pot, while others remain nicely compact, and work well in combination with others.

A small-scale cutting garden on a patio or balcony is constantly on show, and must be fertilized at least once or twice a week throughout the growing season with a high-phosphate fertilizer to encourage flower production. You will be able to cut flowers all summer long, and still have lots of others blooming in your pots and planters.

Cut flowers will last longer and look better if they are well treated from the beginning. The best time to cut them is in the early morning or late evening, when the air is cool. Plant stems are less able to take in water during the heat of the day, and this often results in wilted flowers. Stems should be cut with sharp secateurs or special flower cutters and placed in lukewarm water immediately after picking. If they are left without water for too long the ends will dry out, making it harder for them to absorb water; if this happens they should be recut.

Plants with woody stems, such as shrubs, often have trouble absorbing water. In this case the ends of the stems can be lightly crushed with a hammer, or split lengthwise with a sharp knife. Any leaves that will be submerged in water should be removed. This will allow more room for the stems, and will help to prevent the water from becoming slimy and dirty. Underwater rose thorns should also be removed.

Plants that wilt easily, such as poppies, will absorb water more readily if the ends are either seared with a match or dipped quickly into boiling water. Tulips often look wilted, even when they have been freshly picked. This is the result of an airlock in the stem, a problem that can be overcome by pricking halfway into the stem with a sharp sewing needle at 1-inch (2.5-cm) intervals along its length.

Floral preservatives contain fungicides and bactericides. These help to keep the water clear, resulting in longer-lasting flowers. If you don't use preservatives, change the water every day or two; if this is not possible, add fresh water daily.

Your flower arrangements can be much more interesting if you experiment with using familiar kitchen and household objects as well as vases for containers. Try a tea pot, wine cooler, or saucepan as a container for taller flowers such as delphiniums, cosmos, yarrow, and sunflowers; or an antique tea cup, baby mug, or plastic-lined, small clay pot for sweet peas, pinks, or miniature bulbs. Even milk bottles acquire a certain elegance when they are overflowing with color and greenery.

Setting the scene

The following checklist will help you start creating an imaginative cutting garden on your patio or balcony.

- Six to eight hours of sunshine for most plants, especially the annuals and sun-loving perennials.
- One large wooden planter, at least 5 feet (1.5 m) long and 2 feet (60 cm) wide.
- An assortment of other containers, to fill the space.
- A working table large enough to arrange flowers.
- Flower-arranging tools and equipment—vases, oasis foam, knife, cutting shears—and a sturdy waterproof plastic container under the table for storage.
- A selection of your favorite flowers for the cutting garden—shrubs, perennials, bulbs, and annuals.
- Basic soil mix and high-phosphate fertilizer.
- Watering and lighting systems.
- Basic garden tools and storage.

Since this is the ultimate flower arranger's garden, fill every nook and cranny with pots and flowers—peeking out of hanging baskets, glazed pots, wooden crates, old wicker baskets, and plastic tubs, totally surrounding your large wooden planter. There should hardly be room to move without tripping over flowers.

Plants for a cutting garden through the seasons

Shrubs for year-round foliage

Small evergreen shrubs with good foliage will provide greenery for flower arranging right through the year. These are five good shrubs to use.

Elaeagnus pungens 'Maculata'. See "Design by color."
Euonymus japonicus 'Silver King' (Japanese spindle bush). See "In the shade."
Pachistima myrsinites 'Emerald Cascade' (Oregon boxwood, myrtle boxwood). See "Going native."
Sarcococca spp. (sweet box). See "Old-fashioned fragrance."
Skimmia japonica ssp. *reevesiana*. One of only two self-fertile skimmias, this low-growing evergreen shrub with glossy, rich green leaves produces clusters of tiny white flowers in April and May, and red berries in the fall. It grows to a height and spread of 2 feet (60 cm) and needs shade and plenty of water. Zones 7–9.

Spring perennials: plants and bulbs

Bergenia cordifolia (elephant's ear). See "In the shade."
Convallaria majalis (lily-of-the-valley). See "Old-fashioned fragrance."
Iris xiphium Dutch hybrids (Dutch iris). Dutch iris should be planted 4 to 6 inches

(10 to 15 cm) deep in light, fertile soil and full sun. These are the first of the *I. xiphium* hybrids to flower, from early to mid-June, and there are many attractive cultivars. Perhaps the most stunning is 'White Excelsior', which bears pure white flowers with yellow markings on 16-inch (40-cm) stems. Zones 6–9.

Narcissus **spp.** Miniature daffodils are a welcome addition to early spring. A good choice is 'Tête à Tête', which grows to a height of 10 inches (25 cm) and has long-lasting flowers with rich golden petals surrounding a yellowish-orange cup. They like sun or part shade and well-drained soil. Zones 3–9.

Pulmonaria angustifolia 'Mawson's Variety' **(lungwort, blue cowslip).** Less well known than *P. officinalis,* the leaves of this cultivar are narrow and dark green, rather than spotted, and the funnel-shaped flowers are a deeper blue. It grows to a height and spread of 9 inches (23 cm) and likes sun or part shade. Zones 4–8.

Trollius x *cultorum* 'Alabaster' **(globe flower).** Globe flowers thrive beside pools and streams and in wet, boggy areas, but they will also grow well in containers as long as they are not allowed to dry out. This cultivar produces attractive, round, ivory-colored blooms, excellent for flower arranging. It grows to a height of 24 inches (60 cm) and spread of 18 inches (45 cm). It grows best in sun. Zones 5–8.

Tulipa **spp. (tulips).** Many of the smaller tulip species and hybrids are in full bloom by midspring, and they look especially attractive when they are planted underneath evergreen shrubs. A wide selection of early-blooming tulips are available at most garden centers.

Summer perennials

Achillea **spp. (yarrow).** There are many cultivars of this upright perennial, all good for cutting with long, stout stems, fernlike foliage, and flat flower heads that bloom throughout the summer. Good cultivars are 'Moonshine', light yellow; 'Coronation Gold', strong yellow; 'Gold Plate', deep gold; 'Cerise Queen', bright pink; 'Fire King', deep red; and 'Rosea', soft pink. They grow to a height of 2 to 3 feet (60 to 90 cm), depending on the cultivar, and like sun and good drainage. Zones 2–9.

Alstroemeria **Ligtu hybrids (Peruvian lily).** Peruvian lilies have long-lasting, azalealike flowers that bloom profusely from May to midsummer on leafy stems ranging in height from 2 to 5 feet (60 to 150 cm), depending on the cultivar. Their colors vary from orange and yellow to shades of pink, lilac, red, and creamy-white, and the blossoms are often streaked and speckled with darker tones. They grow best in cool, moist, sandy soil in sun and part shade. Zones 7–10.

Aster sedifolius 'Nana'. This compact aster produces long-lasting, daisylike, lavender-blue flowers with yellow centers during the late summer and fall. It grows to a height of 18 inches to 2 feet (45 to 60 cm), with half that spread, and does best in sun and well-drained soil. Zones 4–8.

Astilbe **spp.** There are many dwarf astilbe hybrids, all excellent for flower arranging with their delicate leaves and tapering flower panicles. They thrive in moist soil, in sun or part-shade, and vary from 12 to 18 inches (30 to 45 cm) depending on the cultivar. Look for 'Bronze Elegance', clear pink with a salmon tinge; 'Praecox Alba', white; and 'Sprite', shell-pink. Zones 3–9.

Delphinium spp. (delphiniums). Delphinium's lovely, tall spires are a welcome addition to any garden, and last well when cut. For container growing it is probably best to look for the *D.* x *belladonna* cultivars, strong, sturdy plants that grow to 2 feet (60 cm) and are not as susceptible to rain and wind damage as the larger hybrids. Good cultivars are 'Bonita', gentian blue; 'Casa Blanca', pure white; and 'Pink Sensation', pink. Zones 3–8.

Dianthus Allwoodii hybrids (carnations, pinks). See "Old-fashioned fragrance."

Eryngium maritimum (sea holly). This is an interesting, spiky-looking plant with blue stems and blue teasellike flower heads, each with a collar of spiny bracts resembling thistles, and gray-green basal foliage. The plant grows to a height of 18 inches (45 cm) or more, and it likes sun and well-drained soil. Zones 5–10.

Heuchera micrantha (coral bells). The large, rounded, hairy leaves of this perennial are often tinted or marbled with silver and the tiny, bell-shaped flowers rise above the foliage on wiry stems. 'Palace Purple' has heart-shaped, deep metallic-purple leaves and sprays of small white flowers that last for weeks as cut flowers. The plants require sun or part-shade, and well-drained, fertile soil. They grow to a height of 12 inches (30 cm). Zones 4–9.

Kniphofia 'Little Maid' (poker plant). This hybrid is much more attractive than its name implies. It bears dainty, slender, flower spikes of pale cream-yellow in summer and grows to a height of 24 inches (60 cm). It requires sun and good drainage. Zones 5–9.

Liatris spicata (gayfeather). See "Backyard wildlife."

Scabiosa caucasica (pincushion flower). Often expensive to buy in flower shops, this plant is prized for its attractive, tightly compact, pincushionlike flower heads in soft shades of blue, red, lavender, or violet. It grows to a height of 2 feet (60 cm) and likes sun and well-drained, limy soil. Zones 3–9.

Winter perennials

Helleborus spp. (Christmas and Lenten roses, Corsican and stinking hellebores). The best hellebores for cutting are the green-flowered stinking and Corsican hellebores. See "In the shade." The flowers last well indoors as long as you make a small slit in the side of the flower stem, near the base of the flower, and avoid putting them in rooms that are too warm. Other hellebores can be a little trickier; cut them in full bloom only. Zones 7–9.

Annuals

Annuals can be divided into two groups: those that can be grown easily from seed (although you may prefer to buy some of them as small plants) and those that are usually bought as established bedding plants. New and interesting cultivars seem to come into garden centers all the time, and this list should help you search for some of the more unusual ones, as well as the tried and true. The most important thing to remember is that the more you cut annuals the more they will flower—a definite advantage when you have a cutting garden.

Annuals from seed

Unless specified, these annuals require full sun and a well-drained soil and are easily grown from seed sown outdoors in early spring.

Calendula officinalis (pot or English marigold). See "A taste of Provence."

Centaurea cyanus (cornflower). The well-loved, bright blue cornflower is also available in other shades of blue, pink, plum, yellow, and white, and the flower forms vary, depending on the cultivar. They vary in height from 8 to 36 inches (20 to 90 cm).

Clarkia amoena (godetia, farewell-to-spring). This is always a favorite, with delicate, cuplike blossoms in soft shades of pink, white, red, and lilac, clustered on 6- to 12-inch (15- to 30-cm) stems.

Consolida ambigua (annual delphinium, larkspur). Now there are compact cultivars of this well-loved cutting flower, with its tall spires of feathery flowers in shades of blue, salmon, rose, lilac, purple, or white. One good form is 'Frosted Skies', semidouble, white with a blue edge to the petal. It grows 12 to 18 inches (30 to 45 cm) in height.

Cosmos bipinnatus (cosmos) and *C. sulphureus* (yellow cosmos). Their single, showy flowers are produced over a long period, right up to the first fall frosts, making them a really good addition to the planter. Look for smaller cultivars, such as 'Sonata', white with a gold center, to 24 inches (60 cm); and 'Sunny Gold', golden, semidouble, to 18 inches (45 cm). Sow outdoors after all danger of frost is past.

Lathyrus odoratus (sweet pea). See "Old-fashioned fragrance."

Nigella damascena (love-in-a-mist). Resembling a more delicate version of the cornflower, this annual also comes in many shades of white, pink, mauve, and blue. 'Dwarf Moody Blue' grows to a height of 6 to 8 inches (15 to 20 cm). The seed heads are interesting in dry flower arrangements.

Papaver spp. (poppy). There are many annual species and cultivars of poppies suitable for containers. One of the best for flower arranging is the *P. rhoeas* 'Shirley' series (Shirley poppy). Flowers may be single or double, in attractive shades of pink, white, rose, salmon, and crimson; plants grow to 24 inches (60 cm) high. Another attractive seed strain is 'Mother of Pearl', with unusual pastel blooms, including gray, soft blue, lilac, pale peach, white, and speckled; it grows to 12 inches (30 cm). To make them last when cut, pick them just as the nodding buds become erect, before they open, and dip the freshly cut stems into boiling water or sear them with a match. Sow seeds in the fall to bloom in spring and early summer.

Rudbeckia 'Becky Mixed' (coneflower). Most cultivated coneflowers are perennials, but some are annuals. 'Becky Mixed' is an annual dwarf cultivar ideal for container growing. Its yellow and orange flowers with dark-eyed centers are up to 6 inches (15 cm) across, although the plant only grows to a height of 8 to 10 inches (20 to 25 cm).

Half-hardy annuals

Often in full bloom when home-grown seedlings are a long way from flowering, half-hardy annuals give instant color to pots and planters. Resist the temptation to plant them outdoors before the third week of May, when the weather is usually reliably warm, although you may get away with it if you have a sunny, protected spot. A small cold frame is a good place to store plants until the weather cooperates.

Antirrhinum majus (snapdragon). Among the best flowers for sunny borders and for cutting, snapdragons are perennials, but are usually grown as annuals. They bloom from late spring through summer and need sun and a rich, well-drained soil. They grow from 8 inches to 3 feet (20 to 90 cm), depending upon the cultivar.

Callistephus chinensis (China aster). A single species of half-hardy annual has given rise to a large number of cultivars with many different flower forms, including quilled, curled, ribbonlike, and pompon flowers; they are excellent for cutting. Colors range from white to pastel pink, rose-pink, lavender, blue, wine, and scarlet, in sizes ranging from 1 to 3 feet (30 to 90 cm). They require rich soil and sun.

Cobaea scandens (cup-and-saucer vine). If you have room for one climber, this is it. It has white, cup-shaped blossoms that change to greenish-purple and violet as they mature, and it blooms vigorously from July to September, requiring full sun and a rich soil.

Gaillardia pulchella (blanket flower). Blanket flower has large flowers that vary in form from daisylike to quilled or ball-shaped, depending on the cultivar. Colors range from creamy-white to yellow, rust, and red. Many are bicolored. They grow to about 18 inches (45 cm) and love the sun.

Matthiola incana (common stock). Common stock cultivars flower in many soft colors and can vary in height from 1 to 3 feet (30 to 90 cm). They need sun and well-drained soil to grow. They are worth growing for their sweet fragrance.

Moluccella laevis (bells-of-Ireland). The 2- to 3-foot (60- to 90-cm) stems have green bells along their entire length and are an interesting addition to both fresh and dried flower arrangements. They need lots of sun to grow well.

Nicotiana alata (flowering tobacco plant). See "Old-fashioned fragrance."

Osteospermum cultivars (Cape marigold, African daisy). A daisylike plant that is excellent for cutting and has a long blooming season, it is available in a wide range of hybrids in various shades of white, pink, or purple. 'Whirlygig' is an interesting cultivar with bluish-white flower heads resembling whirlygigs. It grows to a height of 2 feet (60 cm) and needs lots of sun and well-drained, fertile soil.

Salpiglossis sinuata (**painted tongue**). A relative of the petunia, it has trumpet-shaped, often speckled flowers in interesting shades of gold, scarlet, mahogany, and blue. It grows 2 to 3 feet (60 to 90 cm) high and requires sun and protection from wind.

Zinnia **cultivars**. These well-known, colorful annuals, with their tight, dahlialike flower heads, are a great addition to summer planters. There are many dwarf, medium, and tall cultivars available, including a favorite—lime-green 'Envy', which grows to a height of 2 feet (60 cm). Three dwarf zinnias planted in a small terracotta container make an attractive centerpiece for the table.

Planting a small-scale cutting garden

This planting plan is designed to provide a basic framework for any mixed shrub and flower garden on a small, sunny balcony measuring approximately 6 feet by 20 feet (1.8 m by 6 m). It can be adapted easily to a smaller space by making the wooden planters smaller and reducing the overall number of containers. It includes plants that flower in winter, spring, summer, and fall, so that there will be something interesting to cut and arrange for many months of the year.

Most cutting flowers are sun-loving and require a minimum of six hours of sunshine a day during the growing season. However, if your patio or balcony is in the shade, there are still many attractive plants you can grow and use for flower arranging, including such lovely plants as monkshood, columbine, lady's mantle, violets, and primroses. See the plant list for "In the shade" for more ideas.

Materials

- Containers:
  — One wooden planter (A), 10 feet (3 m) long, 30 inches (75 cm) wide and 10 inches (25 cm) deep, or two 5-foot (1.5-m) long wooden planters to fill the same space.
  — One wooden planter (B), 4 feet (1.2 m) long, 12 inches (30 cm) wide and 10 inches (25 cm) deep.
  — One wooden planter (C), 3 feet (0.9 m) long, 12 inches (30 cm) wide and 10 inches (25 cm) deep.
  — Five round, five-gallon (23-L) plastic containers or equivalent size in terracotta or concrete pots (D, E, F, G, and H).

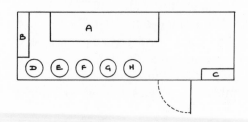

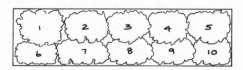

Planter A

Planter B   Planter C

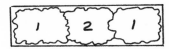 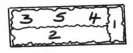 

- Potting mixture: basic soil mix with some controlled-release fertilizer added, and additional liquid fertilizer for use during the growing season, especially a high-phosphate formulation for good flower production.
- Plants:
  — A: (1) several *Consolida ambigua* (larkspur); (2) one *Achillea* 'Moonshine' (yarrow); (3) one *Eryngium maritimum* (sea holly); (4) three *Gaillardia pulchella* (blanket flower); (5) one *Kniphofia* 'Little Maid' (poker plant); (6) one *Dianthus* Allwoodii hybrid (modern pink); (7) one *Aster sedifolius* 'Nanus' (aster); (8) one *Osteospermum* 'Whirligig' (African daisy); (9) one *Lavandula angustifolia* 'Munstead' (dwarf lavender); and (10) one *Carex morrowii* 'Aurea Variegata' (variegated Japanese sedge).
  — B: (1) two *Sarcococca hookeriana* var. *humilis* (sweet box); and (2) one clump of *Convallaria majalis* (lily-of-the-valley).
  — C: (1) one *Cobaea scandens* (cup-and-saucer vine); (2) six *Lathyrus odoratus* (sweet pea); (3) six *Narcissus* 'Tête à Tête' (dwarf daffodil); (4) three *Iris xiphium* Dutch hybrids (Dutch iris); and (5) one *Hedera helix* cultivar (ivy).
  — D: three *Cosmos bipinnatus* (cosmos).
  — E: one *Helleborus foetidus* (stinking hellebore).
  — F: one *Astilbe* 'Bronze Elegance' (astilbe).
  — G: one *Alstroemeria* Ligtu hybrid (Peruvian lily).
  — H: one *Rosa* 'Cecile Brunner' (rose).
- Other: a good watering system, preferably a drip system that waters each pot and planter simultaneously; and trellis and twine for the climbing plants in planter C.

Method

Partially fill the planters and pots with the soil mix and plant them up, according to the planting plan given, so that the level of the soil is about one inch (2.5 cm) below the rim of each container. Water all the plants in well. Prepare a trellis for the climbing plants in planter C and attach the plants to the trellis as they grow.

Aftercare

Keep the plants well watered and fertilize once a week during the growing season with liquid fertilizer. In spite of regular fertilization the soil will become depleted and will need to be enriched at the end of the year with a rich, organic material such as compost or well-rotted manure. It is best if you can change the soil completely every two years and divide the perennials every two to three years.

Backyard wildlife

This collector's garden is strictly for the birds and butterflies

FEW THINGS BRING AS MUCH SIMPLE PLEASURE AND INTEREST TO A SMALL garden as the sight and sound of birds and butterflies. All you need to do is provide the right conditions and environment and you will be rewarded with a lively and colorful display of these lovely creatures. You will also be helping to conserve their numbers as they compete for survival in our increasingly urbanized world.

Their needs are really very simple. If you provide birds with food, water, shelter, and a place to raise their young, they will happily visit even the smallest garden, and you may be surprised at the many kinds you can attract. Butterflies can be harder to please, but if you make a garden that has the right plants and conditions you should be able to attract several species of adult butterflies.

This is one theme where the untidy gardener has a distinct advantage. Birds and butterflies like a little chaos in the garden and are happiest in an environment that is as much like their native habitat as possible, with a diverse selection of plants. One of the best environments is a native garden, where the foliage is layered to provide maximum cover and shelter for the birds (see "Going native"), and the plants will attract local bird and butterfly species.

Birds and butterflies are quite specific about their needs, and as you develop your garden you should keep this in mind. The plants suggested here are applicable to a wide range of birds and butterflies throughout most areas of North America. However, you will find that you can attract even more local species if you know which ones live in your area, and the plants they like. You may want to visit your local library or nature store for more help and information. This theme is an excellent one if your neighborhood already has lots of native plants for butterflies, and trees and shrubs to provide cover and food for birds.

When butterfly eggs hatch, the larvae (caterpillars) live and feed on specific plants, known as host plants, which vary according to the species of butterfly. Red admiral larvae, for instance, feed on nettles, and cloud sulphurs eat clover and alfalfa, so if you do not have any of these host plants nearby you are unlikely to have many of these butterflies in your neighborhood. In larger gardens it is possible to have a nettle or clover patch at the bottom of the garden; if your patio or balcony is large enough, you may want to grow one pot of them in a corner of your balcony, as an experiment.

If there are any adult butterflies in the area, they will be easier to attract if you grow lots of nectar-producing flowers, since nectar is the favorite food for most butterflies. Many flowers produce nectar, but some are clear favorites with the butterflies. These include such aptly named plants as butterfly bush (*Buddleia davidii*) and butterfly weed (*Asclepias tuberosa*). Choose a selection of plants with different flowering times so that there is something to attract the butterflies throughout the growing season. The plant selection for this theme includes plants that grow well in containers and are attractive to most butterflies.

Equally important is the general environment and habitat of your garden: it must be sunny, sheltered, and pesticide-free. Butterflies need sun in order to grow, flourish, reproduce, and feed, and the flowers they feed on will grow best in full sunshine, producing more nectar. The butterflies need to be sheltered from cooling breezes that sap their energy, especially in the spring and fall. Most important of all, butterflies are killed by pesticides, and this includes the commonly used bacterial insecticide BT (*Bacillus thuringiensis*). If you need to spray, try to use only an organic repellent (see "Practical Details: Pests and diseases"). Pesticides also cause a great deal of harm to local bird populations, yet another reason to grow your plants organically.

In a small space it is hard to grow enough food for all the birds you might want to attract. Luckily there are many bird feeders you can make or buy, and they make excellent decorations for your patio or balcony. Wild birdseed mixtures that are high in corn, millet, and sunflower seeds provide the calories and nutrients the birds need. It's important to keep feeders clean and fresh to avoid spreading diseases among birds. Position the feeders so that birds will be safe from cats and protected from wind, snow, and rain. In winter you can decorate trees and shrubs with garlands of edible fruits, nuts, and berries as a special treat for the birds. Popcorn, cranberries, grapes, kernels of corn, and peanuts are especially popular.

Water, especially running water, will attract many birds into your garden for a drink or a bath. A wall-hung water feature, such as the one discussed in the water garden theme, is ideal but not essential. Birds will be just as happy with a shallow bowl placed either on the ground or raised up, as long as it is safe from cats and kept filled with clean water. A three-inch (7.5-cm) depth of water is ideal for bathing. If the water is any deeper the birds will be wary of it and will probably only use it for drinking.

Birds rely on trees and shrubs for shelter and protection, as well as for food. Almost anything leafy will give them shade or a temporary place to perch, but they will need more substantial plants for nesting and for protection against harsh weather, especially in winter. It is not really possible to provide birds with this kind of cover if you are relying on container-grown trees and shrubs, but if you can make your patio or balcony as enticing as possible with feeders, bird baths, and fruit-bearing plants, you will still have lots of temporary visitors. If your patio or balcony is overhung by taller trees, they will provide the long-term protection that you cannot and may also make excellent nesting sites for some of the birds.

When it comes to birdhouses and nesting boxes, birds are fussy. Each species has its own idea of the ideal place to make a nest and raise its young, and some birds prefer to make a nest in the open, rather than in a birdhouse. Swallows and robins, for instance, prefer an open shelving arrangement, whereas wrens and chickadees like birdhouses. The size of the birdhouse, the diameter of the entrance, and its height from the ground are all important factors and will determine whether or not a particular bird will nest there.

Before you make or buy a birdhouse or nesting shelf, make sure that the dimensions will be right for the birds you want to attract and that you can provide a good spot for it, protected from the elements. Nesting boxes can easily be attached to an upright wooden stake and sited under a canopy of leaves, or attached to the wall with an overhang for protection.

Spring and fall migrations bring a change in the bird species that frequent any given area. Some species will overwinter in very cold climates, even as far north as the Yukon and Alaska, and their cheerful presence is a welcome sight when all is cold and white. Birds that winter in your area will really appreciate a feeding station, especially if you provide a consistent supply of food all winter long.

Some of the most interesting and creative gardens for birds are those that use unusual and unconventional feeders, bird baths, nesting boxes, and shelving to meet the needs of the birds. For instance, rural mailboxes make great nesting boxes, either closed, with a hole cut out of the end for an entrance, or with the flap open for birds that prefer an open plan. Old fly-fishing creels, hung under an overhang for protection, will suit some birds, while others will be happy to nestle into crevices in a pile of rocks. Folk-art pieces, decoy ducks, weathervanes, and other collectable pieces are also fun and add to the general ambiance.

If you only have room for one container, consider a small, upright, cutleaf or lace-leaf maple—the birds will enjoy hiding in its attractive foliage in summer, and you can hang edible garlands on it during winter. Hang a feeder nearby and add a bird bath or water bowl. The larger your space, the more fruit-bearing trees and shrubs you can plant, and the more adventurous you can make your playground for birds. The plant list below—trees and shrubs that are popular with many common birds—should give you a good starting point for your own bird garden.

Setting the scene

The following checklist will help you start creating a paradise for birds and butterflies on your patio or balcony.

- Sun or semishade if you are growing plants for birds, and six to eight hours of sun a day—the more the better—if you want to attract butterflies.
- A birdhouse, nesting box, bird feeder, and bird bath, if you have room for them all.
- Large containers for trees and shrubs that the birds like. The containers should be at least 24 inches (60 cm) in diameter, and if possible 16 to 18 inches (40 to 45 cm) deep.
- Various containers, large and small, for nectar-producing flowers for butterflies.
- Plants chosen from the selection below.
- Basic soil mix and fertilizer.
- Watering and lighting systems.
- Basic gardening tools and storage.

Lots of mess and clutter is acceptable! Remember to add those pots of weeds in the corner, and strings of edible foods for birds on your trees and shrubs in the wintertime. Tiny ceramic birds, peeking through the shrubbery, are a pretty touch. Include a large, comfortable chair, binoculars, and books about your local birds and butterflies.

Nectar plants for butterflies

The following plants grow well in pots and are extremely attractive to many adult butterflies. All the plants need at least six to eight hours of sunshine a day. Choose plants that will give you continuous bloom throughout the spring, summer, and fall, so that your garden is a reliable source of nectar at all times.

Asclepias tuberosa (butterfly weed, pleurisy root). This midseason flowering perennial is an erect, tuberous plant with long, lance-shaped leaves. It bears small, five-horned, bright orange-red flowers in summer, followed by narrow pointed pods. Increasing scarcity of some butterfly species is directly related to the disappearance of this plant in the wild. It grows to a height of 30 inches (75 cm) and prefers fairly dry, sandy soil. Zones 4–9.

Aster novi-belgii and *novae-angliae* cultivars (Michaelmas daisy). There are many different asters in varying shades of white, pink, orange, and purple. They are perennials that bear clusters of small, daisylike flowers in late fall and grow anywhere from 1 to 4 feet (0.3 to 1.2 m) tall, depending upon the cultivar. Zones 2–9.

Aubrieta x cultorum (purple rock cress). This is a compact, early-flowering perennial that spreads, forming a flat, trailing carpet of leaves and flowers over the edges of walls and containers. It bears many small purple flowers in spring. Zones 5–8.

Buddleia davidii (butterfly bush). This vigorous arching shrub can grow to a height and spread of 15 feet (5 m). It has long, lance-shaped, dark green leaves and bears dense clusters of fragrant, tubular, violet-purple flowers from midsummer into fall. Zones 5–9.

Coreopsis lanceolata (lance coreopsis) and *C. verticillata* (threadleaf coreopsis). These spreading, clump-forming perennials can be grown as annuals and have daisylike, double, bright yellow flower heads in summer. Grow the species plant for butterflies; they reach a height of 2 feet (60 cm). Zones 3–9.

Echinacea purpurea (purple coneflower). Purple coneflower is an upright perennial with lance-shaped, dark green leaves. Its large, daisylike, deep crimson-pink flower heads with conical brown centers are borne singly on strong stems in summer. Purple coneflowers and related species used to grow in profusion in the prairie and grassland areas of North America. It grows from 2 to 2 1/2 feet (60 to 75 cm). Zones 3–9.

Eupatorium purpureum (joe pye weed). This stately, upright perennial bears terminal heads of tubular, pinkish-purple flowers in late summer and early fall. It grows to about 5 feet (1.5 m). Zones 3–8.

Heliotropium arborescens (common heliotrope). An evergreen, bushy, tender perennial that is grown as an annual in most climates. Its semiglossy, dark green leaves are finely wrinkled, and it bears dense, flat clusters of purple flowers from late spring right through to the frost. Grows to 2 feet (60 cm). Zone 10.

Hylotelephium spectabile syn. *Sedum spectabile* (stonecrop). From late summer into fall this compact perennial produces flat heads of pink flowers over a mass of fleshy, gray-green leaves. A good cultivar for butterflies is 'Brilliant'. It grows to a height and spread of 18 to 24 inches (45 to 60 cm). Zones 4–9.

Liatris spicata (gayfeather). This clump-forming perennial bears spikes of rose-purple flower heads that rise from basal tufts of grasslike, green foliage in midsummer. It grows to a height of 2 feet (60 cm). Zones 3–9.

Monarda didyma (bee balm, bergamot). A lovely native perennial herb that bears whorls of hooded flowers above neat mounds of aromatic foliage all summer long. Native species are pink and mauve, and there are some excellent pink and red cultivars, especially 'Gardenview Scarlet', brilliant red, and 'Marshall's Delight', hot pink. Butterflies prefer the species, rather than the cultivars. Zones 3–9.

Rudbeckia fulgida (black-eyed susan, coneflower). A moderately fast-growing, erect, branching perennial that bears daisylike, golden-orange flowers with brown centers in summer and early fall and grows to a height of 3 feet (90 cm). It prefers moist soil and full sun. Zones 3–9.

Syringa patula (small-leafed lilac). See "Old-fashioned fragrance."

Trees and shrubs to attract the birds

Amelanchier spp. (serviceberry). There are many attractive members of this genus of deciduous trees and shrubs and they all flower profusely in the spring, have attractive foliage that is frequently brightly colored in the fall, and bear edible fruits that attract birds. They vary enormously in size and growth habit, from compact shrubs to spreading trees, so be sure the one you buy will fit your container for the long term. *A. alnifolia* (Saskatoon serviceberry), an upright shrub to 10 feet (3 m), and *A. laevis* (Allegheny serviceberry), a spreading tree to 20 feet (6 m) are two possibilities. Zones 5–9.

Cotoneaster spp. These are deciduous, semievergreen or evergreen shrubs grown for their attractive foliage, white or pink flowers, and red fruits. Some are hardier than others and many make excellent specimen plants for containers. *C. hupehensis* is a deciduous, arching shrub to 6 feet (1.8 m). Zones 5–8. *C. microphyllus* (little-leaf cotoneaster) is a small-leafed, evergreen shrub growing to 3 feet (0.9 m) with a spread of 6 feet (1.8 m). Zones 6–8.

Crataegus spp. (hawthorn). In the fall hawthorn berries are a tasty treat for birds, and the berries can also be made into an excellent pancake syrup. Many hawthorn trees are rather large for containers. Two of the smaller ones, with a height and spread of about 15 feet (4.5 m) when mature, are *C. macrosperma* 'Acutiloba', zones 4–8; and *C. pedicellata,* zones 6–8.

Elaeagnus pungens 'Maculata'. See "Design by color."

Ilex crenata 'Convexa' (dwarf Japanese holly). See "In the shade."

Pinus spp. (pines). See the plant lists in "Santa Fe-style" and "The art of Zen" for a good selection of pines. Although they are unlikely to form mature pine cones with pine nuts for the birds, they do provide good cover for small birds in winter and summer.

Prunus spp. (cherry, plum, almond, peach). There are more than 400 species of *Prunus,* and they are among the most popular of the spring-flowering ornamentals. Some interesting smaller cherry cultivars are suitable for containers. 'Amanogawa' is an attractive columnar tree, 20 feet (6 m) high, spreading to 6 to 8 feet (1.8 to 2.4 m). It bears semidouble, slightly fragrant, soft pink flowers. 'Shirotae', also called 'Mt. Fuji', grows to 15 feet (4.5 m) tall, with a 20-foot (6-m) spread when mature, less in a container. It has large, white double flowers in early spring. *P. subhirtella* 'Autumnalis' is a pretty, delicate tree that flowers in late fall and continues sporadically through the winter. It grows to a mature height of 20 feet (6 m). Zones 6–8.

Pyracantha cultivars (firethorn). These evergreen, spiny, summer-flowering shrubs have attractive foliage, flowers, and fruits. They can be pruned into a compact form, especially when trained and espaliered against a wall. Attractive forms are 'Golden Charmer', with bright orange berries, and 'Golden Dome', orange-yellow berries. Zones 6–9.

Symphoricarpos albus (snowberry). This dense, deciduous shrub forms a 6-foot (1.8-m) mass that is partly upright, partly arching. It has rounded, dark green leaves and pink bell-shaped flowers in the summer, followed by large, marblelike, white fruits in the fall. It is attractive underplanted with bulbs for spring flowering and white or pink pansies for color in the summer. Zones 4–7.

A planter for butterflies

Materials

- Container: either a wooden planter or terracotta pot at least 18 inches (45 cm) in diameter and 12 inches (30 cm) deep.
- Potting mixture: basic soil mix and controlled-release fertilizer.
- Plants: three *Aubrieta* x *cultorum* (purple rock cress); one *Asclepias tuberosa* (butterfly weed); three *Heliotropium arborescens* (common heliotrope); and two *Hylotelephium spectabile* (stonecrop).

Method

Half-fill the container with the soil mixture and position the butterfly weed in the center, towards the back, loosening the rootball and making sure that the top of the rootball sits about 1 inch (2.5 cm) below the rim of the container. Gradually fill in with more soil and place the heliotrope and stonecrop plants around the butterfly weed. Finally fill in around the edge with the rock cress so that it can trail over the edges. Water the pot well.

Aftercare

Water regularly and fertilize with liquid fertilizer every couple of weeks during the growing season. Do not let the pot dry out. Remove the heliotrope in the fall and discard. Replant with fresh heliotrope the following spring.

The winter garden

Form and structure delight the eye in a winter landscape

WINTER IS PERHAPS THE MOST CHALLENGING SEASON OF ALL IN THE garden. The brilliant colors of fall are already a memory, leaves have fallen, and the branches of deciduous trees and shrubs are bare, stripped of their glory for another year. Annuals are finished, perennials have died back, and the bare earth gives no hint of the spring that will inevitably come. Instead, the short days and long nights send us scurrying indoors, away from winter rains and snow storms, cold and wind.

This may sound quite dreary, and yet there is much to enjoy and appreciate outdoors, wherever you live. Even in the largest city there is a unique quality to the winter landscape, one that is enhanced by the simple forms of nature. In city parks and streets, deciduous trees reveal the graceful lines of curved and arching branches, the architectural balance of forms, and the colors and patterns of different tree barks. Frost etches the margins of winter foliage, and outlines the remaining fruits and berries with a powdery whiteness. When snow falls it coats naked branches, creating a delicate tracery, a double image of dark and light that stands out against nearby buildings and the night sky.

Evergreens bring energy to this monochromatic environment. Their many different colors and forms give us an amazing array of plants in shades of green tinged with metallic and silvery blue, purple, copper, red, yellow, and gold. When snow falls on their covered branches it reinforces their vibrant forms and brings life even to the bleakest landscape.

Perhaps the greatest joy of all are the plants that flower in the winter months, even when snow is still on the ground. These include the autumn-flowering cherry, several early-flowering rhododendron species and cultivars, and fragrant, winter-blooming shrubs such as Chinese witch hazel, *Viburnum* x *bodnantense*, and wintersweet. There are also some lovely early-flowering bulbs and perennials, and when you see bright yellow winter aconites, stately Christmas roses, delicate snowdrops, and cheerful dwarf iris poking their bright heads up through the earth, then spring cannot be far behind.

Creating a winter garden on a patio or balcony is just as possible and potentially pleasing as it is in a larger garden. For inspiration, take a look at the natural vegetation that grows in your area. Most likely there are more plants than you realize that are at their best in winter and can survive temperature extremes. For instance, the attractive snowberry shrub (*Symphoricarpos albus*) is hardy to zone 4 and looks lovely when its delicate bare branches are laden with luscious white berries. The berries hang on throughout the winter, providing food for many species of birds (see plant selection in "Backyard wildlife").

The key to creating a successful winter garden is simplicity. In winter the structure of a garden is exposed, and enduring features, such as trees, shrubs, ornaments, and containers, become doubly important. Simple, elegant forms, well maintained, will add a touch of class to even the smallest space, whereas containers that are still planted with last year's annuals will be a sorry sight. For a container winter garden to be most effective, therefore, it is important to plan pots carefully, with this in mind.

Before you decide which trees and shrubs to plant, it is worth taking a good look at the trees and shrubs growing in your local botanical garden, and find out what is available in the garden center. Remember that plants in containers will be much more vulnerable to cold weather than they would be if planted in the ground. Even if your containers are very large, you will still need to insulate them in some climates, and mulch the soil surface (see "Practical Details: Winterizing").

Check the shape and form of trees and shrubs carefully, bearing in mind that they will get bigger as they mature. It may be that you have room for a tall, umbrellalike tree, but not for a smaller, bushier shrub. Some forms will really appeal to you when their branches are bare, while others will not, and it is a good idea to choose plants that offer something of interest throughout the seasons. For instance, the star magnolia is a lovely tree all year round. It has attractive, bud-tipped, bare branches in winter and bears lovely, star-shaped, white flowers in spring, followed by handsome, green leaves that last all summer long and into the fall.

Many plants that have been described in other themes are especially attractive in winter months. Evergreens and interesting topiary forms maintain their look and form throughout the year and can be dressed up with tiny, white lights for an added seasonal touch, or with garlands of fruit and berries for the birds.

Well-chosen ornaments and statues can make quite a difference to the charm and appeal of a winter garden. Nothing could be simpler or more attractive than a plain Japanese garden lantern, covered with a soft skiff of snow, sitting in a bed of large, round river rocks. This arrangement has a very calming, pleasing effect (see "The art of Zen"). There is, indeed, a certain Zen quality to the garden in winter, especially when the first big snowfall comes and a breathtaking stillness pervades the land. Then winter offers us a chance to slow down, enjoy the simple pleasures, and appreciate the natural beauty of the world around us.

Setting the scene

The following checklist will help you start creating an attractive winter garden on your patio or balcony.

- Large wooden, terracotta or concrete containers, big enough for trees and shrubs. They need to be 18 to 24 inches (45 to 60 cm) in diameter and 18 inches (45 cm) deep.
- A selection of plants that provide color and interest in winter.
- Basic soil mix, amended as necessary, and fertilizer.
- White outdoor fairy lights, or other small tree lights for nighttime decoration.
- Outdoor ornaments and statuary, such as stone garden lanterns, Italian terracotta figures, or simple piles of rocks or stones.
- A watering system.
- Basic garden tools and storage.

Since the essence of a winter garden is simplicity, try to keep it that way, and do not be tempted to clutter it up with too many distracting elements.

Plants to grow for winter interest

These plants are all particularly attractive during the fall and winter months, whether it is for their form, color, fruit, or general structure. Remember that many plants mentioned in other parts of this book, especially the evergreens, maples, grasses, and native plants, are also interesting during the winter months.

Trees and shrubs

Callicarpa bodinieri 'Profusion'. A deciduous, bushy shrub that bears tiny, lilac flowers in midsummer, followed by clusters of small, richly colored purple berries in midwinter. It grows from 6 to 8 feet (1.8 to 2.4 m) with a 4-foot (1.2-m) spread and prefers a sunny, sheltered position and fertile, well-drained soil. Zones 5–8.

Chimonanthus praecox (wintersweet). An outstanding winter shrub, wintersweet has glossy, dark green leaves and produces sweetly fragrant, cup-shaped yellow flowers on bare branches from midwinter to early spring. It grows to 8 feet (2.4 m) with a 5-foot (1.5-m) spread, prefers filtered sun, a sheltered position, and fertile, well-drained soil. Zones 7–9.

Cornus alba 'Elegantissima' (red osier dogwood). This dogwood is a vigorous, deciduous shrub whose naked, bright red shoots stand out dramatically against the snow in midwinter. It has attractive white-edged, gray-green leaves and bears small, creamy-white flowers in late spring and early summer, followed by white fruits in the fall. It can grow to 10 feet (3 m) with a spread of 5 feet (1.5 m) and prefers a sunny position and fertile, well-drained soil. Zones 2–8.

Corylopsis pauciflora (buttercup winter hazel). One of the loveliest of the early-flowering shrubs, it bears fragrant, tubular to bell-shaped pale yellow flowers on bare branches in late winter and early spring. Depending on the species, it grows to a height of 5 to 10 feet (1.5 to 3.0 m) with a slightly wider spread and looks lovely underplanted with white crocus and blue iris. It prefers filtered sun and a fertile, well-drained soil. Zones 6–9.

Cryptomeria japonica 'Elegans Compacta' (Japanese cedar). This is a dwarf form of the evergreen, with soft, fibrous, red-brown bark, and needlelike mid- to dark green leaves that turn copper-colored in winter. It grows to a height and width of 6 feet (1.8 m) and prefers a sunny position. Zones 6–9.

Hamamelis mollis 'Pallida' (Chinese witch hazel). See "Old-fashioned fragrance."

Lonicera fragrantissima (very fragrant honeysuckle). This honeysuckle is a deciduous, bushy, spreading shrub that grows to 6 feet (1.8 m) with a slightly larger spread. It has oval, dark green leaves, and bears fragrant, short-tubed, creamy-white flowers in winter and early spring. It flowers best in semishade, and likes fertile, well-drained soil. Try growing clematis through its branches for summer interest. Zones 5–8.

Magnolia stellata (star magnolia). A slow-growing, bushy, dense shrub that can be pruned to remain reasonably compact at a height of 8 to 10 feet (2.4 to 3 m) and spread of 5 to 8 feet (1.5 to 2.4 m). It bears fragrant, star-shaped, white flowers with many narrow petals. The flowers open on bare branches from furry buds in early to midspring. In winter the star magnolia's elegant branches are bare, except for the attractive flower buds at their tips. The leaves open once the flowers are finished. It prefers full sun and a fertile, well-drained soil. Zones 5–9.

Mahonia x media 'Charity'. This evergreen, upright shrub has dark green, spiny foliage and bears long spikes of fragrant, lemony-yellow flowers from late fall to early spring. It is a good plant for a tight corner and grows to 6 feet (1.8 m) with a spread of 3 feet (0.9 m). It prefers semishade and a moist, fertile soil. Zones 6–9.

Nandina domestica (heavenly bamboo). See "In the shade."

Rhododendron spp. The *Rhododendron* genus has been discussed at some length in "The art of Zen" and "In the shade." Several species and cultivars bloom in winter and early spring and are worth growing for their form and winter color. They include 'Christmas Cheer', clear pink blooms from January to March, to 4.5 feet (1.4 m); 'Cilpinense', pink blooms in March, to 3 feet (0.9 m); *R. dauricum*, lavender blooms from December to March, to 4 feet (1.2 m); and 'Olive', pink blooms in February and March, to 5 feet (1.5 m). Zones 7–8.

Viburnum x bodnantense. For both color and scent, this is one of the best of the winter-flowering deciduous shrubs. It has a strongly upright form and bears very fragrant double clusters of rose-pink flowers, or white flowers tinged with pink in the bud, on bare branches from December through into February. It grows to 8 feet (2.4 m) and several cultivars are available; the most desirable is 'Dawn'. Zones 7–9.

Perennials

Anemone blanda (windflower). A pretty, early-spring-flowering, tuberous perennial that spreads into a clump 4 to 6 inches (10 to 15 cm) across. Flattish blue, white, or pink flowers with narrow petals are borne on 2- to 4-inch (5- to 10-cm) stems above deeply toothed leaves. Look for a white cultivar such as 'White Splendour'. Zones 6–9.

Eranthis hyemalis (winter aconite). This clump-forming tuberous perennial can be slow at first but does well once it is established. It flowers profusely, bearing cup-shaped, stalkless, bright yellow flowers from late winter to early spring. It grows to 2 to 4 inches (5 to 10 cm) in height and spread and prefers partial shade. Zones 3–8.

Hacquetia epipactis. This is a clump-forming perennial that spreads by short rhizomes and bears yellow or yellow-green flowers in late winter and early spring before the leaves appear. It grows to 2.5 inches (6 cm), with a spread of 9 inches (23 cm) and likes a well-drained, fertile soil. It may be hard to find, but it's worth the search. Zones 5–8.

Helleborus niger (Christmas rose). Hellebores are a must for the winter garden if they can grow where you live. See "In the shade."

Ophiopogon planiscapus 'Nigrescens'. This exotic-looking perennial has distinctive, grasslike, clump-forming black leaves which last all year in milder climates. It grows to 12 inches (30 cm) in height, with a wider spread, and bears lilac-colored flowers in summer, followed by black fruits. It prefers partial sun and well-drained soil. Zones 6–10.

Bulbs

Many bulbs can be grown indoors, and they are a welcome and cheerful sight in the dreary late winter months. It is also worth planting some in containers outdoors for extra color in early spring.

Crocus spp. The early-flowering species crocuses may be hard to find, but they are worth the search. *C. longiflorus* is deep lilac with an orange throat and is strongly scented. Zones 5–8. *C. chrysanthus* is golden-yellow, while *C. tomasinianus* and its cultivars, 'Barr's Purple' and 'Whitewell Purple', are mauve to deep mauve. Zones 3–8.

Galanthus spp. (snowdrops). *G. nivalis* is the common snowdrop, and bears its delicate, nodding white flowers on 4-inch (10-cm) stems from January onwards, depending on the climate. Another species, the giant snowdrop, *G. elwesii,* has stems up to 10 inches (25 cm) tall. Zones 3–9.

Iris reticulata (netted iris). See "There are fairies at the bottom of the garden."

Planting a pot for winter

If you only have room for one large container, and you would like it to be easy-care and attractive year round, it makes sense to plant it with one tree or shrub and underplant it with spring bulbs. Plant annuals and perennials around it for summer color. The container may need to be insulated during the coldest part of winter.

The planting arrangement below is a most appealing one and looks good at any time of the year, especially since the elegant branches of the star magnolia are perfect for hanging tiny white fairy lights, and garlands of red cranberries for the birds in midwinter.

Materials

- Container: one large concrete or wooden container, at least 18 inches (45 cm) in depth and diameter.
- Potting mixture: basic soil mix and controlled-release fertilizer.
- Plants: one *Magnolia stellata* (star magnolia); twelve *Anemone blanda*; and twelve *Iris reticulata*.
- Add in the spring: five pink impatiens (if container is in the shade), or pink petunias (if container is in the sun). Look for some of the newer compact and more interesting cultivars of these plants.

Method

Take the star magnolia out of its pot and loosen its roots. Make sure that the container is large enough to hold the whole rootball with at least 2 inches (5 cm) to spare around the bottom and sides.

Remove the magnolia and put a good layer of soil into the bottom of the container. Place the magnolia on top of the soil so that the top of the rootball is about one inch (2.5 cm) below the rim of the pot. Fill around the plant with soil, planting the anemones and iris about 2 to 3 inches (5 to 7.5 cm) below the surface of the soil. Water well.

Aftercare

Water regularly so that the soil does not dry out. Around the third week of May, plant impatiens or petunias in the container for summer color.

Fertilize the annuals with liquid fertilizer every other week, and deadhead regularly to maintain good bloom throughout the summer.

The art of becoming a gardener

An appreciation for the rich and varied experience of older gardeners

A PASSION FOR GROWING PLANTS OFTEN BEGINS VERY EARLY, WHEN A young gardener-to-be first sees a seed spring into life and watches it turn, miraculously, into a plant. Eager and earnest, the fledgling gardener begs for a small corner of the family garden to call her own. Within weeks, fat, round, red radishes are ready to be harvested, followed by tall, green pole beans that wind over a teepee of bamboo poles, making a cool hiding place in the heat of summer. By late summer cheerful, yellow sunflower heads tower majestically over the bed, and the young gardener is well pleased with her efforts.

Unfortunately, the joys of these early gardening years are short-lived. Soon the teenage gardener is unable to tell the difference between a tulip and a daffodil, can't even find the parsley or mint when it is needed for the kitchen table, and is heard to remark that she plans to live in an apartment, with no grass to cut, when she finally leaves home. Quite possibly her only interest in plants revolves around excursions with friends into the woods for wild mushrooms, and the growth of exotic hothouse plants that might contain substances more stimulating than chlorophyll.

All is not lost, however. Suddenly the reluctant gardener has a garden of her own, and once more begins to till the earth with great enthusiasm. More knowledgeable this time, she heads for the local gardening store and fills her cart with flats of bedding plants and seed packets. Soon every nook and cranny in her garden is overflowing with colorful plants, a floral excess that is as energetic as the owner herself. Bright red geraniums, hot pink petunias, yellow French marigolds, and blue ageratums vie with each other for space.

This, too, is a passing phase and it is soon replaced by a period of austerity and restraint. In one energetic and ruthless clean-up session in the fall, all color is stripped from the garden, and the garden purist spends the winter making lists of all the white-blooming plants she can find, in order to turn her beds into a symphony of white and green. In the spring she plants not only things that are supposed to be white, like snowdrops and lily-of-the-valley, but also things that usually are not, like white lavender, white lilac, and white pinks. The quest for white is tireless, and in the evening the white gardener enjoys the calm and serenity of her tranquil garden, as all those whites shine with a luminous intensity.

After a while even this becomes boring and, with palate cleansed, the experimental gardener embarks on a quest to redefine her garden. She searches for interesting plants in muted, harmonious colors, and includes benches, arbors, pergolas, new beds, and pathways to add form and structure to her garden. She plants fewer annuals, all in soft pastels, and for the most part the garden is made up of perennials and nicely shaped shrubs.

Finally, and with many years of successes and failures behind her, the experienced gardener begins to specialize, searching with ever-increasing intensity for the rare, the unusual, and the different. Now she knows the botanical name of every plant in her garden, and she knows what she likes and where to find it. She propagates nearly everything she grows herself. An active member of local garden clubs, she is consulted more and more frequently for her knowledge about rare and unusual species, and people come from miles around to visit her garden.

Around about now, these truly exceptional gardeners find it is time to move into a smaller place, an apartment or townhouse with only a small patio or balcony for a garden. At first they despair. But soon they are visiting the garden centers, buying the biggest pots they can find, and filling them with interesting arrangements of plants. Their flair for the unusual brings them compliments from everyone who comes to visit, and they spend their days happily puttering among the pots, propagating what they can, and savoring the many pleasures they have always had in growing plants.

The plant selections below will help you make the kind of interesting and unusual pots that some of these experienced gardeners might create. Most are easy to make, and most of the plants they contain are well known, yet they are eye-catching combinations that will bring pleasure for many months of the year. They look best if given plenty of space, so that each pot can be appreciated individually. If you do not have much room on your patio or balcony, consider setting off one of these pots against a backdrop of greenery, such as a row of conifers or some bamboo, which will allow the colors and forms of the container plants to stand out.

Even though it might take a little extra effort to find some of these plants, and some will need to be brought indoors for the winter, the effects they can give are well worth the trouble. If you know of someone special who is moving into an apartment for the first time, consider making up one of these pots as a gift. He or she will appreciate it for a long time to come.

Setting the scene

The following checklist will help you start creating a garden of interesting and unusual plants on your patio or balcony.

- Sun or partial shade, depending upon the needs of the plants.
- Large concrete or terracotta pots, as specified for each planting given below, and put onto casters so that they can be moved around easily.
- Plants: as specified, below, for each pot.
- Basic soil mix and fertilizer.
- A watering system; perhaps the most elegant watering can you can find, such as a Haws watering can with a rose-head attachment, and a rain barrel for a water supply.
- A lighting system.
- Basic gardening tools and storage.
- If there is room, comfortable chairs with lots of soft pillows, and a table.

This garden is for an expert, so you will want to have many gardening books, magazines, and catalogues to read, and a cosy, warm, and comfortable corner to do it. Add a thick, soft, warm blanket to curl up in. The ideal patio or balcony would be well protected and, if possible, covered with a glass or plexiglass roof so that its owner can sit out whatever the weather, especially if there is a patio heater for extra warmth.

Unusual and familiar plants

Agapanthus africanus (lily-of-the-nile). An evergreen, clump-forming perennial that grows to a height of 3 feet (90 cm) and has light green, strap-shaped leaves. The leaves cascade downwards to make a soft mound of green. Deep blue, light blue, or white flowers are borne on the end of tall, erect stems in summer. It grows best in full sun and moist, well-drained soil, and will need to be brought indoors in most climates for winter. A white cultivar would be especially attractive in the "Summer skies" pot below. Zones 9–10.

Amaranthus caudatus (love-lies-bleeding). An exotic-looking bushy annual that grows quickly to a height of 4 feet (1.2 m) and is covered with oval, pale green leaves. In summer and fall it carries a profusion of tassellike crimson-red flowers that hang down in 18-inch-long (45-cm) panicles. It likes full sun and well-drained soil.

Argyranthemum frutescens syn. *Chrysanthemum frutescens* (marguerite). This is an attractive plant and easy to grow as an annual although it is actually a tender, evergreen perennial. It has pale green, fernlike leaves and bears many daisylike single, white, yellow, or pink flowers all summer long. It grows to a height of 3 feet (90 cm) and likes full sun and a well-drained soil. Look for yellow cultivars such as 'Jamaica Primrose' for the "Mellow tones" pot.

Dahlia hybrids (dahlia). Prolific and long-flowering, dahlias have long been a cutting garden favorite, and people either like them or hate them. All of them need a sunny position and rich, well-drained soil. Their tubers must be lifted in the fall and stored in a frost-free place; replant them in the spring once all danger of frost is past. 'Bishop of Llandaff' has bronze-green leaves and single, open-centered, dark red flowers; 'Vicky Crutchfield' bears soft pink, waterlily-shaped flowers. Both bloom from late summer into the fall and grow to a height and spread of 3 feet (90 cm).

Felicia amelloides 'Santa Anita' (blue marguerite). This tender, evergreen, bushy shrub bears daisylike, vivid blue flowers with bright yellow centers from late spring to fall, making it a valuable addition to a container. It needs full sunshine and well-drained soil. 'Santa Anita' is an attractive cultivar and grows to 10 to 12 inches (25 to 30 cm) in height and spread.

Foeniculum vulgare (fennel). See "A taste of Provence." Choose bronze fennel for the "Mellow tones" pot.

Fritillaria michailovskyi (fritillaria). This small garden or rockery species plant has deep purplish-brown bell-shaped flowers edged in bright yellow, and lance-shaped grey leaves. It blooms in spring and grows to a height of 4 to 8 inches (10 to 20 cm). Zones 4–8.

Fuchsia hybrids (fuchsia). Fuchsias are often overlooked by serious gardeners because they are grown so often in containers, and yet if they are used wisely they can be quite stunning. A good cultivar for the "Summer heat" pot is 'Thalia', an upright shrub with long, slender flowers with orange-red petals and red tubes that open into small, red sepals. Its velvety foliage is a dark maroon color. It grows to a height and spread of 3 feet (90 cm), takes full sun, and needs a well-drained soil. It will not survive freezing temperatures, but can be propagated easily from semihardwood cuttings taken in late summer. Zones 9–10.

Helichrysum petiolare 'Limelight' (licorice vine). This tender, evergreen shrub forms mounds of trailing, silver-green shoots and lime-yellow leaves. It has creamy-yellow flowers in summer and is usually grown as an annual for edging in containers or as a ground cover. It can be propagated easily from semihardwood cuttings. It needs full sun and a well-drained soil.

Lilium spp. (lily). See "Old-fashioned fragrance." For the "Summer skies" pot you will need six 3-foot-tall (90-cm) lilies in various shades of pink. If possible, choose ones with different blooming times, such as two Asiatics, two trumpets, and two Orientals.

Limnanthes douglasii (poached-egg plant). This bright little annual makes an excellent ground cover. It is slightly fragrant, with cup-shaped, yellow flowers edged in white, and it blooms all summer long. It grows to a height of 6 inches (15 cm), and likes full sun and a well-drained soil.

Mimulus 'Malibu Series' (monkey flower). This fast-growing, branching perennial is grown as an annual in all but the warmest climates. It is very effective in containers, particularly in hanging baskets. A good selection is usually available in most garden centers in late spring. It has flared, tubular flowers in shades of red, yellow, and orange; for the "Mellow tones" pot choose yellow-flowered plants. It needs sunshine and a moist soil and grows to a height and spread of 6 to 12 inches (15 to 30 cm).

Nicotiana alata (**flowering tobacco plant**). See "Old-fashioned fragrance." Choose wine-red hybrids from the 'Sensation Series'. They will grow to 2 1/2 to 3 feet (75 to 90 cm).

Pelargonium **spp. (geranium)**. These well-known, easy-to-grow plants can cause you to look again when they are combined in new and interesting ways. Although they are evergreen perennials, geraniums are usually grown as annuals; they can be propagated easily from softwood cuttings taken in late summer. Most geraniums require full sun and well-drained soil; ivy geraniums may scorch in hot afternoon sun. Keep removing dead flower heads and the plants will keep on blooming. For the "Summer skies" pot you will need trailing and upright geraniums.

Petunia x *hybrida* **'Star Series' (petunia)**. Petunias are one of the plants most widely used for containers. Perennials that are grown as annuals in most places, they are available in a wide range of colors and forms. The 'Star Series' hybrids are striped; choose ones in crimson-red with white stripes for the "Summer heat" pot. Grow them in fertile, well-drained soil in a sunny position, sheltered from wind. They grow to a height and spread of 6 to 12 inches (15 to 30 cm).

Salvia purpurea (**purple sage**). The purple form of common sage; see "A taste of Provence."

Tulipa **hybrids (tulip)**. There is a wide selection of tulips to choose from in the fall. 'Queen of the Night' flowers in the late spring. It is the darkest of all the tulips and has long-lasting, deep maroon-black flowers on strong, 2-foot (60-cm) stems. 'Angelique' is also late spring-flowering, and bears slightly fragrant, pale pink flowers on 16-inch (40-cm) stems. Zones 4–10.

Viola x *wittrockiana* (**winter-flowering pansy**). Grown as an annual although it is really a perennial, winter-flowering pansies provide cheerful color if the winters are reasonably mild. They are available in a wide range of colors and color combinations; choose creamy white or maroon and white hybrids for the "Summer heat" pot spring planting.

Planting some special pots

Summer heat

This is a striking combination that even wins a few hearts among those who don't like red in the garden. With a bit of care, there will be something in bloom from early spring to late fall.

Materials

• Container: it should be at least 24 inches (60 cm) in diameter and 20 inches

(50 cm) high. Try to find an old and weathered terracotta pot.

- Potting mixture: basic soil mix and controlled-release fertilizer.
- Plants:
    — For the spring: eighteen *Tulipa* 'Queen
      of the Night'; and ten creamy white
      winter-flowering pansies.
    — For the summer: one *Amaranthus
      caudatus* (love-lies-bleeding); six crim-
      son and white *Petunia* 'Star Series'; one
      Dahlia 'Bishop of Llandaff'; one upright
      Fuchsia hybrid, such as 'Thalia'; and
      three wine-red *Nicotiana alata* 'Sensa-
      tion Series' (flowering tobacco plant).
      All the plants must have at least six
      hours of sunshine a day.

Method

Prepare the container and partially fill it with soil. Put the summer plants into the pot,
arranging them according to the illustration, with the tops of their rootballs about an
inch (2.5 cm) below the rim of the pot. Fill in around the plants with soil, up to the
tops of their rootballs, and water the pot well. If necessary add a little more soil and
top with a layer of fine gravel so that the surface remains about an inch (2.5 cm)
below the rim of the pot.

Aftercare

Keep well watered throughout the summer months and fertilize weekly with a liquid
fertilizer, or once a month with a granular fertilizer. Take cuttings from the fuchsia in
July. In the fall, dismantle the arrangement. Take the dahlia bulb out of the pot and
store the tuber in a cool place, in dry peat moss, during the winter. Plant up the pot
with the tulips and winter pansies.

When the bulbs have finished flowering the following spring you can remake the
pot using the fuchsia cuttings, the dahlia, and fresh annuals, or try a completely different arrangement.

Mellow tones

This container is a delightful combination of yellow and purple plants; a soft and
understated arrangement.

Materials

- Container: it should be rectangular, about 30 inches (75 cm) long, 15 inches (37.5 cm) wide, and 12 inches (30 cm) deep and could be made from terracotta, concrete, metal or wood. Wrought iron would be an attractive choice.
- Potting mixture: basic soil mix and controlled-release fertilizer.
- Plants: One bronze-leafed *Foeniculum vulgare* (bronze fennel); two *Helichrysum petiolare* 'Limelight' (licorice vine); one *Argyranthemum frutescens* 'Jamaica Primrose' (yellow marguerite); one *Salvia purpurea* (purple

sage); three yellow *Mimulus* 'Malibu Series' (monkey flower); three *Limnanthes douglasii* (poached-egg plant); and three *Fritillaria michailovskyi* (fritillaria).

Method and aftercare

Follow the method and aftercare outlined for the "Summer heat" pot. In many climates the fennel, sage, and fritillarias will overwinter happily in the container, and more bulbs can be planted for additional color in the spring. Take cuttings from the tender perennials in July for use the following year.

Summer skies

This is an elegant pot, cool and warm at the same time.

Materials

- Container: it should be at least 24 inches (60 cm) in diameter and 20 inches (50 cm) high, in terracotta or concrete.
- Potting mixture: basic soil mix and controlled-release fertilizer.
- Plants:
  — For the spring: eighteen *Tulipa* 'Angelique'; and ten blue pansies.
  — For the summer: one white *Agapanthus africanus* (lily-of-the-nile); three dark pink, upright *Pelargonium* spp. (geraniums); three hot pink trailing *Pelargonium* spp. (geraniums); two *Felicia amelloides* 'Santa Anita' (blue marguerite); one *Dahlia* 'Vicky Crutchfield', or other warm pink dahlia hybrid; and six *Lilium* spp. in soft pink, two early-blooming, two mid-season, and two late.

Method and aftercare

Follow the method and aftercare outlined for the "Summer heat" pot. Take cuttings from the geraniums and blue marguerite in July. When the dahlia has finished blooming, remove and store the tuber in a cool place, in dry peat moss, ready for planting again the following spring. Bring the lily-of-the-nile indoors for the winter if you live in Zone 8 or below; the lilies can probably be left in the pot, depending upon your climate. Add blue pansies and 'Angelique' tulips to the pot for spring color.

Practical Details

Getting started

By now your mind is probably buzzing with ideas and exciting possibilities as you look at your potential mini-garden with new eyes. Now you know that even the most bleak and awkward corner has potential, whether it is a shady stairwell leading to a basement suite, a deserted parking lot, a window ledge, a patio or balcony, an exposed rooftop, or even a hook on the wall. Wherever there is space to put a pot or hang a basket, you can make a garden.

This is the most critical moment, for it is time to translate your ideas into a workable reality. Many factors will influence the choices you make and the final look of your garden. You may find you are attracted to several different themes or ideas, and want to incorporate elements from each into your place. Or you may find that you are even more confused than you were before and haven't a clue where to start.

Take your time; there really is no hurry. Try not to feel pressured into buying any containers or plants until you are absolutely sure what you want—and are able—to do. If you follow the guidelines given below, they should bring you through the planning and developing process and help you make the garden you want.

Design and planning

Often the most helpful thing to do first is to measure your space and draw up a plan of it, to scale, on marked graph paper. Make detailed notes and take photographs of the space from every possible angle, at different times of the day, so that you can see just how much sun and shade different spots get during the course of twenty-four hours. Remember that the angle of the winter sun will be different from that of the summer sun. Using newspaper, make shapes in the sizes of containers you would like to have, and see how they will fit together in your space. Is there room to move around your containers so that you can cultivate the plants? Will you still have space for a patio chair or two, a small table, an umbrella? How wide can your plants grow and still leave space for you?

What kinds of containers appeal to you, and will they look aesthetically pleasing in the location you have in mind? Although terracotta pots are an integral part of the landscape in many countries of the world, they may not be in others. For instance, in Spain and Italy they can be found in an endless range of shapes and sizes, sitting in courtyards, gardens, and patios, and beside houses that are roofed with tiles made from the same local clay. On the other hand, in areas where wood is the most commonly used building material, planters are more likely to be made from it; and in the jungle highrise complexes of large cities, gray concrete containers in simple forms often look the best and seem to blend with their background. The look of your containers, and the materials from which they are made, will have a big effect on the overall aesthetic of your garden.

Correct proportions are critical. Plants and containers should be in scale with each other, with the location, and with their immediate surroundings. This is one important aspect of design that is commonly overlooked. Often containers are too small for the space, and they are filled with small plants and placed at ground level. This arrangement is easily lost in its surroundings. Try grouping various sizes of pots together at ground level so that the pots and their foliage are at different heights, and place at least some pots at waist level. This type of arrangement is more interesting and has greater impact.

Pedestals, wooden boxes, tables, benches, chairs, walls, and window ledges can be used to house various containers at different levels. For safety reasons, it is important that these supports are all level and firmly anchored. Hanging baskets should be attached to bolts that are screwed into supports, and they should be hung at chest level or above six feet (2 m), so that people won't walk into them.

The opportunities for making a wonderful garden in a large space are endless. If you have the room, try to add some screening features, such as arbors, pergolas, and trellises, to your plan. These also make excellent supports for climbing plants. You may be able to include built-in seating, such as wooden benches, and do consider making some raised planters so that plants can be brought closer to the eye and nose. This is especially important for fragrant plants, such as herbs.

Choosing a theme

Once you have an idea of the space you are working with, how many containers you can put into it, and what size and shape they can be, it is time to choose the theme or themes you would like to try in your space. At this point it is important to consider your own likes and dislikes, the amount of money you are able to spend to realize your ideas, the amount of time you will actually be able to devote to gardening, and the exposure and amount of sunshine or shade your garden receives. Be realistic.

The themes in the book are meant as guidelines for developing your own ideas. Use the themes, but give yourself freedom to experiment with many kinds of plants and containers, to imprint your unique personality into the design of your garden.

Money—or the lack of it—is obviously a prime consideration. The less you have, the more you will have to make and grow things from scratch, and the more inventive you will have to be. However, lack of money should not stop you from making a good garden; it's amazing how much you can achieve with very little. Plants can be grown from cuttings and from seed, and you can make your own containers very cheaply from recycled materials, especially in wood and plastic. All you really need is a container that is weatherproof, nontoxic to plants, and has a bottom opening for drainage. You can even grow plants directly in "Grow Bags" without using containers at all. (Grow Bags are an English invention, recently introduced into North America, that allow you to grow plants directly in bags of specially formulated, prefertilized soil.)

If lack of time is your problem, keep it simple and make a garden that needs a minimum of water and long-term care. Grasses and seaside plants are some of the best choices under these circumstances, and you can also produce very pleasing results with a simple Zen garden of rocks, raked sand, and a backdrop of bamboo.

Your climate and the exposure and location of your site will determine to a large extent the plants you can grow and themes you can follow successfully. A shady garden can be as beautiful, if not more beautiful, than a sunny garden, but it is important to ensure that sun-loving plants receive sunshine and shady plants are located mostly in the shade. This may seem self-evident, but many gardens come to grief when this simple fact is ignored.

Bylaws, rules, and regulations

If your garden is located above ground level, you will need to take the weight of your plantings into consideration. Containers filled with soil can be very heavy, particularly when wet. For example, a half-barrel filled with wet soil can weigh over 200 pounds (100 kg). If you are planning an extensive container garden above a garage or on a balcony, check with a structural engineer before you begin. An engineer can counsel you on the soundness of the surface and the measures that must be taken to distribute the weight evenly.

Not only do the acceptable loading capacities for existing buildings vary from community to community, they also depend upon the local building code in force at the time of construction. Some buildings are planned specifically to bear extra-heavy rooftop construction. If you are in doubt about the load-bearing capacity of your building, your local municipal building department should have a record of it. If you are only planning a few containers, you probably do not need to be too concerned, although it is always a good idea to locate large planters as close to the building as possible, or above supporting walls and posts.

If your home is part of a strata unit development, find out if there are any weight restriction bylaws for your strata, and design accordingly. In addition, you will probably need to discuss your garden plans with members of your strata counsel. Needless to say, if you are renting, check with your landlord to confirm that your plans do not contravene any bylaws, rules, or regulations. Most landlords and strata groups are only too happy to see their property beautified, especially if you have some interesting ideas and attractive, unusual plantings.

Containers

The question of containers—which ones to get and why—is one of the most important things to consider when you are making a container garden. Not only do your plants depend, quite literally, upon the right containers for their survival, but the containers define your space and set the scene for the effect you are trying to create. The three most common materials used for containers are terracotta, wood, and concrete.

Terracotta pots have many advantages. The clay "breathes" well, which plants like; the pots come in all shapes and sizes; many are relatively inexpensive; and they look very attractive when arranged in groups. They work especially well if your surrounding environment makes use of red brick and white stucco, or if you are aiming to re-create a Mediterranean, Californian, or Southwest atmosphere. They evoke sun, rather than shade. On the negative side, many are not frost-proof, although the better-made ones are. If you live in an area where the winters are cold, you will probably have to empty your pots in the fall and move them into a sheltered spot, refilling and replanting them in the spring. If you want to garden year round in a harsh climate, consider using wooden planters (discussed below) or concrete containers.

Concrete containers come in various interesting shapes and sizes, and many of them are so well made they can be mistaken for stone containers. They are especially effective with contemporary architecture, such as the balconies or rooftops of downtown highrise buildings, or an exposed aggregate patio of a new townhouse complex. Many concrete containers are replicas of the stone urns and vases that are so popular in Italian, French, and English gardens. The main disadvantage of concrete is its weight. Large concrete pots are very heavy, and you will need to be especially careful to check weight-bearing capacities and loading restrictions.

Containers are also made from fiberglass and plastic. Fiberglass containers are less commonly used, probably because they are harder to make aesthetically interesting, and they are also expensive. They are, however, the lightest of all the containers—a distinct advantage under some circumstances. Plastic pots are also light and are relatively inexpensive. Glazed ceramic pots can be a great addition to an outdoor container garden, especially if you have chosen to follow an Oriental theme.

You can use just about any weatherproof container as long as it is nontoxic to plants and has a hole in the bottom for proper drainage. Many strange things have been used as planters, including old shoes, wheelbarrows, mailboxes, fly-fishing baskets, pieces of driftwood, milk pails, and leather hats.

Whatever containers you use, it is very important to raise them up from the ground by an inch or so (2.5 cm). Nail strips of wood to the underside of wooden planters; place strips of wood beneath terracotta or concrete containers, or place them on small blocks or a few pebbles—anything that will allow air to circulate underneath the base of each container. This prevents wooden decks and planters from rotting, and discourages slugs, sow bugs, and other pests and diseases from lurking in moist corners.

Containers can be heavy even when empty. When they are full they are impossible to move unless they are on wheels. It is a good idea to put large terracotta and concrete pots onto small platforms or dollies with casters so that they can be moved easily. Permanent casters can be attached to the bottom of wooden tubs and planters.

Not only will this make it easier to move them, it will also lift the containers off the ground, with all the advantages already noted.

Planters

Wood is an excellent natural material for planters, especially if you live in an area where trees are a dominant feature of the environment. The planters can be as informal as a few boards nailed together, or quite formal, such as a Versailles tub, making them very versatile in form and function. Wooden planters retain moisture well, are easy to make, can be painted or left natural, and make for very flexible planting. Wooden half-barrels are the perfect size for many trees and shrubs and for water gardens. Old apple boxes and wooden packing crates also make excellent containers.

You do not have to be an expert woodworker to make attractive planters. With a few simple tools and a good set of instructions you can build them in just a few hours. There are many excellent do-it-yourself books to consult: try your local library or bookstore. Planters can be made from many species of wood, such as pine, spruce, hemlock, fir, redwood, and cedar. Cedar and redwood can be left to weather naturally and do not need any protective paint or stain, but they are also the most expensive to buy. If you plan to paint your planters, use one of the less expensive woods.

A simple wooden planter, basically a rectangular box with four legs, is ideal for many situations: hanging over the edge of a balcony, used as a window box, fixed by brackets onto the wall, or simply sitting on the ground. It can be used for vegetable garden beds, perennial borders, shrubs, or any other use that calls for simple wooden planters. It can be turned into a raised planter by extending the length of the legs and attaching a shelf underneath for stability and storage.

A Versailles tub is a more ornate version of a simple planter. It is usually about 2 feet (60 cm) square in size, and each side is made from vertical wooden slats fitted into a square frame. On the top of each corner post sits a round wooden ball—a distinctive feature of the Versailles tub. The planter is painted white, which gives it an elegant and formal appearance. Versailles tubs were first made for the formal French gardens of the palace of Versailles, outside Paris.

Structures

Trellis, pergolas, fencing, shelving, and seating

Even the smallest balcony or basement stairwell can be improved with the addition of architectural forms and structures. They help to define the space, give some privacy and protection from wind, and provide support for climbing and rambling plants. A blank wall, for instance, takes on a completely new look when it is covered with a trellis supporting your favorite climbing roses, sweet peas, clematis, ivy, or runner beans. A tiny arbor will support fruiting and flowering vines, shrubs, or trees, and separates the space into different areas. Freestanding structures such as pergolas and gazebos can be cool and welcoming on a sunny day, and lattice and bamboo screens can be used to hide ugly neighboring structures.

Hardware stores, garden stores, and lumber yards carry an increasingly wide range of arches, pergolas, trellises, gazebos, benches, and other garden structures that are of good quality and ready to assemble. You can also make them yourself. Work out approximately what you think you will need and then see what is available. Look through gardening magazines and books for more ideas. If you are uncertain, take the time to draw what you want on paper, and try to imagine what effect it will have on the garden when it is in place. Does it block sun from sun-loving plants? Does it really provide privacy from the neighbors? Does it protect your plants from wind? Does it obstruct your view?

Trellis is usually made from 1/4- to 1/2-inch-wide (0.6- to 1.25-cm) wooden slats, arranged in either a horizontal or a diagonal grid to form prefabricated panels. Standard sections are typically 2 or 4 feet (60 or 120 cm) wide and 8 feet (2.4 m) tall. The weave of the panels can be quite open or dense, depending upon how closely the slats are arranged to each other. The lattice can be edged with heavier wood to give it a more finished appearance. The best woods to use are redwood and cedar since they can be allowed to weather naturally and do not need an exterior layer of paint or stain.

If you are likely to move fairly often you can make panels that are easy to dismantle, remove, and reassemble. Simply make a freestanding frame that is sturdy and will stand upright, even in a wind, and fit the center of the frame with prefabricated trellis. You can place your pots in front of the frame and plant them with climbing plants. If you are clever with a paint brush and want to add to your theme, fill the frame with plywood and paint a trompe l'oeil scene on it.

Shelves are an excellent way to conserve space and give yourself extra growing room. They can be freestanding or attached to a wall. Make sure that the space between the shelves is large enough to accommodate both the pots and the mature plants and allow the plants to get plenty of light. Shelves are a good way to display small plants, especially if the shelving is at eye level.

If you have the space, you may want to include a simple wooden bench in your structural design. A plain bench, backed by a wall or railing and flanked by planters, is a lovely place to sit and read on a sunny afternoon. It can be made very simply from planks of wood nailed onto a supporting base.

Flooring

The flooring of most small patios or balconies is practical and utilitarian—usually slab concrete, asphalt roofing, or exposed aggregate. These surfaces are functional and hard-wearing, but not usually aesthetically appealing. However, there are many ways to improve the look of the floor without jeopardizing the building's construction or contravening the bylaws. First, and most importantly, whatever the subfloor you are dealing with, make sure it is in good repair and will not leak. If you are in any doubt, be sure to have it looked at by a competent professional. It is much cheaper to do repairs before you have brought in your plants and flooring materials than at a later stage. Watch for plant roots that escape from the base of the pot, and trim them back before they burrow into the building.

Gravel, pebbles, and stones make excellent flooring materials for a small space. They are easy to bring to the site, easy to install, and easy to remove if you relocate. Larger stones can be used for edging around low pots, grow bags, or even piles of earth. They give an informal, natural look, and provide design flexibility. Old bricks, tiles, or interlocking pavers can be most effective too. You can create some interesting designs with them, and use them to establish formal seating areas or paths. The main disadvantage of all these hard materials is that they are heavy, so be sure your patio or balcony can handle the extra weight before you install them. A good substitute material is plastic floor tile, which is comparatively light and is now available in some well-made and attractive forms.

One of the best flooring materials is wood. A wooden deck is lightweight and is easily assembled in modular units. Each unit can be taken up quickly to check the flooring underneath, and boards can be replaced if necessary. Wood decking distributes weight evenly over a wide area, which makes it a particularly useful surface underneath heavy pots and barrels. You can make different patterns and designs from the wood, and this will change the look and feel of your space. The main disadvantage of wood is that it can become mossy and slippery if your garden area is too wet and shady.

Once you have chosen your flooring materials you are ready to begin. Before you start, make sure you know where the drains are and which way the floor slopes. Otherwise you run the risk of blocking the drains and preventing the water from draining away from the building properly. Even if it is not necessary, it is a good idea to use a protective layer of heavy plastic sheeting. This will protect the subfloor and prevent staining and wear, even if the subfloor is made of concrete.

If your building will not support the weight of additional flooring material, consider using paint to create the desired effect. For example, a coat of sandy-colored paint sprinkled with sand will give the feel of a Southwestern desert, or imitation wooden planks painted on the floor will evoke the lakeside. Do get permission first, though!

Lighting

Outdoor lights can create a mood or change the ambiance of your outdoor space. Some cast a warm, soft glow that brings an atmosphere of intimacy and romance to the simplest spot. Others radiate spooky shadows that dance and flicker in the moonlight. From traditional to funky, there are lights to suit every mood. Lights are mentioned in the different themes, such as the strings of tiny white lights that decorate trees and shrubs in the wintertime, the tall flame torches that burn brightly for hours and add a touch of drama to a lakeside theme, colored strings of rabbits, cows, and chili peppers, and traditional Santa Fe lumières.

These are just some of the many ways lights can be used to make a difference to your outdoor garden, whatever its size. You may have room for only one pair of candles on a small table; or you may be able to install an electrically controlled lighting system with spotlights for every tree, but whatever you do you can enhance the atmosphere of your space with the right kind of lighting.

First decide what you will be using the lights for. You may want to have lights bright enough to use for reading and will need a fairly strong light source, ranging from an electric light to an old-fashioned kerosene lantern. Ambient light can be provided by strings of lights, lumières, flame torches, hanging lanterns, candles, or even battery-powered torches. If it is summertime and you feel extravagant, you may want to assemble all the candlesticks you own and fill them with beeswax candles. The smell of the melting beeswax, mingled with the evening scents of plants, will give you fragrant memories that will last long after winter has driven you back indoors.

Patio heaters

If evenings are cool, making it uncomfortable to sit outdoors, outdoor patio heaters can make quite a difference. Hardware stores are carrying an increasingly interesting range of free-standing or wall-mounted heaters made especially for outdoor use. Rather than heating the air, these radiant heaters warm objects around them. They are powered by gas, propane, or electricity and are available in various sizes. Although the initial cost can be quite high, depending upon the heater you choose, operating costs are relatively inexpensive and they are well worth it for the extra pleasure they bring.

Water and watering systems

Plants in pots need water. How much and how often depends upon the size of your containers, the materials they are made from, the composition of the soil, the requirements of the plants themselves, and various environmental and climatic conditions such as hours of sunshine, wind, and air temperature.

Plants may or may not let you know in time if they are receiving enough water. Plants with young, tender leaves and flowers, such as annuals and vegetables, will wilt as soon as they become short of water, but trees and shrubs may look fine for a long time, even though they are suffering from water shortage. They will not thrive as they should and are likely to become susceptible to damage by pests and diseases. It is important, therefore, that plants in containers are watered well and consistently—

which can be anything from twice a day to once a week.

As a general rule, plants in containers should be watered as soon as the top inch (2.5 cm) of soil has dried out. Water thoroughly, until the water runs freely out the bottom of the container. This encourages the plants to produce roots well below the surface of the soil. A light sprinkling of water on a more frequent basis encourages plants to make roots closer to the surface, where they dry out more quickly.

The best times of day to water are in the evening or the early morning. In hot, dry weather, try to water in the evening so that the soil has the rest of the night to absorb the moisture, and the leaves can absorb water before it evaporates too quickly. In climates where the evening air is cool and damp, even in summer, try to water in the early morning so the leaves will be dry overnight. This helps to discourage the spread of fungal diseases, such as tomato blight and powdery mildew.

Try to avoid watering at all during the heat of the day unless you have no choice. When water sits on the leaves of plants it acts like a lens, concentrating the sun's rays and burning the foliage. When the temperature is high, the water evaporates quickly and the soil dries out before the roots have had a chance to benefit from the watering. If pots or hanging baskets do dry out, soak them in a sinkful of water or a rain barrel.

There are many methods of watering. If you have just one or two flower pots, a watering can with a rose attachment is fine. However, if you have a lot of pots you will find it much easier to use a garden hose with a watering wand attached to the end of it. Aluminum wands vary in length from 2 to 4 feet (60 to 120 cm) and are supplied with round or fan-shaped sprinkling attachments. The longer wands are particularly useful for watering hanging baskets and pots that are at or above eye level.

Ideally, a garden hose should be attached to an outside tap, but if you do not have an outlet there are special hoses and fittings sold for attaching to kitchen taps. Make sure this is what you use, or water will leak all over the kitchen floor. If you use a hose it is well worth investing in a hose reel to keep it neat and tidy.

A drip irrigation system connected to a timer is indispensable if you have a large patio or balcony, or are away for many days or weeks at a time. Drip irrigation systems dispense water directly to the plants through a network of plastic tubes. These lead to drip heads supported by spikes that are stuck into the containers. The water drips gently into the containers without disturbing the soil, and the timing mechanism makes sure that the plants are watered efficiently and effectively when desired. Additional spike heads and tubing can be purchased and added when they are needed.

Various drip irrigation systems and water timers are available in most hardware stores and garden centers. Take a plan of your garden design to the store, and make sure you have marked on it the locations and measurements of your containers. Then you will be able to determine exactly what you need: the lengths of hoses, number of spikes and drip heads, and timing mechanism. If you are clever at this sort of thing you will probably be able to custom design and make your own drip system, once you have looked at them in the stores. If not, ask a knowledgeable assistant in the store if he or she can help you; you'll often find someone who can rise to the challenge.

If you have room, it is always a nice idea to use rainwater collected in a watertight container for watering your pots. Even if you don't have room for a rain barrel, during dry summer months it is worth keeping a container full of tap water at hand. Let the water sit for twenty-four hours before using it; this cuts down substantially on the amount of chlorine in the water and the plants will benefit.

One way to conserve water in containers is to add mulch to the soil surface. There are many different types of organic material, such as well-rotted mushroom manure, compost, seaweed, straw, bark mulch, and two-year-old sawdust. Even a one-inch (2.5-cm) layer of mulch will make a big difference.

Garden tools

Container gardeners do not need a lot of tools but it helps to choose the ones you want carefully, getting the best quality you can afford. The right tools, well maintained, will make it easier to care for your containers and will increase your enjoyment. In the long run it is cheaper to buy a few good tools that will last a lifetime than to replace poorly made tools every few years.

With storage space at a premium, start with the minimum of tools and supplies and add more only as the need arises. You will need a clean, dry place to store them when they are not in use, preferably somewhere out of sight. Raised planters can be designed with a storage shelf underneath them, or you can install a tall, narrow cupboard that fits against the wall and is big enough to house the tools you need. You can even keep them in a large plastic garbage can or storage box, or fix a rack to the wall and hang the tools neatly on it. Just be sure that the tools are under an overhang, protected from the weather. The following list should be all you need for a container garden, whether it is large or small.

- For digging, planting, weeding, and cultivating: there are some excellent basic tool kits for container gardening, consisting of two or three hand-held tools such as a narrow and a wide trowel and a fork. This may be all you need for light digging, transplanting, weeding, and turning soil. If you are planting trees and shrubs, a small shovel is useful, and a hand rake to keep planters free of garden debris.
- For pruning and cutting: a good pair of secateurs are indispensable for any size of garden. You can use them for removing faded flower blossoms and taking off dead and unwanted branches and foliage. If you have topiary plants you will also want a good pair of pruning shears and special bonsai pruners for fine work.
- For hauling: getting tools, soil, pots, and supplies in and out can be a major challenge. A collapsible wheelbarrow stores easily and is invaluable for hauling, especially if you are bringing supplies via an elevator to an above-ground apartment. You can also use a collapsible wire shopping cart lined with an extra-strength garbage bag, a flat trolley on wheels, or a small cart with a handle. A lot of apartments

will have large hauling equipment on hand to help people on moving day, but it is well worth having a small one of your own.

- For storage: plastic pails, plastic containers with lids, and plastic garbage cans are all useful for storing soil, fertilizers, and small tools.
- For watering: watering cans; a hose and attachments, including a watering wand; a watering system; or rain barrel if you have room (see "Water and watering systems," above).
- For vegetative recycling: a worm bin is excellent (see "Making your own worm bin," below). If you have a large patio garden, you can also make or buy a small compost bin.
- Miscellaneous supplies: a folding garden stool for weeding raised planters; an outdoor broom; garden gloves; sturdy canes for staking; garden twine or string; blank plastic labels and waterproof markers to make labels for your plants; a bird bath and feeder; an apartment-size cold frame for starting plants from seed, overwintering tender plants, and getting a head start on a vegetable garden (see "Winterizing," below).
- Finally, don't forget your garden journal. Keeping a journal, with photos, is a great way to learn from your successes and failures. You can record everything you buy and plant, weather conditions, and the progress of your garden year by year.

Soil and amendments

Basic soil mix

Plants grown in containers require a lighter, more porous soil than those grown directly in the garden. The soil must be able to absorb water more quickly and drain more easily than garden soil, without becoming hard and compact. This allows the roots to obtain water and nutrients efficiently from the soil. The soil should have a higher-than-usual percentage of a light, porous material, such as vermiculite or perlite; some good-quality, sterilized topsoil; organic or inorganic fertilizer; and moisture-retaining materials, such as peat moss or ground wood bark.

There are many prepackaged soil blends available through garden centers, and some of them are specially formulated for container growing. These mixes may be more expensive than those you make yourself, but they are easy to use, properly sterilized, and may save you time and effort in the long run. If you are using a mix, purchase a high-quality one from a garden center you can trust. If you want to make your own blend, it is simple to do and has the advantage that you can custom-make each batch for the particular needs of the plants you are growing. For example, rhododendrons and azaleas prefer a peaty, acid soil, whereas roses and clematis thrive in a more alkaline soil mix.

You can make an excellent basic soil mix using the recipe given below. The ingredients are all readily available from your local garden center. Blend the mix directly in the container, mix it on a large plastic sheet on the floor, or use a baby bath, garbage bag, or garbage pail. You will need:

- 1 part good-quality topsoil.
- 1 part vermiculite or perlite.
- 1 part well-moistened peat moss, ground pine bark or fir bark (these are important for their conditioning and water-retaining properties, but do make sure that they are well-moistened first or they will not hold water properly).
- 1/4 to 1 cup of the appropriate fertilizer, depending upon the plant and the size of the container (for recipes see below).
- Sand or fine gravel for bonsai, penjing, and alpines.

Simply stir all the ingredients together. You can cut down on the weight by reducing the amount of topsoil: some experts say you can eliminate soil altogether. Many mixes use ground tree bark and sawdust as a conditioner, as well as or instead of peat moss. This makes a lot of environmental sense, since overharvesting of peat moss is leading to the rapid disappearance of peat bogs in Europe and North America. However, do make sure that the mix does not contain too much sawdust, since it has a tendency to break down rather quickly. Moderate amounts are fine. Since peat moss and ground wood products tend to be fairly acidic, a mix high in these ingredients is ideal for growing acid-loving plants. Add some dolomite lime if you are growing plants that prefer sweeter soil.

Vermiculite and perlite lighten the soil and make it more porous. Vermiculite is a mica that has been "popped" under heat and pressure. It is extremely light and sterile and absorbs water easily. It has a neutral pH and contains small amounts of potash. Perlite is a volcanic glass that forms a lightweight material when it is expanded by heat. It drains water quickly, is sterile, and is often used instead of vermiculite. Sand can also be used in soil mixes, especially for seaside plants, grasses, bonsai, penjing, and other plants that prefer a sandy, very well-drained soil.

Fertilizers

Plants must obtain many different nutrients from the soil in order to grow properly. If any one is lacking, the growth of the whole plant will suffer. In nature, plants adapt to local soil conditions, and the kinds and sizes of plants that grow in a particular area are largely determined by the natural fertility of the soil and climatic factors. However, when plants are grown in the garden, and especially in containers, the soil is unlikely to have all the essential ingredients they need for healthy growth. Also, many cultivated plants are hybrids; high-performance plants with higher nutritional needs than the species plants. Thus it becomes important to add the right balance of nutrients to the soil regularly, in the form of fertilizers.

The three minerals required in the largest amounts are nitrogen (N), phosphorus (P) and potassium (K). Nitrogen allows the whole plant to grow strongly and is responsible for the health, size, and strength of the leaves; phosphorus is especially important for good roots, abundant flowering, and healthy fruiting; and potassium helps to develop storage carbohydrates so that the whole plant will be robust and healthy.

All packages of fertilizer, whether organic or chemically synthesized, will have three numbers on their packaging indicating the relative percentage by weight of these three components. For example, one commonly used high-potency fertilizer is a commercial preparation known as 20-20-20: it contains approximately 20 percent N, 20 percent P, and 20 percent K (the three minerals are always listed in this order). Because it is so high in nutrients, this fertilizer is a powerful stimulant to the overall growth of the plants—their roots, leaves, shoots, and flowers.

Plants also need to have trace amounts of several other minerals in order to grow properly. The most important ones are calcium, magnesium, sulfur, iron, boron, manganese, copper, zinc, and molybdenum. A well-balanced fertilizer, whether it is organic or inorganic, will also contain all these trace elements. Read the package carefully for details.

Each type of fertilizer has its advantages and disadvantages. Controlled-release formulations such as Nutricote and Osmocote release their nutrients slowly over a period of months; the speed of release is dependent on soil temperature and moisture content. Formulations such as 14-14-14 are good controlled-release fertilizers to add to the soil before you plant trees, shrubs, perennials, hanging baskets, and annuals. Controlled-release fertilizers are, however, all synthetic and cannot be made at home.

Granular fertilizers are available in both organic and commercial forms (such as 6-8-6 and 8-20-20). They tend to last about four to six weeks, and should be watered in each time they are used. Granular fertilizers are good for trees, shrubs, and perennials, to help with their health and growth during the growing season. Do not use them more than once a month, or they could burn the plants.

If you are growing herbs and vegetables, mix an organic granular fertilizer, rather than a controlled-release formulation, into the basic soil mix. An organic fertilizer can be custom-mixed, combining the ingredients in proportions that meet specific planting needs. Listed below are three mixes, with suggestions on how to use them.

Soluble fertilizers are a good solution for weekly or twice-weekly watering of annuals, vegetables, and hanging baskets. Fish and seaweed (kelp) fertilizers are the most commonly used organic ones, and commercial formulations include 15-30-15, 8-24-12, and 20-20-20. For annuals and hanging baskets it is a good plan to start with a very high-phosphate fertilizer such as 15-30-15 to encourage strong root development, and then switch to 8-24-12 to encourage flower as well as root production. For herbs and vegetables it is always best to use organic fertilizers.

If plants are dry, be sure to water them well before fertilizing them; fertilizer can burn plant roots if it is applied directly to dry soil.

A watering can is ideal for applying liquid fertilizers to a small number of containers. However, if you have a large garden, consider adding an inexpensive siphon device (available at most hardware stores or garden centers) to your garden hose. The siphon is attached between the hose and the tap, and a tube extends from it into a concentrated solution of fertilizer. When the water is turned on, the siphon action sucks the solution into the hose and meters it out in the desired concentration.

Organic fertilizers

The formulations given here can be mixed and blended according to your needs, and stored in labeled containers. Since you will probably have to buy more of the raw ingredients than you can possibly use in a year, why not make up extra batches for friends, and give them away for birthday and Christmas presents? Gardeners really appreciate this kind of gift.

Basic grow mix: especially good for annuals, vegetables, herbs, and perennials.

- 3 parts blood or fish meal (especially high in nitrogen).
- 3 parts steamed bone meal (especially high in phosphorus and calcium, and quite a bit of nitrogen too).
- 1 1/2 parts K-Mag (also known as Sul-Po-Mag, a great combination of potassium, magnesium, and sulfur).
- 1 part kelp meal (contains at least 62 trace minerals, and potassium, amino acids, and natural growth-promoting hormones).

High potassium mix: encourages root growth.

- 2 parts cottonseed meal (all-purpose balanced fertilizer).
- 1 1/2 parts steamed bone meal.
- 2 1/2 parts K-Mag.
- 2 parts kelp meal.

Acid mix: for plants that require a low pH, such as rhododendrons and azaleas.

- 4 parts cottonseed meal.
- 1 1/2 parts K-Mag.
- 1/2 part steamed bone meal.
- 1/2 part kelp meal.

Making your own worm bin

A worm bin is an environmentally friendly way to recycle vegetable waste and add nutrients and organic matter back into your soil. A worm bin is easy to make. It is not smelly and can be easily tucked into a corner of your apartment or balcony, as long as air can get into the holes on the top. The nutrient-rich organic matter produced in a worm bin will help keep your containers healthy and well fed, and you can be proud you are doing your bit to help recycle organic waste.

Materials

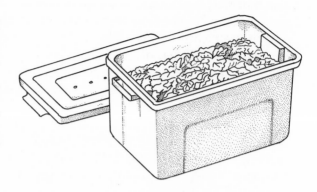

- One heavy plastic storage box with lid, about 2 feet (60 cm) long, 18 inches (45 cm) wide, and 9 inches (23 cm) deep.
- About half a pound (275 g) of garden worms. If you can't get worms from a friend's garden, ask a bait shop or garden center for sources of supply.
- Some topsoil.

Method

Drill holes in the lid of the box. Fill the box about two-thirds full of soil and add the worms. Chop vegetable scraps, the finer the better, and bury them several inches (8 or 10 cm) deep in the soil. Worms don't like onions and garlic, but just about any other vegetable and fruit scraps, coffee grounds, and eggshells are fine. After a while the compost material compacts and becomes very heavy and dense. At this point, place the box, with the lid off, in the sun. The worms will tend to go towards the bottom of the box, and the soil they have made can be taken off the top. The rest of the soil/worm mix is ready to use again.

Caring for plants in containers

The three most critical factors for successful pot planting are drainage, nutrients, and water. If plants do not obtain the nutrients or the moisture they require, they will not thrive. But if they become too wet and water sits in the pot, their roots will become waterlogged and they will die.

If plants are to receive adequate moisture and not become waterlogged, water must be able to percolate evenly through the pot, and excess water must be able to drain out easily. There are several different opinions about the best way to achieve this. Many books recommend putting a layer of coarse drainage material, such as fine gravel or small stones, in the bottom of the pot. However, surface tension created between the water and the drainage materials will often hold the water in the base of the container, rather than allowing it to drain through. Also, if the soil becomes compacted, water will tend to make channels through it, so that some of the roots and soil will be well watered while other parts will not receive any moisture at all.

Here, then, are the steps to follow to ensure that containers have good drainage. First, make sure the container has lots of drainage holes in the bottom and is raised up at least an inch or two (2.5 to 5 cm) from the ground.

Place a piece of fine plastic mesh over the drainage holes. This will prevent the soil from running out the bottom of the pot. If you don't have any plastic mesh, you can use a couple of layers of newspaper or some moss, although the mesh is the best. Fill your planter with soil and plants, adding extra sand and fine gravel to the top two or three inches (5 to 7.5 cm) of soil. This makes the top layer more porous so that water will spread right across the pot and percolate evenly down through the soil. The bigger the pot, the better the drainage. Finally, cover the soil with a thin layer of organic mulch to help retain moisture.

Many plants that come from the nursery have lived too long in their pot, and their roots can be seen circling the inside of the pots. As you prepare to repot them, loosen the rootball with a small hand fork or chopsticks. This will allow the roots to grow outwards into the fresh soil. Once all the plants have been firmed into their new location, water them until excess water runs out of the bottom of the pot. It is always helpful to add a little transplanting solution to this water to minimize transplant shock.

Commercial transplanting solutions are available in garden centers, but one of the best, and least well known for this purpose, is Rescue Remedy, a subtle combination of flower essences that works in very small quantities for any state of shock, whether in plants, animals, or humans. It is available through many health and herbal stores under the product line of "Bach Flower Essences." To use for plants, add twenty drops of the essence to a gallon (4 L) of water, stir well, and water the plants in with it.

Leave the pots until the top inch (2.5 cm) of soil is dry and then make sure to water and feed your pots as necessary. Slow-growing trees and shrubs will not need to be fed very often, if at all, since too much stimulation will result in overproduction of roots, shoots, and leaves, and the plant will soon outgrow its pot.

Even without fertilizers, there will come a time when perennials, shrubs, and trees will be too big for their original containers and will need repotting. As a general rule, this is best done in the early spring, just as the plants are beginning to break dormancy. Remove the plants carefully from their pots, shake off any loose soil, and tease out the roots with a small fork or chopsticks. Prune out any dead or rotting roots, being careful not to damage healthy roots. If you have to prune some healthy roots, be sure to leave most intact and only remove as much as is necessary. Clean out the container and refill with fresh soil before repotting the plant: you may need to use a larger pot. Prune the foliage, taking away at least as much foliage as you did root, or the plant will suffer. Clumps of spreading perennials should be divided.

Good pruning is important for all plants, but it is especially important for plants in containers. The arts of topiary, bonsai, and penjing depend upon pruning for visual and aesthetic effect, but all trees and shrubs in pots need to be pruned carefully to maintain their health. The extent to which the roots can grow may limit top growth. This is less true for annuals since they complete their life cycle in one season and so do not usually outgrow their space; remove their blossoms as soon as they are spent, so the plant will continue to produce flowers in an attempt to reproduce. Here are some basic pruning guidelines.

- Annuals: prune off all blossoms once they are spent and cut flowers for decoration indoors. The more you cut, the more they bloom.
- Perennials: cut off the blossoms once they are spent, and bring some flowers indoors for decoration. Perennials have a specific blooming season and will not usually bloom again outside their usual pattern.
- Flowering shrubs: the best time to prune is just after they have flowered. Spring-flowering shrubs should be pruned in the late spring, and fall-flowering shrubs in the late fall or winter.
- Flowering trees: usually pruned during their dormant period from late fall to late winter, depending upon the time they break dormancy in the spring; late winter is usually the best time since there are fewer organisms around to infect wounds.
- Conifers: these are usually pruned two or three times a year.

Do not prune anything if the temperature is below freezing (except for cutting back perennials).

Layering spring bulbs

Spring-flowering bulbs grow well in many different kinds of frostproof containers as long as their particular needs are met. In milder climates, large containers can be left outdoors all winter long and the bulbs will be protected from freezing by the soil surrounding them. If containers are too small, cold will affect the growth of the bulbs.

In colder climates, bulbs planted in the garden are protected from frost damage by a blanket of snow, but bulbs planted in containers may not have the same protection. You will need to insulate the containers from the cold (see "Winterizing," below). It is a good idea to group small containers together and cover them with an overturned wooden or cardboard box that is insulated with a layer of peat moss or styrofoam chips. Remember to keep the bulbs moist; do not allow the soil in the pots to dry out.

Where the winter is very wet, such as in the Pacific Northwest, place containers under a roof or overhang out of the rain, if at all possible, and make sure they have good drainage so bulbs do not become waterlogged. Don't forget to place the containers on bricks or blocks to raise them up and allow excess water to drain out properly.

If bulbs are layered correctly, and you plant a selection of early, mid-, and late spring bulbs, you will have a lovely show of color in the spring. Larger bulbs should be planted deeper than smaller bulbs. As a rule of thumb, the correct planting depth for a bulb is three times its diameter. Thus tulips and daffodils should be planted at a depth of 8 to 9 inches (20 to 23 cm) below the surface of the soil, whereas crocuses should be planted only 2 to 3 inches (5 to 7.5 cm) below the surface.

Fill the container with basic soil mix and then remove the top 10 inches (25 cm) of soil, placing it beside the pot. Add sand or perlite to this soil, using about a quarter of the volume of the soil mix. This will improve drainage around the bulbs. Put about

2 inches (5 cm) of this soil back into the container, spread a thin layer of bone meal over the soil surface, and then add another inch (2.5 cm) of soil. Place the larger bulbs, such as daffodils and tulips, on the soil so that they are at the correct depth. Cover them with 2 or 3 inches (5 or 7.5 cm) of soil, and add another thin layer of bone meal and a bit more soil. Then plant the smaller bulbs, and cover them with soil to within one inch (2.5 cm) of the top of the container. The smaller bulbs, such as snowdrops, crocuses, iris, and winter aconite, will bloom first. As they finish, the stems of the larger bulbs will emerge and cover the foliage of the smaller bulbs.

Take the bulbs out of the pots once they have finished blooming and remove the flower head. Place the bulbs in damp peat moss, preferably out of sight, until their foliage has died back. Store the dried bulbs in a dry place ready for replanting in the fall. The container can then be planted for the summer.

Plant selection and hardiness zones

By now you will have chosen your theme and assessed all the advantages and drawbacks of re-creating that theme in your space. You will have chosen many of your pots and containers and prepared your patio or balcony so they can be put in place. Now you are ready for the most enjoyable part of all—selecting your plants.

The first step is to find a reputable, well-established nursery or garden center and talk to the staff about the plants that are available and will grow in your area. Don't hesitate to ask questions. Take this book with you, mark the plants you would like to buy, and then find out if you really can grow them where you live. This is not usually a problem with annuals, or with tender perennials that are grown as annuals, but if you want to keep trees, shrubs, and perennials outdoors from year to year you need to know how hardy they are in your climate.

The hardiness zones given for each plant are a good guide, but no one can agree on the hardiness of different plants, and in truth it can vary greatly even within one zone. Hardiness zones are given based on the plant's ability to withstand both winter cold and summer heat, and this means there are always some compromises: for example, parts of Florida and parts of Victoria, British Columbia, are classified as Zone 9, and yet there are plants that do fine in Victoria but cannot withstand the summer heat of Florida. Microclimates can exist in protected spots, and you may be able to grow plants that even your neighbor can't. This is why you need to talk to the locals. They will know what will actually grow where you live, not what the hardiness zones say. It is always worth giving it a try if you like the plant. Remember that plants grown in pots are much more susceptible to cold than those grown directly in the ground. For example, if you live in zone 7 and have a bad winter you may lose plants hardy to zone 7 unless their roots are very well protected.

Read the labels carefully. Size, shape, and color are all important. If you choose a plant that grows to 5 feet (1.5 m) and you need one that grows to 3 feet (0.9 m), you will change the relative balance between container and plant and alter the overall effect. A plant that is too bushy for the pot will crowd out others, and dwarf more delicate plants; and three clashing reds in a pot will have a very different impact from the cool blues and yellows you had in mind.

Of course, sometimes breaking the rules can bring a more attractive result than you expected and, as always, we learn more from our failures than our successes. The best advice is still to ask for help and consult books; if you are still uncertain, ask again. Plants are expensive. Money doesn't grow on trees. All of this we need to re-member when going to the garden center.

Pests and diseases

Advice about control of pests and diseases is the same whether you have a 5-acre (2-ha) garden or a couple of pots on the patio. If you keep your garden clean and follow good garden practices it will be healthy; if not, it won't—an ounce of prevention is worth a pound of cure. Here are some general guidelines to follow.

- Buy only healthy plants and good-quality seeds and bulbs. Look for disease-resis-tant cultivars.
- Make sure the plants you buy are suited to the sites you choose for them, and that all their requirements are met. A plant under stress is much more susceptible to pests and diseases.
- Keep your containers tidy and weed-free. Rotting plants can be a source of infec-tion and will attract pests to the garden. Clean up and destroy all infected plant material.
- Prune out dead and diseased branches, and remove overcrowded and crossing branches to ensure that trees and shrubs have adequate ventilation.
- Prepare the soil properly for your containers and follow the instructions carefully for any given plant so that it has the conditions it needs to thrive.
- If a plant is not thriving, and is diseased or continually attacked by pests, get rid of it and plant something else. Avoid pesticides if at all possible.
- When insects appear, and you don't know them, watch them for a while. They may be beneficial, such as green lacewings or ground beetles, who feed on other in-sects, not on plants. Slugs, snails, sow bugs, weevils, and other harmful, large creepy-crawlies can be removed by hand, especially at night with the help of a flashlight, and eliminated.
- If your harmful insects are small, try to dislodge them by washing infested plants with a high-powered jet of water, especially on the undersides of leaves. If that doesn't work, give them a soapy wash with an environmentally friendly product such as Safer's Insecticidal Soap or Trounce. Even dishwashing liquid can be better than nothing.
- Insect repellents sometimes help keep pests away from plants. You can make your

own organic repellent by adding 1/4 ounce (about 7 g) tobacco, 4 peeled cloves of garlic, 2 tablespoons (30 mL) of liquid soap, and 2 tablespoons (30 mL) of household ammonia to a quart (1 L) of boiling water. Let steep for several hours, strain, put into a spray bottle and use on vulnerable plants. You can eat herbs and vegetables the day after you spray them, but rinse them well with cold water first.

- Search your local garden center for good organic controls: there are many on the market today, such as Tanglefoot, a sticky substance used to trap climbing insects; floating row covers, such as Reemay, that protect young seedlings; yellow sticky traps for flying insects; and diatomaceous earth (sharp particles that cut up snails, slugs, aphids, cutworms, and other soft-bodied insects when they crawl across it).

- If you have an insect or disease you cannot identify, collect a specimen and take it to a nearby garden center or botanical garden. They should have knowledgeable personnel on hand who can identify it for you and suggest environmentally friendly controls you can use.

Propagation: *How to take your own cuttings*

Propagating plants by making cuttings is an easy and rewarding activity. A cutting is more or less what its name suggests: a small part cut from a mature plant and prepared and treated in such a way that it can grow into a new plant.

There are different types of cuttings, but with plants that can go on from year to year, such as geraniums (*Pelargonium* spp.), and for shrubs, such as lavender, rosemary, and box, the simplest way is to start with stem cuttings. July is usually the best time to take them, when the plants are putting on lots of new growth and the plant stem will still bend, but is not dry enough to snap. Cuttings are an excellent way for container gardeners to overwinter many tender or semihardy perennials.

Method 1: Softwood cuttings

This method works very well for many plants that are usually grown as annuals but are in fact perennials, such as geraniums and impatiens. If you take cuttings of these plants towards the end of the summer and follow the instructions below, you will have lots of healthy, small plants the following year. It will save you money and is easy to do. You will need to buy some rooting compound, available from garden centers.

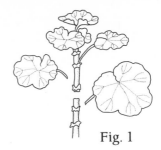

Fig. 1

Choose a healthy shoot without flowers or flower buds. Using a sharp knife, cut the shoot off just below a node, so that the cutting is 3 to 4 inches (8 to 10 cm) long. Remove the lower leaves, but leave at least three leaves per cutting (Fig. 1).

Fill 3-inch (7.5-cm) pots three-quarters full with potting mixture, and make a hole for the cutting with a pencil or piece of dowel. Dip the end of the cutting in rooting compound, shake off the excess, and drop it into the hole. Press it firmly in place and add more potting mixture. Water it well and then keep it on the dry side, giving it a little water when necessary so that it does not wilt. Water sparingly during the winter months and keep in a cool, bright room (Fig. 2).

Harden off in April or May, either by setting plants out during the day and bringing them in at night or by placing them in a cold frame. Plant out in the garden at the end of May.

Fig. 2

Method 2: Semihardwood cuttings

This is an excellent method for propagating lavender, hebe, rosemary, skimmia, euonymus, senecio, and many other woody perennials and small shrubs. First ensure that the plant is healthy. Remove a side shoot about 6 inches (15 cm) long from the main stem so that a thin sliver of bark and wood from the old stem, the heel, also comes away at the base of the cutting (Fig. 1).

Trim the heel with a sharp knife and remove the lower leaves (Fig. 2). Then pinch out the growing tip and dip the base of the cutting in rooting compound. Make a hole in the potting soil, which should be moist, but not wet. Make a mini-greenhouse for the cutting by placing the pot inside a large, clear plastic bag that is tied at the top. Place stakes around the cutting so the plastic does not touch it. Check the cutting daily and keep it moist but not too wet.

Once they have rooted, the cuttings can be kept in a cool, light place indoors during the winter, hardened off in the spring, then planted outdoors for the summer.

Fig. 1

Fig. 2

Winterizing

Protecting plants in winter

Before buying any plants, whether they are herbs, perennials, shrubs, or trees, it is worth finding out whether they will survive the winter outdoors in your climate. Take a long hard look at tender and semihardy plants before you buy them. Think about the size of your townhouse or apartment. Unless you have room to overwinter the plants successfully indoors, or have a friend who can keep them for you, you may want to reconsider your decision to buy. It can be expensive to replace choice plants year after year, and it may make more sense to substitute hardier plants for the ones you have chosen. Another solution is to take cuttings of plants in July, as described above, since cuttings take up less space than mature plants. Cuttings can be kept inside during winter, ready for planting out next spring.

The roots of plants in containers are much more vulnerable to extremes of temperature than they would be if they were planted in the ground, and even the hardiest plants may need additional protection in cold weather. One effective method is to move the container into a sheltered location, such as next to a building, or into a garage or shed. Wrap the container and plant in a layer of burlap. Place the wrapped container inside an insulating box made from wood or cardboard lined with styrofoam sheets, and fill the space between the box and the container with an additional layer of insulating material, such as straw, styrofoam chips, moss, or bubble wrap. Old packaging material works well for this.

Alternate freezing and thawing causes the most winter damage to plants. It is worth keeping this in mind, particularly if your patio or balcony faces east. On a clear, frosty day there will be a rapid rise in air temperature as the warmth of the sun hits the plant. It will thaw, but it will freeze again just as quickly when the sun disappears and the temperature drops. This cycle is very destructive to some plants, especially tender shrubs, so try to protect them from the sun whenever outside temperatures fall below freezing.

Where winters are rainy, container plants can suffer from soggy bottoms, and eventually the plants drown. This is caused by a settling of the soil mixture to the bottom of the container. The water is unable to drain completely from the bottom layer of the rootball. Potbound plants are particularly vulnerable, so check the roots of large plants yearly. You can do this by running a large knife between the container sides and the soil, laying the container on its side, and sliding the whole plant out. Check the rootball and cut out any roots that wind around and girdle the pot. If necessary, move the plant into a larger container. Otherwise, repot into the same container, shaking out some of the old soil and adding fresh.

After a heavy snowfall, be sure to shake excess snow off all trees and shrubs. This will prevent the branches from breaking due to the weight of the snow. If you are concerned about overwintering plants in containers outdoors in your area, call a botanical garden or good garden center near you. Their advice will be based on many years of first-hand experience with the same climatic conditions.

Particular care should be given to your water garden as winter approaches. There are very few parts of the continent where a small tub or container of water plants can be left outside without risk of loss. As water lilies and other deciduous plants begin to die back for the winter, lift them out of the water and check them. Divide and replant them if they have become rootbound. Bring the container indoors (or use another container that you already have indoors), replenish the water, and put the plants back into the container. Most oxygenators will keep working at inside temperatures as long as they receive plenty of light, and they make a very attractive indoor pond. Fish will remain active and will need to be fed, although not as often as you would feed them during the summer. If you used a water pump, disconnect it, check for worn parts, clean it, and store it indoors for the winter.

Using hot and cold frames

For the adventurous, hot and cold frames are an excellent way to extend the season and overwinter plants that would otherwise be vulnerable to winter cold. It is easy to make a basic frame. It is simply a rectangular form that can be anywhere from 1 to 3 feet (30 to 90 cm) high, covered with a piece of glass or acrylic that is hinged to the back of the frame and can be lifted up and down

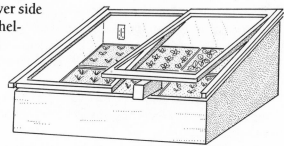

during the day. Often the frames are higher on one side than the other, with the lower side to the south for maximum sun and shelter. During the day the lid is propped open so that air can circulate around the plants inside the frame, and it is closed again at night. This protects plants from cold weather and is, in effect, a mini-greenhouse.

You can make the basic frame from wooden boards and the lid from an old window, still in its frame and hinged at the back. You can also buy some excellent ready-made acrylic frames that will pack away flat when not in use. If you plan to grow a lot of vegetables, for instance, it makes sense to construct one of the planters with removable, high wooden sides and a clear lid made from glass, acrylic, or heavy plastic. It can be used in the spring and fall for a cold frame.

A hot frame is a cold frame that has heating coils in it. The coils are either around the sides of the frame or underneath a raised platform on which you can place trays of seeds, seedlings, or cuttings. Hot frames make it possible to keep your plants from freezing in even the coldest weather, and they really give you a jump-start in the spring. You need an outside source of power in order to have a hot frame.

A final word

I hope the ideas in this book will help you enjoy your own outdoor space and create the garden of your dreams. I would love to hear about your successes—and your failures—and wish you many happy hours of puttering, potting, and planting.

Selected bibliography

Birren, Faber. *Color and Human Response.* New York: Van Nostrand Reinhold, 1978.

Bond, Sandra. *Hostas.* London: Ward Lock Ltd., 1992.

Brickell, Christopher. *The Gardener's Encyclopedia of Plants and Flowers.* London: Dorling Kindersley, 1989.

Burke, Ken. *Gardening in Containers.* San Ramon, Ca: Ortho Books, 1984.

Chan, Peter. *Better Vegetable Gardens the Chinese Way.* Pownal, Vermont: Garden Way Publishing, 1985.

Chan, Peter. *Bonsai. The art of growing and keeping miniature trees.* New Jersey: Chartwell Books Inc., 1985.

Clausen, Ruth Rogers and Nicolas H. Ekstrom. *Perennials for American Gardens.* New York: Random House, 1989.

Druse, Ken. *The Natural Shade Garden.* New York: Clarkson Potter, 1992.

Eliovson, Sima. *Gardening the Japanese Way.* London: George G. Harrap and Co. Ltd., 1971.

Elliot, Jack. *Alpines in the Open Garden.* Portland, Oregon: Timber Press, Inc., 1991.

Evison, Raymond J. *Making the most of Clematis.* England: Floraprint Ltd., 1979.

Fell, Derek. *Annuals: How to Select, Grow and Enjoy.* New York: HP Books, 1983.

Fitch, Charles Marden. *The Complete Book of Miniature Roses.* New York: Hawthorn Books Inc., 1977.

Fogg, H. G. Witham. *Vegetables Naturally: An organic-gardening guide.* London: Crescent Books, 1976.

Gault, S. Millar and Patrick M. Synge. *The Dictionary of Roses in color.* In collaboration with The Royal Horticultural Society and The Royal National Rose Society. London: Rainbird Reference Books Ltd., 1971.

Genders, Roy. *Scented flora of the world.* London: Robert Hale Ltd., 1977.

Grieve, Maud. *A Modern Herbal.* New York: Dover Publications, Inc., 1971.

Griffiths, Mark. *Index of Garden Plants.* Derived from *The New Royal Horticultural Society Dictionary of Gardening.* Portland, Oregon: Timber Press Inc., 1994.

Hammer, Patricia Riley. *The New Topiary. Imaginative Techniques from Longwood Gardens.* London: Garden Art Press Ltd., 1991.

Hart, Rhonda Massingham. *Northcoast Roses.* Seattle: Cascadia Gardening Series, Sasquatch Books, 1993.

Hightshoe, Gary L. *Native Trees, Shrubs, and Vines for Urban and Rural America.* New York: Van Nostrand Reinhold, 1988.

Hoffman, David. *The Holistic Herbal.* England: Element Books Ltd., 1983.

Ingwersen, Will. *Manual of Alpine Plants.* London: Cassell Publishers Ltd., 1978.

Joyce, David and Christopher Brickell. *The Complete Guide to Pruning and Training Plants.* London: Simon and Schuster, 1992.

Keeling, Jim. *The Terracotta Gardener.* London: Headline Books Publishing, 1991.

Keswick, Maggie; Judy Oberlander; and Joe Wai. *In a Chinese Garden: The Art and Architecture of the Dr. Sun Yat-Sen Classical Chinese Garden.* Vancouver: The Dr. Sun Yat-Sen Garden Society, 1990.

Kraft, Ken and Pat. *Grow your own dwarf fruit trees*. New York: Walker and Company, 1974.

Kruckeberg, Arthur R. *Gardening with Native Plants of the Pacific Northwest. An illustrated guide*. Seattle: University of Washington Press, 1982.

Lowe, Duncan. *Growing Alpines in raised beds, troughs and tufa*. London: B.T. Batsford Ltd., 1991.

Morris, Edwin T. *The Gardens of China. History, Art and Meanings*. New York: Charles Scribner's Sons, 1983.

Newton, Judy. *The Complete Guide to Vegetables for Amateurs and Experts*. Vancouver: Whitecap Books, 1991.

Reader's Digest. *Encyclopaedia of Garden Plants*. London: The Reader's Digest Association Ltd., 1978.

Reader's Digest. *Illustrated Guide to Gardening. Pruning and Training a Horizontal Espalier*. London: The Reader's Digest Association Ltd., 1978.

Ridge, Antonia. *For Love of a Rose*. London: faber and faber, 1965.

Rix, Martyn and Roger Phillips. *The Bulb Book*. London: Pan Books Ltd., 1981.

Stevens, Elaine; Dagmar Hungerford; Doris Fancourt-Smith; Jane Mitchell; and Ann Buffam. *The Twelve Month Gardener. A West Coast Guide*. Vancouver: Whitecap Books, 1991.

Swindells, Philip and David Mason. *The complete book of the water garden*. New York: The Overlook Press, 1990.

Taylor, Nigel J. *Ornamental Grasses, Rushes and Sedges*. London: Ward Lock Ltd., 1992.

Thomas, Graham Stuart. *Perennial Gardening Plants* or *The Modern Florilegium*. London: The Orion Publishing Group, 1976.

Tolley, Emelie and Chris Mead. *Herbs*. New York: Clarkson N. Potter, Inc., 1985.

Trehane, Piers. *Index Hortensis*. Wimborne, England: Quarterjack Publishing, 1989.

Van Pelt Wilson, Helen. *Color for your winter yard and garden*. New York: Charles Scribner's Sons, 1978.

Vertrees, J. D. *Japanese maples*. Portland, Oregon: Timber Press, 1978.

Warner, Christopher. *Climbing Roses*. London: Cassell Publishers Ltd. 1987.

Welch, H. J. *Dwarf conifers: A complete guide*. London: faber and faber, 1966.

Index

Main entries are in **boldface**.